Walls Within Walls

Entry to a home deep within the Walled City.

Walls Within Walls

Life Histories of Working Women in the Old City of Lahore

Anita M. Weiss

OXFORD

UNIVERSITY PRESS

Great Clarendon Street, Oxford OX2 6DP

Oxford University Press is a department of the University of Oxford.
It furthers the University's objective of excellence in research, scholarship,
and education by publishing worldwide in

Oxford New York

Auckland Bangkok Buenos Aires Cape Town Chennai
Dar es Salaam Delhi Hong Kong Istanbul Karachi Kolkata
Kuala Lumpur Madrid Melbourne Mexico City Mumbai Nairobi
São Paulo Shanghai Singapore Taipei Tokyo Toronto

and an associated company in Berlin

Oxford is a registered trade mark of Oxford University Press
in the UK and in certain other countries

© Oxford University Press 2002

The moral rights of the author have been asserted

First published in 1992 in the United States of America
by Westview Press, Inc., 5500 Central Avenue, Boulder, Colorado 80301-2847,
and in the United Kingdom by Westview Press, 36 Lonsdale Road,
Summertown, Oxford OX2 7EW

ISBN 0 19 579761 2

This edition by Oxford University Press, Pakistan, 2002

Printed in Pakistan by
Mas Printers, Karachi.
Published by
Ameena Saiyid, Oxford University Press
5-Bangalore Town, Sharae Faisal
PO Box 13033, Karachi-75350, Pakistan.

For Farrukh Raza, Janice Weiss,
and
the women of the Walled City of Lahore

Contents

Illustrations

Maps

Photos

Following page 13
Bazaar outside Lohari Gate
Breakfast in a Walled City bazaar
Rehra used for transporting goods
Men smoking a *hookah*
Rebuilt area leading into Kashmiri Bazaar
Preparing food in Suter Mandi
Bridegroom and his band on their way to
    bride's family's house
People sleeping on roofs
Kucha near Kashmiri Gate
Selling prepared foods in a bazaar

Following page 80
Interior of two-room home
Preparing *samosas* for sale
Parandas on sale in Kashmiri Bazaar
Woman buying dry goods
Sehras on sale in Kashmiri Bazaar
Girl cutting out shoe pieces
Boys assembling plastic horns
Stringing flowers

Preface and Acknowledgments

"Power? Taking off a *burqa* and putting
on a *chadar*: now that's power!"

--*A woman in Kucha Kakazaiyan*

The interrelationship between women and development in Pakistan is one of the most compelling socioeconomic discourses confronting the country at this time. Following over two decades of frustrating results from development planning, only a small group of economists and other social scientists are seriously confronting the reality that Pakistan's development experience has been seriously compromised by not incorporating women's active participation into the variety of schemes which have been attempted in the past. On those infrequent occasions when attempts to include women in development planning have occurred, planners have virtually "second guessed" the circumstances of women's lives. However, before a viable attempt can be made to rectify the matter of truly making women "partners in development," we must first identify how Pakistani women view various issues affecting them. Only with their input regarding their situation and problems which confront them can we explore the relationship between their economic activities and social relations and understand the kinds of changes occurring within their practical lives, social orientations, and values. From their stories, we can take a step closer to understanding the interplay between Islamic religious ideals and traditionally embedded orientations on the one hand, and practical economic needs on the other, especially as these forces concern women's roles in the cultural context of development.

This book is based on life history accounts that I collected from a representative sample of working women resident in the old Walled City of Lahore during the summer of 1987. I focussed in particular on women who engage in some sort of labor for which they or their families receive monetary compensation. The encouragements, constraints, and reconciliations with tradition they experience while working as well as the ramifications of their working status on their personal power and social environment emerge through these life history accounts. Their stories do not speak for all Pakistani women, or even for all women

xi

living in Lahore.[1] Their personal histories reflect the parameters bounding the lives of poor urban women within which there are degrees of freedom of movement but we see today more limitations than possibilities for expansion. In meeting with these women in the Walled City, in talking with them, I was struggling to understand their intrinsic values, their own moral vocabulary and orientations, as opposed to socially imposed ones. Do they in fact subscribe to the dominant, prevailing themes of patriarchy and women's separation because it is a part of a socially constructed moral universe, or are they essentially compelled to accept such circumstances out of fear of retribution and/or social expulsion?

The techniques of life history accounts circumvent specific research problems which arise when addressing women and labor throughout the world. For example, official estimates in the 1981 National Census Plan claim that only 3.5 percent of all Pakistani women work.[2] This extremely low estimate, which only includes women's economic participation in the formal sector, underscores the need for a qualitative assessment of poor urban women's activities that contribute to economic gain for themselves and their families. As ideal Muslim women are physically veiled, so too are their productive contributions "veiled" in popular cultural assessments and official documentation. Idealized notions in which Muslim women are cared for by the men in their families so as to preserve the family's *izzat* (respectability) and *sharafat* (honor) are often inconsonant with the realities of everyday life for many women and the actual roles they perform. There have only been a few studies (Hafeez, 1983; Weiss, 1984; Hooper, 1985; Shaheed & Mumtaz, 1983; World Bank, 1989) conducted on the objective circumstances of working women in Pakistan. From this limited body of research, however, ample proof emerges to question the low numbers of women said to be engaged in remunerative labor in existing official documentation and to question the popularly held view that most women would rather not work if given a choice.

The situation of the invisibility of women's labor is not unique to Pakistan, for women's contributions remain dismally underreported in many parts of the world.[3] In most Third World cities, the sexual division of labor is marked by the majority of working women participating in marginal sectors of the economy, with relatively few working in the formal labor force.[4] While this remains true within the Walled City of Lahore, women here are confronted with an additional dilemma in that sociocultural mores virtually exclude them from many of the informal sector activities in which their counterparts engage in other countries such as selling roadside snacks or raw fruits and vegetables from pushcarts. Instead, women are primarily occupied as piece-rate workers in home-based cottage industry, but with a remarkable social "twist": they essentially do the exact same work which men do in the bazaar, but solely within the walls of their own homes and for significantly less remuneration.

My research was conducted in two stages. The first stage began with the assistance of colleagues from the Lahore Development Authority who provided me with essential grid maps of the Walled City from which I could generate a random sample population.[5] This was necessary as the homes in the Walled City usually have no telephones or even specific street numbers (multiple floor dwellings often have only one address although more than one family resides in them) from which a computerized random sample could be generated. Two experienced female interviewers, native to Lahore, administered the surveys in Urdu or Punjabi to women in one hundred households. The survey administered in this first stage served two important purposes: (1) it provided basic demographic information about women and socioeconomic life within the Walled City; and (2) it identified a population of working women from which I could then draw a representative sample. In the second stage of my research, I met nearly a quarter of the women surveyed and recorded the life histories of twelve of them.

I recognize that there are always limitations associated with representing the lives of other people, whether from one's own natal culture or from another. In the life history interviews, I took great care to really listen and understand what the women were trying to convey. Between the awareness of the caution necessary in any form of cultural representation and by living within the Walled City -- experiencing daily life in as cogent a context as possible -- I trust that many of these issues have been realistically and appropriately addressed and reconciled, and thus potential pitfalls avoided.

My random sample data not only further substantiates the argument that women's productive contributions are severely underreported in the country (fully two-thirds of the women in my sample either do work or would like to work), but it adds a qualitative dimension to the actual work they do, the conditions under which they do it, and how this affects the contours of the domestic domain in this rapidly changing society. The life history accounts augment this with detailed descriptions of the circumstances of women's lives: how they grew up and were married, how decisions in their lives have been made, and what their aspirations are. The stories of these women's lives have been topically arranged in the coming chapters because, in truth, it is not the individual who is our concern but rather that her story is representative of the experiences of many, many women within the Old City's walls. It is also for this reason, as well as to preserve the anonymity and hence *izzat* of my informants, that all the women's names used herein are pseudonyms.

Allama Iqbal contended that Islamic tradition can accommodate social change as its very nature is based on change (Adams, 1982: 122). This becomes evident through the life stories presented here, as we come to understand the complex changes that have been brought about in various dimensions of women's personal and public empowerment due to the twin factors of industrialization in Lahore and sociopolitical events affecting women everywhere in Pakistan. I focus on the women's own views of the kinds of changes they see occurring in their lives and what they regard as both preferable and possible in the context of development so as to generate ideas for alleviating the problems they confront. These ideas are discussed in the conclusion and have been presented to the Ministry for Women's Development of the government of Pakistan with the hopes that they will someday be implemented into viable projects from which the women of the Walled City will benefit.

I am very thankful to the many people and organizations which have facilitated this research. My research in the Walled City was funded through a three-month Senior Fulbright Islamic Civilization Research Grant. I gratefully acknowledge Sabeeha Hafeez's support of my request to be affiliated with the then Women's Division of the Cabinet Secretariat, as the fact of affiliation consistently encouraged me to see through my fieldwork despite temperatures reaching 130 degrees Fahrenheit; I was and remain hopeful that it will result in an applied benefit for the women in the Walled City. Sociologists from the Lahore Development Authority, particularly Fauzia Roohi, were extremely helpful in providing me with various maps and copies of research they and others had conducted within the Walled City. I am grateful to Khawar Mumtaz, Khokhar and Tauqir for introducing me to Miss Gohar Bano and Mrs. Parveen Akhtar, my fine research assistants, who administered the hundred surveys in the first stage of my research.

I am unable to personally acknowledge everyone who helped and supported me while I was conducting my fieldwork, but I would at least like to thank them. Special thanks go to Rani and her family for all they did; all my dear ones from Rajoa, Sahiwal, and Therkhanwala; to Nan for helping me to remember who I was; and most of all, to the wonderful family on Fane Road that treated me as one of their own. A most special note of acknowledgment and thanks goes to Miss Nasim Hussain, my very special research assistant and now sister, who accompanied me all over the Walled City, put up with my constant enthrallment over her natal home, and helped me see the fieldwork through to its end.

Many people helped in generating ideas for this research and in the period of analysis that followed. In particular, I would like to warmly thank Hina Jilani, Asma Jehangir, Khawar Mumtaz, Kamil Mumtaz, Robert Bellah, Gerry Berreman, Shahid Javed Burki, Mark Juergensmeyer, Diana Martin, Hanna Papanek, Bruce Pray, and, most especially, Barbara D. Metcalf. While I was a Lecturer at the University of Hong Kong, Conoor Kripalani-Thadani and the Centre of Asian Studies were consistently supportive and helpful; I am grateful to CAS for providing funding for Cecilia Poon to conduct bibliographic research prior to my fieldwork. I am very thankful for the support of my colleagues in Eugene, especially Cynthia Brokaw, Gerry Fry, Galen Martin, Valmik Ahuja, and Nancy Worthington. I greatly appreciate the University of Oregon Summer Study Award and the Oregon Committee for the Humanities Summer Award that enabled me to write up the results of this research while in residence as a Visiting Fellow at the Institute of Development Studies, University of Sussex during the summer of 1989. I would like to thank IDS for their invitation, and all those at IDS who, through their interest in this research, raised issues I had not previously considered and who certainly contributed to its timely conclusion.

Finally, I would like to thank, once again, all the women of the Walled City who participated in this research, who shared their dreams, struggles, and prayers with me. *Insha'allah*, all these dreams will someday be realized.

Anita M. Weiss

Notes

1. Good overviews of the circumstances faced by Pakistani women in general include Hafeez (1983), Shah (1986), and Mumtaz & Shaheed (1987).

2. The World Bank estimates this labor force participation rate was 6.0 percent in 1981. Refer to World Bank (1990: xxxi) for these and additional statistics comparing women's status in Pakistan to that in five other Asian countries.

3. General analyses include Rogers (1980), Bay (1982) and Buvinic et al., (1983). Comparisons with Pakistan can also be raised with analyses of working women elsewhere in the Muslim world, e.g., see Youssef (1974), Beck & Keddie (1978) and Papanek (1981).

4. This issue has been pursued by Beneria (1982) and Fawcett et al. (1984) and Thorbek (1987). Research on women's informal sector activities include Mies (1981), Jules-Rosette (1982), March & Taqqu (1982), and *IDS Bulletin* (1982).

5. The LDA had surveyed approximately 70 percent of the Walled City, which they had divided into 237 sections of 1/4 hectare each. I randomly selected grid no. 6, and then chose the 34th grid that followed, resulting in the selection of seven grids: 6, 40, 74, 108, 142, 176, and 210. We determined that ten interviews would be conducted within each grid. We then evaluated the areas of the Walled

City which had been excluded. Working from a larger Walled City map, I selected a locale inside Bhati Gate for ten interviews and selected four locales within which five interviews each would be conducted: Kucha Talian, Chuna Mandi, the Waterworks by Masti Gate, and another locale by Masjid Wazir Khan. My research assistants were instructed to randomly select a house in which to conduct an interview in each of the twelve areas. They were then to leave six residences and conduct the next interview with the household residing on the next level of the building until their quota for a given area was filled.

Preface to the Second Edition

It has been fourteen years since I lived in Gali Sirki Bandan, inside Lohari Gate, and conducted the initial field research for this book you have before you. I have returned many times, and still greet the same shopkeeper, *chik* maker, *istrywala* (ironer), and various box makers. The women in my *kucha* who had young children then are now thinking of their marriages. The drains are covered, but the noise and air pollution is more unbearable than ever for the local inhabitants.

The cultural richness that I had tried to capture in this book still pervades many parts of the Walled City, but is increasingly endangered. As I wander along the main bazaar inside Lohari Gate, I see the kinds of changes that underscore significant structural transformations occurring throughout the Walled City. Shops which were once open to the cool night air are often now encased in glass, although the shop owners are nowhere to be seen because most no longer live in the Walled City. Globalization is evident nearly everywhere, with goods originating from around the world available in Walled City bazaars. The World Bank's Walled City Redevelopment Project has covered many of the open drains that meandered through the kuchas and muhallas for hundreds of years and which had contributed to airborne and waterborne diseases, particularly in the hot summers. Despite this physical improvement, however, the overall health of the Walled City's residents does not seem to have improved markedly. Indeed, the promise of physical improvements has had problematic results for renters here. They have seen their landlords sell property in unprecedented numbers as land prices have risen astronomically with the expansion of the Azim Market wholesale cloth bazaar. Havelis which had housed multiple households in such areas as Chuna Mandi and Mochi Darvaza have been torn down and replaced by wholesale merchant shops, all in the name of 'progress' and economic growth. Residents of many such areas have been forced to seek accommodation elsewhere in the city of Lahore.

To do so, however, changes the shape of community. The social ethos of the Walled City has long stood apart from the rest of the city of Lahore. But as Walled City residents disperse to Lahore's new environs, women in particular now face challenges they had never known before. Economic pressures markedly increased as Pakistan underwent economic restructuring in the 1990s, with a concomitant rise in domestic and public violence against women. Home-based work—be it sewing, embroidery, stringing flowers, or tutoring—described in this book that supports women in the Walled City, is difficult to find in these new environs. When women can find such work, they are now more isolated in their efforts, unlike the more communal exchanges which generally occurred in the Walled City. When they cannot find such work and are forced to leave their homes in search of other employment in the wake of economic pressures, they must learn to navigate transport systems, crowds, and the legalities inherent in working in the formal sector of the labor force. Importantly, too, they must navigate new arenas of gender relations, for they now often work beside men who might be customers, colleagues or supervisors. In a context where women had limited contact with any men outside of their own family until their marriage, and then highly limited and restricted contact with unrelated men following their marriage, the social implications of such changing gender dynamics are enormous.

While gender relations are shifting, economic options for women remain marginal. In the past decade, a greater percentage of women have entered the formal sector of the labor force than ever before, though in official estimates they comprised only 28 per cent of the labor force (the lowest percentage of any South Asian country) in 1998.[1] Most of these opportunities, however, exist for women from middle and upper class backgrounds who are well educated; formal sector labor for working class women hailing from the Walled City consists mainly of factory-based production. In 1999, 39 per cent of all working women in Pakistan earned less than Rs. 1500 monthly; just 12 per cent earned more than Rs. 4000 monthly.[2] While the home-based work described within continues to dominate women's economic options, a far greater percentage of women engage in such work because of the economic restructuring that Pakistan has undergone. With the devaluation of the rupee (at the time of writing this, it is approximately Pak Rs. 66 = US $1) there has not been a concomitant rise in earnings, and hence absolute income for many households has fallen.

The resultant rise in women's economic participation has brought greater attention to the reality of violence against women in various domains. The Government of Pakistan's Ministry for Women's Development is now commissioning baseline studies to identify the prevalence of domestic violence. However, as I have frequently returned to the Walled City in these ensuing years, I hear more accounts of public and domestic violence against women than ever before. Changing gender roles, and the subsequent social power women gain from earning an income, are being constructively renegotiated in many homes, though not in all. As men increasingly find themselves unable to support their families financially and must 'live off the labor of their women', there is ample confusion about how to navigate these new social realities. At a meeting I held with some two dozen men inside Bhati Gate, virtually all of the men understood the economic necessities that were propelling the women in their households to seek remunerative work. But many of their images of how women were to do this were unrealistic, ranging from being sequestered (often alone!) with no interactions with males whatsoever at the workplace, to being able to offer tutoring to children in their homes and earn a substantive income (despite there being so much competition to do this).

Many men finally admitted their anger to me over having to contend with the new economic uncertainties. In our group, however, the frank discussion took an unanticipated turn. Some started to verbally assault one of the men at our meeting for beating his wife. They clearly knew who the perpetrators of domestic violence were, but given social norms of relations between non-kin, they rarely interfere in each other's domestic matters. In this instance, they took the opportunity to engage in a public, collective action and hence no one man could be singled out as the primary interloper.

The political atmosphere for women has also transformed substantially since I first conducted the field research for this book. As you read about women's hopes and dreams for the future, you will see how, in 1987 under the waning years of the late dictator General Ziaul Haq, the promise of a better future under a government led by Benazir Bhutto captured the imagination of many of these women. They often saw her as an important role model, a woman who could help fix the country's social and economic wounds. Today, she and many compatriots from her Pakistan People's Party—including Jehangir Badr, the working class hero from the Walled City—along with a wide berth of politicians from many other parties, are being charged with corruption and having accumulated substantial wealth disproportionate to their known sources of income. On the ground, this manifests as further disillusionment with politics and politicians. The recent allegation in August 2001 by international lenders that Rs. 30 billion is missing from Pakistan's failed Social Action Programme serves to strengthen sentiments such as those expressed by a widow in this book that only politicians and bureaucrats are served by social welfare programs, to the detriment of the poor. Alienation from the political process coupled with the economic transformation described above contribute to a greater sense of despondency than I had expected, or had hoped, would exist among Walled City inhabitants at the dawn of the 21st century.

There is a beacon of hope, however, that has already started to empower some women in the Walled City. Since the late 1980s, Pakistan has witnessed an extraordinary rise in the quantity—and quality—of Non-Government Organizations (NGOs) throughout the country. In the Walled City, the local Business and Professional Women's Association has established a literacy, health, and skills training center inside Yakki Gate; other NGOs offer free legal aid counselling and basic health care assistance. At the provincial and federal levels, the major political parties as well as the government have also made some efforts in this regard. By the early 1990s, each of the major political parties included mandates in their election platforms outlining their goals to empower women by addressing women's socio-economic needs and connecting these to long-term national objectives. By the February 1997 elections, they each placed women's empowerment, in some way, at center stage of their political agenda. An unprecedented 29 women contested seats in the National Assembly in that election; five women were actually elected.

At the federal level, an alliance has emerged between NGOs, donor agencies, and the state, which had relied heavily on NGO activists in developing its National Report for the UN women's conference in Beijing and in clarifying Pakistan's position on the then-proposed Platform for Action. The Beijing Follow-up Unit (BFU) became a collaborative effort to maintain the energy and momentum for women's empowerment that characterized the preparatory process and to integrate key themes into Pakistan's planning strategies for the Ninth Five-Year Plan, 1998–2003. The position paper on women's development for the Ninth Plan stated:

> Pakistan has made a firm commitment towards the empowerment of women, both through the ratification of the Convention on the Elimination of All Forms of Discrimination Against Women (CEDAW), as well as its commitment to the Platform for Action adopted at the Fourth World Conference for Women in Beijing. Women's development should, therefore, be viewed as a key element in the approach to the Ninth Plan. It must be remembered that women are not a 'group', but account for half the population of Pakistan, and their concerns need to be addressed in every sector.

The Government of Pakistan took a step further and ratified CEDAW, the UN Convention on the Elimination of All Forms of Discrimination Against Women, on 12 March 1996. The following year, it finalized the National Plan of Action outlining, in detail, how it planned to implement the Beijing Platform for Action throughout the country. In 2000, it constituted a permanent National Commission on the Status of Women (NCSW) to identify discriminatory practices and other challenges confronting women in the country. The devolution of power plan formulated by the present government of Pervaiz Musharraf has reserved one-third of elected seats in the local elections for women. In Lahore, there was no dearth of female applicants contesting such seats. Plans too are underway, championed by women from various quarters in Pakistan, to ensure one-third representation of women in the national assembly elections that are to be held in late 2002, although these are not yet finalized. Also not finalized is the National Policy on Women that is being vetted throughout the country at this time, which will provide a vision for where Pakistan hopes to proceed to provide an enabling environment for the empowerment of its women.

The implications of most of these various policy changes on women's lives in the Walled City of Lahore remain ambiguous at this time. Indeed, such policy changes will not necessarily result in implementation of empowering projects for women. However, for Pakistan, a country that has both neglected human development and has a limited history of non- governmental social activism (especially prior to 1988), this heralds a decisive stage. This kind of interactive, collaborative process— providing opportunities for a range of voices and opinions in Pakistan's planning strategies—holds great promise to further facilitate the rise of a civil society in the various social domains of Pakistan, which will in turn serve to empower women to participate in it. The legitimacy now placed on women to participate actively in the political process, either at the local level to serve as a nazim or in future national assembly elections, may indeed prove to be the most decisive policy change of all.

The women whose lives are recounted in the following pages are strong women whose distinct visions of survival strategies and empowerment are shared herein. Enabling such women to gain a political voice—and be listened to—may well herald an entirely new chapter in the lives of all women in the Walled City of Lahore.

Anita M. Weiss
September 2001

Notes

1. Source: World Bank, 2000. *World Development Indicators 2000*. Washington, D.C.

2. Mahbub ul Haq Human Development Centre, 2000. *Human Development in South Asia 2000: the Gender Question*, Oxford University Press, p. 71.

1

Walled City Life

The Walled City of Lahore -- the *andaroon shahar*, the inner city -- comprises approximately one square mile sequestered within parameters delineated by thirteen ancient gates. (Refer to Map 1.1.) Over a quarter of a million people live within the area encompassed by the old walls which houses the largest concentration of urban poor in the country. This is a vibrant center of economic, social and political activity for both Lahore and the greater Punjab, and is widely considered the cultural heart of the province.

Life here appears to the outsider to exist in the public space of the male world: men hawk fruits, vegetables and *samosas* (spicy potato-filled dumplings) from small carts; run sewing machines in their tailoring shops; sell dry goods to a largely male clientele; work by hand fabricating tools in workshops and seem to congregate endlessly around tea stalls. Natural forces have not yet been conquered by technology as water usually only runs a few hours a day, load shedding of electricity seems to exist year round,[1] and dust is everywhere. This is a dynamic culture in action: social gatherings are held in public places; children are carrying covered trays with hot curries or *chana/kulcha* bought in the bazaar; hawkers sell their wares wherever they can find a temporary place to sit; and kites and homing pigeons fly from so many rooftops, plagued by the mass of electric wires hanging everywhere. Everyone simmers in the summertime, drinking hot tea throughout the day and taking care not to eat "heat-producing" foods such as eggs or red meat. The choked gutters, animal wastes and moat which surrounds parts of the Walled City become particularly aromatic in the heat. The smoky haze left by the *jamadars* who sweep the streets every morning but Sundays[2] dissipates by mid-afternoon. Men still sit outdoors at the bazaar in the winter, but now huddle around kerosene heaters or wood-burning fires, shawls wrapped snugly over their heads and bodies. Time is structured by its relationship to the five daily prayers announced by the *azan* in each of the many mosques, thereby making a watch virtually redundant. The

1

2

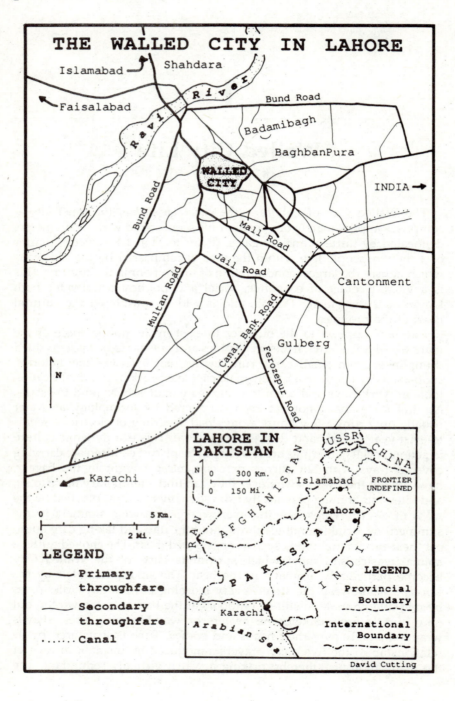

noise, the crowds, the tumult, the cramped alleyways, the horses/
camels/donkeys/oxen pulling or carrying things while drivers urge
people in their path to save themselves, the *halwa/puri* and *nihari* (spicy
meat curry) food stalls, the blaring Hindi film music, are all a part of this
accessible public sphere of life. But what is not, what is conspicuously
absent, is the presence of women.

Most of the Walled City is now framed by the Circular Road which is
about three miles in circumference. Johnson (1979: 197) argues that the
Walled City has retained its essential character as a pedestrian enclave.
Except for the entrance at Shah Alami Gate leading to the wholesale
bazaar at Rang Mahal and the cloth bazaar at Azim Market, there is no
true two-way thoroughfare. Trucks, cars and motorized rickshaws at best
can navigate with difficulty in only limited areas near most entrance
gates, necessitating horse-drawn or hand-pulled carts to transport people
and goods within the city walls. One notices the unusually high
proportion of white horses in use; they can also be hired out to carry the
bridegroom at weddings.

Lahore is widely regarded as a city of gardens, but that is only now
true far away from the walls of the old city. While there were once
Mughal gardens adorning it, there is now ample decay of old, rotting
buildings. Lahoris take great pride in their city's physical beauty -- there
is an Urdu saying that if you have not seen Lahore you have not yet been
born -- but the spaciousness which marks the rest of Lahore is in noted
contrast to the high density existing within the old city's walls. Looking
up, the observer sees a panorama of historical magnificence, of arched
Hindu *jharokas* and latticed balconies, often in various states of disrepair
but frequently still in use. Looking laterally, there is a bustling, lively city
of foodsellers, shopkeepers and craftsmen. But it is in looking down that
we are reminded of Sir John Lawrence's statement made in 1852 that
Lahore presents "such peculiar sanitary difficulties," for conditions today
are not all that different from 137 years ago (Latif, 1892: 251). The
unpaved, dusty streets are the least of the sanitary problems: the open
drains and the refuse which piles up throughout the day awaiting the
street sweepers' morning visit contributes to a fairly unhealthy physical
environment.

Density is extremely high at 1100 persons per hectare compared with
160 persons per hectare for the metropolitan area of Lahore as a whole
(LDA, 1980: 11). Floor space is sometimes only 18 square feet per person
(LDA, 1979: 3). Wachowali bazaar, between Shah Alami Gate and Lohari
Gate, has a density of 786 people per acre, or 804,864 per square
kilometer (Johnson, 1979: 197). This compares to average densities per
square kilometer of 9,930 in Dhaka, 29,393 in Cairo, 88,135 in Calcutta,
and 8,772 in downtown New York City.[3] Such high densities, however,

are not a new feature in the Walled City. An early twentieth century account describes the city as being overcrowded and already in a decrepit shape and that "the streets of the Old City are narrow and tortuous, and are best seen from the back of an elephant."[4]

Large living areas had originally been constructed so as to accommodate many levels of extended kin living together. For purposes of economy today, these former *havelis* have been sectioned off into *katras*, which encompass smaller living units. In 1980, there were nearly 40,000 households in the Walled City, with an average household consisting of 7.2 persons (LDA, 1980: 109). One third of the women we surveyed in the Walled City live in households of six to eight persons while nearly half live in households of nine people or more; therefore, four-fifths live in households of six or more people. However, over half live in homes of only one or two rooms; more than three-quarters live in homes of one, two or three rooms, despite the large number of people per household.[5]

The city was laid out hundreds of years ago with thin streets and galis lined by high buildings providing cooling relief to the inhabitants below while seemingly eternally hiding the pavements in shadows. Minimum space exists for movement along the narrow walkways, causing buildings to be occupied usually by a shop or workshop on the ground level, with two or three levels of family living quarters above, and topped with a latrine and a flat roof.[6] It is difficult to recognize people in the darkness of the alleyways, in the inner sanctum of some *kuchas*. The high buildings enable social exchanges to be carried out on rooftops, where people sleep in the summer and from which they greet each other year-round.

The pre-Islamic history of Lahore similarly lies in shadows. The name is probably derived from one of the sons (Loh) of the Hindu deity Rama: Lahawar means the fort of Loh. But the communities which built the Hindu temple of Loh behind the Lahore Fort as well as many other temples left nearly half a century ago. Fifty years is a fairly substantial period in Lahore's history, as it is doubtful that Lahore is an ancient city. There is no mention of Lahore in connection with the invasion of Sikander (Alexander the Great) while other cities in the Punjab are cited by name (e.g. Khushab, Sialkot). The first historical record is that of Hiuen Tsiang, a Chinese traveller who describes it as a large Brahmanical city which he visited in 630 C.E. while on his way to Jullunder in East Punjab (Research Society of Pakistan, 1976: 323).

Mahmud of Ghazni did not go to Lahore for more than two decades after his first invasion into the Punjab, presumably due to its lack of importance at the time. He built a fort, Mahmoodpur, near Lahore, after annexing the Punjab in 1021 and left both fort and city in the charge of his counsellor, Malik Ayaz, in 1037. It is said that Malik Ayaz built the walls and fortress of Lahore miraculously in a single night. However he did it, the city was repopulated and greatly expanded by 1040 when it became the capital of the Ghaznivid dominions east of the Indus.[7] Malik Ayaz's tomb still lies near Rang Mahal, though the large garden which was once attached to it apparently disappeared during the Sikh era (Latif, 1892: 226).

By the twelfth century, Lahore was considered a center of learning with a highly educated population. In 1206, Sultan Aibak was crowned ruler of India in his Lahore residence. Most historical accounts (Thornton, 1850; Baqir, 1985) argue that the city was probably not yet centered within the current walls, but may have spread out as far as Icchra and Mian Mir's tomb.

However, after Aibak's death merely four years later, Lahore fell to the mercy of various invaders who repeatedly sacked it. This reduced the city again to a town of little significance for the next few hundred years. About 1421, Syed Mubarik Shah came to Lahore and had the fort and city walls rebuilt. This prompted the beginning of the "renaissance of Lahore" as numerous religious schools and *havelis* were also established (Kamil Khan Mumtaz, n.d.: 4). Mubarik Shah's own *haveli* still lies inside Mochi Gate, and is currently used as a Shi'a *imam bara* (religious sanctuary).

Lahore was to reach its peak in the next century when it became the quintessential Mughal city, the "grand resort of people of all nations and a center of extensive commerce."[8] The first Mughal Emperor, Babur, invaded Lahore in 1524. His famous grandson, Akbar, made the first significant architectural change by enclosing the part of the city housing the bulk of its residents within "a brick wall of considerable height and strength" sometime during his residence there between 1584-1598 (Latif, 1892: 85). Akbar's son, Jehangir, is responsible for making the city famous as he encouraged music, art and drama to flourish during his tenure. He fixed his court there in 1622, and was later buried just on the other side of the Ravi river. The following Mughal emperors built some of Lahore's greatest architectural treasures including the Badshahi Mosque, which is within the Walled City.

By the eighteenth century, the population of the city, including the sizable proportion which had spilled out over the Walls, was about a half million persons. However, following Nadir Shah's invasion of India in 1738, Ahmad Shah Durani's attack on Lahore a decade later, and various skirmishes with the Sikhs, the population of Lahore dramatically decreased in the ensuing century.[9]

Ranjit Singh headquartered his empire in Lahore in 1798, though by then the city had become virtually deserted and many of its buildings and artifacts had been destroyed. The Sikh troops are said to have transformed the Badshahi Mosque into an arsenal storage, and desecrated many of the Muslim shrines. In 1812, Ranjit Singh rebuilt the decaying walls of the Mughals. He ordered the construction of a very tall double wall separated by a moat, with gun towers in the outer wall. In the forty years of his rule, Lahore regained some of its prosperity and population, and the Walled City was physically enhanced by the construction of some more spectacular *havelis* (Kamil Khan Mumtaz, n.d.: 15).

The impact of the British within the Walled City is similarly mixed. After the British annexation of the Punjab in 1849, Lahore's political importance increased while Amritsar's decreased. The indigenous population of Lahore was largely restricted to the Walled City.[10] However, while the British governed it, they themselves rarely lived within the Walled City. Instead, they built up a colonial city around it and only went within the walls when necessary.[11]

In 1859, the British had the moat which encircled the Walled City filled in and planted gardens there instead. The outer defensive wall was totally destroyed, and the inner wall reduced by half. The British effected two changes which significantly improved the lives of inhabitants of the Walled City. The first was the construction of the "Paniwala Tilab," a reservoir set inside Kashmiri Gate. The initial water tank constructed in 1881 soon collapsed, and a new one was finally completed in 1884 (Latif, 1892: 298-99). The second change was the construction of Mayo Hospital in October 1871. While outside the walls, it is within easy walking distance of the most densely populated parts and is widely considered to be the most important hospital to the Walled City's inhabitants. The British colonial government decided to build a new wing (thereby adding on three more buildings) for the hospital to commemorate the visit of Prince Albert Victor to Lahore in 1890. The new wing formally opened in 1892.

Pakistan's independence, achieved on August 14, 1947, occurred in tandem with the partition of the subcontinent. Many parts of the Walled City ended up in flames, especially those *kuchas* historically identified with Hindus and Sikhs. Popular lore estimates that about half of the old city's residents abandoned their homes and fled to India during Partition; new Muslim occupants replaced them. It is assumed that many of the *muhajirs* who settled in the Walled City were poor as it was here that the "evacuee property" was in the least demand (PEPAC, 1987: 19). Some *muhajirs* came with kin, others had to create "kin," and a renewed culture comprising over a quarter of a million people was built upon the rubble of the old.[12]

In the past decade, local and international planners have tried to make substantive improvements, especially in sanitation, within the Walled City, as well as refurbish some of the Gates[13] and other cultural sites. While all concerned are eagerly supportive of these efforts, especially the hygenic improvements, residents and planners are still trying to reconcile how to deliver such new systems and yet maintain the sociocultural integrity and historical legacy existing within the Walls.

Women Within the Walls

Fatima Mernissi (1987: 148) argues that the design of sexual space in Muslim society projects "a specific vision of female sexuality." This vision in the Walled City is one of being protected from the outside world where a woman -- and therefore her family's respectability -- is at risk. Women here live under the traditional constraints associated with *purdah*, which creates very differentiated male and female spheres. *Purdah*, literally translated as "curtain" in Urdu, has come to connote the symbolic, physical and practical separations between the activities of men and those of women (Papanek, 1973). Most women spend the bulk of their lives physically within their homes; they go outside only when there is a substantive purpose. As the culture outside the home traditionally revolved entirely around the actions of men, it was considered shameful for a man to send the women of his family outside to labor.

Historically, however, the actual practice of *purdah* was of greater importance to the propertied classes than to the working masses. Paradoxically, gender restrictions now appear to be less severe for upper-class women, especially where socioeconomic activities are concerned. Perceptions of social propriety have, to a large extent, already been transformed regarding women's actions and participation to include those activities in which upper-class women tend to engage, such as working as journalists, teaching in universities or managing independent businesses. In effect, traditional mores continue to pertain to working class women, although they have been redefined for many upper-class women.

The means by which poor women have been able to act outside of their mandated roles traditionally have been very limited. In the past, only the very poorest of women would engage in labor for compensation. Furthermore, there is a strong distinction between those roles (e.g. midwife, sweeperess, nanny) which were available to Muslim women in the urban setting of pre-partition Lahore and those which may now be available to them in its industrializing, changing environment. However, while women seem to be engaged in new types of work, one aspect appears to remain the same: while their labor does open up opportunities to earn an income, this occurs under discriminatory and highly exploitative circumstances that offer little opportunity for mobility and questionably affects empowerment.

The design of sexual space within the walls of the old city is dramatically different from that existing outside. The latter is marked by bungalows enclosed in gardens bordered by high walls, with each bungalow home to no more than one extended family.[14] Social life can be lived on the lawn, out of doors, but still well beyond the watchful gaze of others outside the family. It is expected that in the course of daily life, all sorts of people will come and go, and community markets were designed to be visited by all family members. Women, therefore, could easily sit outdoors, sleep outdoors, cook outdoors and so forth, separated from the outside world by the walls of their own homes. But everyday necessities (e.g. food, cloth) are not immediately obtainable nor are special events (e.g. marriages, relatives' residences, religious places) close at hand. Women outside the Walled City *must* leave their homes for physical and social survival, and even though their family members may carefully note the movements of female relatives, these women are beyond the inquisitive purview of non-kin.

Such imagery, however, does not articulate life within the Walled City. Women's lives are enclosed within the walls of their homes, and their social activities become largely constrained within the walls of the old city. Perceptions of great distances are relative as most of life's important tasks are performed in a very concentrated parcel of space: food, spices, fresh milk, cloth and household goods are found within a short walk of every *kucha*. People attend weddings nearby as relatives often live nearby, often "2-4" *galis* away ("2-4" is the conventional expression for a small amount of time, space or quantity). Females attend schools nearby, visit doctors nearby, and will visit a saint's shrine regularly if it is also nearby. For example, the shrine of the most important saint of Lahore, Hazrat Data Ganj Baksh, lies near Bhati Gate, but only women living near it reported to me that they visited it on a regular basis. Therefore, overcrowded living conditions themselves have become a form of social control in this environment where women's activities are circumspect. Few women wish to risk drawing additional attention to themselves by leaving the security of the *kucha* where all of their contact with others can be readily observed, monitored and hence win approval. This, combined with a community-based orientation and influenced by Islamic notions of the demarcation of sexual space between male and female activities, leaves little room for women to justify leaving the *kucha*, and certainly not on a regular basis.

Formal data on women living in the fifteen populated census wards (86-100) which comprise the Walled City is limited. All we know from Census data is that females were 46.6 percent of the total population in 1981, and that 12.4 percent were educated to tenth class or greater.[15]

However, other information can provide us with a general understanding of the milieu in which women of the Walled City live. For example, "area of origin" is an extremely important concept in the

Pakistani cultural framework today as tribal affiliation (*qaum*) now hold relatively little meaning to most (though not all) groups. It ties one's family to a still larger group beyond their own *biradari* (clan) and serves as a basis for a group identity. The most important differentiation in the Walled City are those who are native to it versus those whose families are *muhajirs*, migrants from India at Partition. In 1979, the Lahore Development Authority found that 52 percent of their respondents had been born in Lahore (45 percent within the Walled City itself) and 36 percent were *muhajirs*. It should be noted, however, that the informants for this as well as various other socioeconomic surveys which the Lahore Development Authority has conducted in the Walled City over the past decade were male heads-of-households, presumably the senior male in the home.

The origins of the families of the one hundred women we surveyed are similar, though they show a slightly higher degree of identification with being from Lahore: 62 percent of all families had originated from Lahore while 28 percent were *muhajirs*. However, when some of the younger women were questioned further it turned out that some of them identified their families as being from Lahore when it was their grandparents who had been muhajirs. Of the women themselves, 62 percent had been born in the Walled City, 11 percent were born elsewhere in Lahore and only 14 percent are *muhajirs*. (Had we surveyed only the senior-most woman in each household, the latter figure presumably would have been higher.)

Language is another important marker of identity. Lahore is a tri-lingual environment in which Punjabi, Urdu and English are all used for different purposes although Punjabi is native to the city. More than three-fourths of our respondents consider Punjabi as their "mother tongue" while the remaining consider Urdu to be so (i.e., there were no native speakers of Pashto, Sindhi, Baluchi or English). Christopher Schackle (1970: 241) writes that "Urdu was the main literary vehicle of the Muslim elite of India," and it follows that as few women resident in the Walled City are elites, they use Punjabi, and not Urdu, for everyday discourse. This includes women who are descendants of *muhajirs* for whom Urdu was initially a "mother tongue." In addition, that these women commonly use Punjabi implies that there are given cultural domains in which Urdu and English are spoken (mostly concerning politics, economics and current events) which have little or nothing to do with their lives. That they understand Urdu, though, underscores the popularity of Hindi/Urdu films and film music. However, while Punjabi is a colorful and expressive language, women in the Walled City do not seem to have a unique vocabulary among themselves as tends to be the case among secluded women in North Africa and elsewhere.

As noted earlier, four-fifths of the women in our survey live in households of six or more persons, as shown in Table 1.1. We felt it important to identify who it is they actually live with as it enables us to further understand cultural norms and trends. Table 1.2 reveals that extended families continue to be the norm for many -- though not the majority -- of women in the Walled City. Given the presence of patrilocal residence patterns, the high proportion of women living with sisters and daughters is interesting. No respondent lives with more than four brothers as few families have large numbers of sons, presumably because many women begin to control their fertility when they feel secure that they have enough sons. If they do not, they may well continue to "try" for a son, thereby creating large families of females while they wait for a boy. In addition, most women live with their sons for much of their lives: no woman with whom we spoke had a son with whom she no longer lived. The relatively low percentage of respondents living with a mother-in-law is explained because (a) 25 percent of respondents have never been married; (b) a mother-in-law may live with another of her sons other than the respondent's husband; and (c) the mother-in-law might be deceased

TABLE 1.1: Household Size in the Walled City

Household Occupants (number)	Respondents (percent)
One	1
Two	4
Three-Five	15
Six-Eight	33
Nine or More	47

TABLE 1.2: Occupants of Households in the Walled City

Relatives Women Reside with	Respondents (percent)
Husband	60
Either or both parents	24
Mother-in-law	13
Either or both in-laws	22
Sister(s)	18
Brother(s)	19
Son(s)	60
Daughter(s)	60
Other Relatives	34

(as is often the case with older women as this group has low life expectancy rates).

An important distinguishing characteristic of women's lives within the Walled City — their highly limited mobility -- is underscored by how long they have lived in their current home. We found that 18 percent of women in our survey have lived in their current home since birth, and 28 percent have lived there since marriage; i.e., almost half have lived in solely one home for a significant period of their lives.

This is related to the fact that the majority of residents or their close relatives own the building in which they live.[16] However, while nearly three-fourths of the women surveyed lived in buildings owned within their family, the interviewed women themselves accounted for only 4 percent of all owners, as shown in Figure 1.1. Husbands and/or in-laws account for the largest group of owners. This could not be accurately broken down further as many women were unclear as to who precisely owned the building: but they knew it wasn't themselves. The building is generally either an ancestral home (in the family for generations) or was allocated to the family as evacuee property when they migrated from India in 1947. A third of the women surveyed live in an ancestral home (either consanguinal or affinal).

Another insight into the lives of women in the Walled City can be derived from looking at commonly possessed household items and recent purchases. In a 1979 survey, the Lahore Development Authority found that radios, televisions, sewing machines and bicycles were the most common "big ticket" items in Walled City homes. In our survey nearly a decade later, we found that major purchases were concentrated more on televisions, refrigerators, washing machines and fans. However, nearly half of the women stated that their families had not purchased any of these goods in the past five years. While these items are desired, poverty prevents their being acquired.

From the type of goods desired, it becomes apparent that the Walled City is a working class area. Income statistics substantiate this observation (Table A.1, in Appendix). In 1980, the LDA estimated that over two-thirds of all households had monthly incomes below Rs. 1,000 ($60). In 1984, the LDA (1984: 12) estimated that 53.7 percent of heads of households in the Walled City had monthly incomes between 500 and 1,000 rupees; 27.8 percent had incomes ranging between 1,000 and 2,000 rupees monthly. In our survey, 54 percent of the women stated that their husband was the major income earner in their home, 16 percent said it was their parents, and 12 percent stated it to be a brother. Two-thirds of the families have no savings; of those who do, however, half of the women keep some savings separately. We do realize that these figures should be regarded only as approximate for because respondents are generally hesitant to

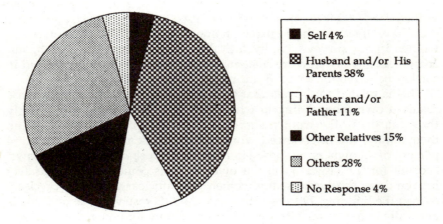

Self 4%

Husband and/or His Parents 38%

Mother and/or Father 11%

Other Relatives 15%

Others 28%

No Response 4%

FIGURE 1.1: Homeowners in the Walled City

reveal their true income, male respondents (in the case of LDA figures) hardly ever include the earned income of women in their families, and many women are unaware of their family's true income and/or given their fluid regard for numbers they often generalize the amount.

Gaining Entrance Through the Gates

A physical infrastructure reflects the social norms, sentiments and vision of a people who built it and then is altered to accommodate change. There are certain associations we can make with the Walled City -- particularly with each gate (*darvaza*, door) and some *kuchas* -- that are relatively stable and speak to us about the cultural orientations behind the layout of the area.[17] (Refer to Map 1.2.) Anyone who has ever ventured through the gates to the Walled City will affirm that they are not merely entryways. They symbolically demarcate the indigenous from the European, a cultural ethos from an alien adaptation.

Each gate is identified with particular sociocultural attributes and generally boasts a unique history. Though most of the wall no longer exists, continuous waves of buildings virtually recreating the wall remain. Therefore, it is through the gates that one still gains entry into the Walled City. Each *kucha* derives a part of its identity from the nearby gate. The cultural cohesiveness of the community which historically populated each *kucha* emerges from the architecture as the majority of buildings pre-date

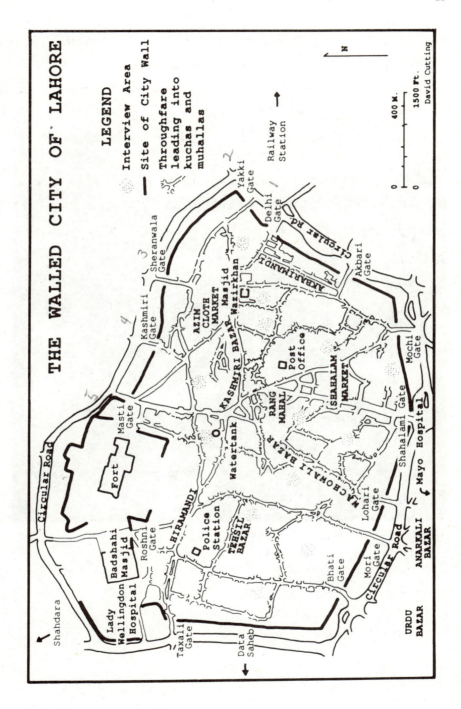

THE WALLED CITY OF LAHORE

LEGEND

Interview Area

Site of City Wall

Throughfare
leading into
kuchas and
muhallas

David Cutting

The busy bazaar outside of Lahori Gate.

Breakfast in a Walled City bazaar on a winter morning.

A *rehra* used for transporting goods within the Walled City.

Men smoking a *hookah* in a *kucha*. The stairs lead up to a one-room residence. A public tap lies in front of them.

An area being rebuilt, leading into Kashmiri bazaar.

Preparing food in Suter Mandi.

A bridegroom accompanied by a bank on his way to his brid's family's house, at the entryway to Lahore Gate.

An early morning view of people sleeping on *charpais* on their roof in the Walled City.

A *kucha* near Kashmiri Gate. The drains on either side of the path have been partially covered by cement.

Selling prepared foods from a cart in a Walled City bazaar. Note the *jharoka* and electric wires.

Partition.[18] To a large extent, this sociocultural cohesiveness remains, as recognized by Lahore Development Authority (1980: 18) sociologists who write:

> Socially it is a well integrated society with roots and family ties which bind clans, frateries, guilds, ethnic and religious groups which provide every resident a sense of security and belonging. The incidence of crime is extremely low and the one quality that strikes any visitor to the Walled City is the friendliness and hospitality of its residents.

The grand aged buildings, now in a state of severe decline, have witnessed many changes in the city's face, most significantly the demolition of its outer fortifying wall after the British takeover in 1857 and the destruction of large parts of Shah Alami bazaar and other Hindu areas in the violence accompanying Partition. Few of the wooden buildings have been repaired to their former splendor. There are many vacant lots where buildings were demolished long ago but now only rubble remains; no new structure was ever built. When owners have constructed new buildings, these are usually plain concrete edifices devoid of former balconies, *jharokas*, carved wooden doors bordered by Kufic script, and other aspects of the architectural majesty which we associate with many old city buildings. Commendable efforts are  underway to redevelop selected parts of the old city and install new water and sewage lines, but the task is formidable.[19]

The gate best known to historians -- but for practical purposes least important to the inhabitants of the Walled City -- is Roshni Gate. Providing an entranceway to the city between the Badshahi Mosque and the Lahore Fort, Roshni Gate is hardly even considered a gate today as few people use it for their daily comings and goings. Latif (1892: 85) writes that historically "it was most frequented by the omerahs, courtiers, royal servants, and retinues; and, as the quarters about here were profusely lighted up at night, it was called the "gate of light," or "gate of splendor." The fort, however, is no longer home to those who rule Lahore. They have instead moved to the Upper Mall, to large multi-storeyed houses set in courtyards with high walls. Except for mid-day prayers on Fridays, Eids and other holidays of note when men come to offer their prayers, mostly tourists frequent the Badshahi Masjid, the most enthralling mosque of the Mughals. Both groups generally enter the mosque's environs from Circular Road, not from Roshni Gate.

However, the part of the Walled City housed on the other side of Roshni Gate is an area which my survey did not cover as it includes the infamous *kucha* Hira Mandi, known for dancing and prostitution.[20] We decided that although Hira Mandi is an important historical and commercial part of the Walled City (housing a well-known high school in Dhiyan Singh's *haveli*), the life circumstances of women resident there differ dramatically from those elsewhere in the Walled City. Furthermore, we determined that given prevailing mores and values, conducting a survey and interviewing women in this area would threaten our research: none of my Pakistani research assistants would venture into the area, and my own respectability and the degree of freedom I enjoyed to mix with women in the Walled City would be compromised if it became known that I frequented the area. Even from Hira Mandi's architecture, observers know they are in an entirely different social domain and locality: every house has a wide *jharoka* complete with an open balcony framing onto a wide street below, just above the ground floor. Men can easily look up and view the "wares" for sale in the evening; the place is shuttered closed during the day, except for the few craftsmen making tablas and sitars in their shops to accompany the dancing which takes place at night. No other *kucha* had such consistent patterns of open balconies. Everywhere else, living space is private, and where there is a balcony or *jharoka* at all, it will frame into a private area, traditionally inhabited by kin (or fictive kin) in Muslim areas, or *biradari* members in Hindu ones.

Going clockwise around the city, the next gate is Masti Gate. Latif (1892: 85) presumes that this is a corruption of "Masjidi," pertaining to a mosque, probably that of Mariam Makani, Akbar's mother, which is in its immediate vicinity. Also nearby is the mosque of Mariam Zamani, Jehangir's mother, which is one of the most ancient mosques of the city. Surprisingly, few women offered the names of either of these mosques as places that they visit, despite the association of both with women.

Masti Gate is no longer a "gate" in a true sense as it lacks any sort of demarcation archway or pillar, though it serves as a popular entryway. It is possible to drive a car through Masti Gate to avoid the traffic on Circular Road by the Badshahi Masjid, and exit via Taxali Gate on the west. In former times, it used to be a dance area. Now, it is one of the least dense of the inhabited parts of the Walled City; it seems in a great state of uninhabited disrepair. Even the bazaar is uncrowded.

The third gate is Kashmiri Gate, so called because it faces in the direction of Kashmir. The masonry archway is barely wide enough for vehicles though they somehow seem to squish their way through it. Buses, often honking their horns loudly, crowd the exterior of the gate; there is a unique hush upon entering, for the sounds of modern technology are generally left behind.

Chuna Mandi, about a three-minute walk from Kashmiri Gate along paved streets bordered by shops, is both a famous *kucha* and bazaar area inside Kashmiri Gate. The largest *haveli* is that of Jemadar Khushal Singh, near the Sikh gurdwara of Guru Ram Das, the fourth Sikh Guru who was born in Chuna Mandi in 1534. The *gurdwara*, which now houses a free hospital, is towards the southern end of the bazaar. It is evident from its architectural remains that Chuna Mandi had once been an important Sikh area of the city, though it is now populated largely by Punjabi *muhajirs*. The *havelis* and *gurdwaras* have been sectioned off into smaller living quarters for which the government's Auqaf department, which oversees religious properties, charges the residents a nominal rent. Residential rights can be transferred through sale.

One of the informants in this study, Laila, age seventeen, lives in a former Hindu *haveli* which is reached by a very narrow entranceway off the bazaar. Once inside, the *haveli* is reminiscent of a village as women wash clothes by communal faucets, chickens walk about freely, and the high buildings of the city surrounding the *haveli* cannot be seen easily. Most of the residents are from Amritsar and are related to one another. The only non-relatives are *mochis* (shoemakers) from Uttar Pradesh. There is only one "flush" latrine in the entire *haveli*; most occupants use the rather unsanitary dry latrines variously located on the *haveli's* rooftops.

Laila's house consists of two small rooms. Her family pays about seventy rupees per month for the use of their house to the Auqaf department, and they can legally sell their rights to live there. The small entrance room is used as a kitchen. The large room in the rear is quite dark as lighting is provided only by a light bulb in the middle of the room. A large steel box with a red-frilled cover sits beneath two small suitcases in a corner. There is a small television and one bed. At night in the summer, everyone sleeps either outside in the center of the *haveli* or upstairs on the roof. In the winter, they double-up on *charpais* (string beds) which fill both of the rooms. A brick partition just short of the ceiling forms the room's rear wall behind which is Laila's *taya's* (father's older brother's) home. Laila's family can easily hear the many arguments which often rage behind the partition, such as a recent one between her cousins and the Hindustanis, *muhajirs*, who live upstairs because the latter had connected a pipe to the former's water tap to use their water. Her family does not "have marriages" with her *taya's* family because the latter "often fight...and they don't treat us well." Living in such close proximity without even a complete wall to separate the two families, no words go unheard nor actions go unnoticed.

This arrangement, however, is going through a major change. Laila's family recently told us that a legal case between the Auqaf department and a local *pehlwan* ("big" man) which had been pending for years has finally been settled, and that he is buying up a lot of land in Chuna Mandi. He has been paying 55,000 rupees per *marla* for the old residences and is in the process of knocking the buildings down in preparation for construction of a multi-level shopping plaza. While the price they are being paid is higher than many of the residents had expected, most are visibly upset because they cannot afford to buy other land within the Walled City, which, due to the activities of this pehlwan and others, has dramatically escalated in value. This is causing them to have to break up large extended families and move outside the Walls to other working class areas of Lahore, but where there is a different sense of community, a different economic and social environment and where, Laila fears, there will be greater restrictions placed on her movements.

The archway and access path from Circular Road to the fourth gate, Sheranwala, strongly resembles that of Kashmiri Gate. Both are popularly considered amongst the "nicest" parts of the Walled City in which to live nowadays. Latif (1892: 86) claims that it used to be called Khizri Gate, given that the Ravi river

> in former times flowed by the city walls, and the ferry was near this spot. The gate was, therefore, named Khizri, after the name of Khizr Elias (Phineas, a companion of Moses), the patron saint, according to the Muslim belief, of running waters and streams, and the discoverer of the water of immortality.

A short walk past the archway, there is an inner wall towering above the bazaar which sports concrete images of domesticated lions said to have been kept here by Ranjit Singh, hence giving the Gate its nickname the "lions' gate," or Sheranwala. While an automobile can enter through the archway, most soon make a sharp right turn, just after the mosque school, and head towards Khizri Muhalla and Kashmiri Gate as the road ahead is too narrow and crowded to navigate. When we see a large car followed closely by a Mitsubishi jeep behind us and both the foot traffic and motorcycles stopping at once, everyone stepping aside for them to pass, we take a closer look to see who is heading straight ahead. Everyone is turned away, scared to look at Aji Pehlwan, formerly the contractor responsible for collecting the tolls when people crossed the Ravi bridge and who is now said to be the *pehlwan* buying up all that land in Chuna Mandi and elsewhere in the Walled City. We've heard people talking about him as if he is a near-mythical figure, the manifestation of all their fears -- and some hopes, for he is the local boy who has become enormously wealthy and powerful. Is it just a coincidence that his guards in the second vehicle, armed with large rifles, are sitting in such a manner that their rifles just happen to stick out of the jeep windows?

We turn away to head towards Khizri Muhalla, passing the old *haveli* of Prince Naunihal Singh on our right. Ever since the British transformed it into a school, it has remained one of the most popular girls' elementary schools in the area.

Khizri Muhalla beckons closer inspection as it epitomizes traditional living arrangements. Entry into the *kucha* is via a masonry archway; the open sewer line winds its way -- as a river -- to each residence. It still houses a few large *havelis* though in recent years, as in Chuna Mandi, these have been divided up into smaller living units. A long-since disused water pump lies to the left, a place now for children to play. The vegetable seller, the fruit seller, the used metal and newspaper buyer all conduct their business from the unpaved streets calling to the stylized wooden windows above.[21] When the transaction is completed, a child is sent with money (or goods) to the vendor below. The streets are empty except for these vendors.

The next entrance to the Walled City is Yakki Gate, which today often resembles a horse market more than anything. The origin of the name is unclear. Latif (1892: 86) claims that it was originally called "Zaki," that being the name of

> a martyr saint who, according to tradition, fell fighting against the Moghal infidels from the north, while gallantly defending his city. His head was cut off at the gate, but the trunk continued fighting for some time, and at last fell in a quarter of the city close by. One tomb of this champion was consequently built at the spot where the head had fallen, and another at the place where the trunk lay.

This is a relatively minor gate as entry is usually for access to the nearby *kuchas* and not for general access to the city's interior. Population densities here are amongst the lowest in the Walled City at only 30.23 persons per acre (LDA, 1980: 108).

The following entryway, Delhi Gate, is one of the most important entrances to the commercial areas within the Walled City. As its name implies, it opens onto the road that leads from Lahore to Delhi, and today lies opposite the used clothing market, Landa Bazaar. The actual archway was rebuilt by the English Raj and is the widest of the existing traditional-styled entrances. The lead-in to Delhi Gate is a lively bazaar, with tongas, motorized rickshaws, cloth stands, racks of artificial jewelry, a butcher, a baker, and dry goods stands all competing for space. The cloth shops begin just on the other side of the gate, extending the entire distance up to Masjid Wazir Khan and into Kashmiri Bazaar. Kashmiri Bazaar runs nearly the entire breadth of the Walled City, petering out by Hakimwala Tehsil near Taxali Gate. From Delhi Gate, just to the right of Kashmiri Bazaar, runs Azim Market, the largest wholesale cloth market in Punjab and possibly the country.

Kashmiri Bazaar formally begins by Masjid Wazir Khan, one of the most spectacular mosques of the subcontinent. It was built in 1634 by Shah Jehan's royal physician, Wazir Khan, a native of Chiniot (Latif, 1892: 215). To ensure that the mosque would be taken care of in perpetuity, he bequeathed all the property surrounding the mosque for its maintenance. However, a clause that twenty shops surrounding the mosque be used for bookbinders no longer seems to be in force. The area underwent a lot of change at partition, and the bookbinders' shops seem to have been replaced by cloth stores. Latif (1892: 214-215) describes the mosque as an architectural monument of surpassing beauty and elegance. It is entirely covered with arabesque painting and lacquered tiles, and the inlaid pottery decorations and panelling of the walls are as vivid and glowing, as bright and perfect, as ever....the appearance of life and freshness in the variety and profusion of the colouring, as also the excellence and richness of the design, render these decorations the admiration of the spectator.

In recent years, there has been a fairly successful effort to refurbish the paintings and tiles. The stairway to the mosque is reached through an archway, which houses a variety of small shops. Visitors deposit their shoes at the top, and women take care to cover their hair. Entering the actual mosque, we see that it is

divided into five compartments each opening upon a spacious courtyard, and surmounted by a dome, the centre one, like the middle archway, being much larger and higher than the two on either side of it. At each corner of the quadrangle is a minaret of great height, with a gallery round it, from which a magnificent view of the city and suburbs is obtained. A reservoir in the middle of the courtyard of the cathedral supplies water for the ablutions of the faithful who resort to it. (Latif, 1892: 215)

During the heat of the summer, we would often take refuge in Masjid Wazir Khan. Sitting under a marble latticed frame, on a marble floor, we would feel a cool breeze as the water in the tank cooled the hot winds of Punjab's summers. This enclosure covers the stairway leading down to the tomb of Syad Mahomed Ishak.[22] While an occasional women goes down to visit this tomb, it is not the most important one in the vicinity of Masjid Wazir Khan to the women of the Walled City. Instead, they frequent the shrine of Syad Suf, a white-domed tomb in the square fronting the gateway to the mosque. Syad Suf was a contemporary of Syad Ishak, though his shrine wasn't built until 1852 at the directive of a British officer (Latif, 1892: 221). A small building is only now under construction enclosing the tomb. Floral wreaths are sold here for placement at the shrine. A visitor remains unaware that the flowers are strung by women living about a five-minute walk from the mosque.

But if we take that walk through the labyrinth of thin *galis* and open sewer lines, we eventually reach Muhalla Namd Garan, home to Gulzar Begum, another of the women who shared her life story with us. Whenever a visitor arrives in the summertime Gulzar Begum, despite her poverty, sends for a round hunk of ice from the bazaar along with a Royal Crown (RC) Cola. She cuts the ice with a knife on a fairly dirty cloth on the floor: some ice skids off, and then she puts all the ice in a cooler nearby. There are invariably a few neighbors or relatives sitting with her. Her father-in-law's brother is sleeping nearby, behind a door in a galley. He, his wife and their seven children live in two rooms upstairs along with his sister-in-law, Gulzar Begum's mother-in-law.

Gulzar Begum's house, about two *marlas* in size, feels very close and dark, with flowers, stems, petals and seeds covering much of the simple brick floor in the front room. There are a few rough pots and utensils in a corner placed on shelves which have been carved out of plaster in the wall. There is an old copper *hamam* for storing water, apparently from her dowry, on an upper shelf. Two wooden windows facing the *gali* in the front of the house provide some natural lighting. The one electric appliance is a black and white television set which her mother-in-law bought five years ago for Gulzar Begum's children. She and her two daughters, aged ten and sixteen, are eating on a bare wooden table about two feet off the floor and about 10 inches by 14 inches wide. Her cousin's six-year-old daughter is waiting for the elder daughter to finish eating and help her with her studies. The very small rear room appears cramped with a bed and a simple showcase.

Not far from here on the way towards Akbari Chowk live two more of our informants, Farida and Jamila. Farida's house, owned by her in-laws, consists of three storeys. Farida's husband is now a drug addict. Just across a small open space is Jamila's house; Jamila's husband abandoned her a few years ago. The house, in which both her father-in-law and *taya* were born, is well over a hundred years old. As she lives on the upper floor, the roof serves as a veranda from which the whole *kucha* can be viewed. However, the stairway leading up to the home is falling apart and there is a strong smell of dung; the latrine, in a small wooden enclosure in a corner of the roof, is falling apart.

Jamila is overweight, talkative, and very lively. People are always coming and going into her house. The house is actually comprised of one large room divided by a wooden partition making it seem to be two rooms. There is a slightly lower floor in the second room. There are two beds, one in each room, which are both covered by colorful floral sheets. The ceiling is made of plain, unfinished wood. There is a large steel *hamam* in the corner for washing dishes. She uses a steel bucket to take water from the public tap in the *kucha* (she has no running water). There is often no electricity due to load-shedding. Her small son is wearing dirty clothes: a white soiled shirt, white shorts. A soiled bandage is over his right eye, a vestige of an eye problem he incurred when he came down with typhoid a few weeks ago.

Walking back towards the mosque, we can make a left turn and walk towards Akbari Gate from the inside of the city. About halfway there, just by the Taj Mahel hairdresser's shop, we make a right turn by a toy shop to get to Kucha Kakazaiyan. The masonry buildings in this largely residential area all seem ancient. The Lahore Development Authority had selected this *kucha* in the early 1980s as one of two pilot areas for redevelopment.[23] Here we find Hasina, whose rented house is in one of the newer buildings right in the middle of the *kucha*. The landlord lives upstairs while Hasina, her husband, four sons and one daughter live in the three rooms downstairs. All three rooms have been whitewashed. Her bedroom doubles as a drawing room and contains good quality furniture including four upholstered chairs, a bed, a sewing machine, a dressing table, a showcase filled with china, a dining table, and a stool, all of which came in her dowry. Her sons sleep in the second room, which is also used for eating. The third is a tiny kitchen. Her family has the use of a flush toilet, though they must share it with their landlord's family upstairs.

As we make our way to the next entrance, Akbari Gate, we travel through an important, colorful and pungent food and spice market founded by the Emperor Akbar. While corn used to be the major commodity sold here, about the turn of the century Akbari Mandi became -- and remains -- the most important wholesale spice market in Lahore.

Kucha Pir Gillanian is one of the largest neighborhoods inside Akbari Gate. The various *galis* are straight unlike the labyrinths found elsewhere in the Walled City. Kanize's house opens onto a small *gali* off a main street in the *kucha*, and is a short walk to the boisterous market at Rang Mahal. In a corner of her house's large inner yard is a high pole with a black flag at the top, common in this predominantly Shi'a locale where black flags can be seen atop many of the homes. The flag is a symbol of her spiritual guide, Hazrat Abbas Alamdar, who was a half brother of Imam Hussain (the Prophet's grandson) and one of his faithful generals. Kanize, her father and her sister live in the sparsely furnished one room downstairs while her brother, his wife and son live upstairs. The family considers themselves fortunate that they have their own bathing area in their house.

The next entranceway, Mochi Gate, takes its name from the occupation of many of its inhabitants who were traditionally *mochis* (shoemakers).[24] The mosque of Mohamed Saleh, built in 1659, lies at the entrance to the gate. The mosque houses beautiful enamelled frescos decorated with Qur'anic verses. The greatest *haveli* here was known as Mubarak Haveli, built during the reign of Emperor Mahomed Shah. Ranjit Singh had kept Shah Shuja prisoner in this *haveli* from which he eventually escaped but only after giving up the Koh-i-Noor diamond.

Today, the open area outside of Mochi Gate is famous for holding political meetings. It was from here that the Pakistan People's Party (PPP) first took out a procession in 1986 heralding Benazir Bhutto's return to the country. Everyone within Lahore as well as many people throughout the country are aware of the political importance of holding meetings at Mochi Gate; often, there are separate areas sectioned off for women, though few women from the Walled City in fact attend. Nearby, from

Haveli Nawab Saheb, Shi'as begin their annual procession on Ashura (the tenth day of the month of Muharram) which will wind its way throughout the Walled City, and which often turns into a political rally as it heightens tensions between Shi'as and Sunnis.

Kucha Tirgran is reached by walking through a bazaar where small plastic toys -- animals, furniture, and games, as well as elaborate paper kites -- are displayed for sale. Through an archway across from the local PPP office and past a goat tethered by its owner, we come across a group of young boys playing "sandlot" cricket. The wooden buildings here are crumbling, though magnificent *jharokas* remain in use by their occupants. Erum's home is in a corner of the *kucha*. She lives in the middle portion of a three-storey house owned by her in-laws. The house is neatly organized and not overly fancy, with a refrigerator in the corner of the main room and all walls carefully whitewashed. The refrigerator was bought seven years ago; the television set was bought twelve years ago.

Erum was not born in the Walled City, but instead moved here after she was married. She has never really adjusted to living in such a small house in a high density area:

> I want a separate dining/drawing room, and separate bedrooms. I don't like all the disturbances. All the boys of the neighborhood collect below our house. From morning to evening, they play cricket and make a lot of noise. Sometimes even big boys play. They have broken my window panes in the kitchen.

The neighborhood boys sometimes pass comments, but really don't bother her four daughters. Until a few years ago, her family did have a lot of problems with water. When the tap was running downstairs where her mother-in-law lives, no water could reach the second floor where her family lives nor the third floor which houses her husband's brother's family. They bought a pump to increase the water pressure about five years ago. However, water remains a problem as it only runs between 5 - 9 a.m., 11 a.m.- 3 p.m., and 5 - 9 p.m.

There are rat problems in the *kucha* and although Erum is not overly concerned about them, she has placed a rat trap on her stairway and catches one occasionally. While a sweeper comes in the mornings -- and sometimes in the afternoons as well -- the *kucha* gets dirty again quickly.

There is a thin lane from Kucha Tirgran which winds its way towards the next gate, Shah Alami. Entry to this gate is the most different of all, for virtually nothing remains of the original Shah Alami Gate. It was largely destroyed in the riots and fires that occurred at Partition and the entire area nearly up to Rang Mahal has been rebuilt. Until reaching Rang Mahal, there is no visible demarcation underscoring that one is now inside the Walled City: this could just be another crowded area of Lahore, like Gujjar Singh or Lakshmi Chowk. The road begins to narrow as it approaches Rang Mahal, and motorized vehicles generally turn back at this point. This is perhaps the very heart of commercial activity in the Walled City: men selling everything from cloth to brassware to dry goods, either retail or wholesale.

The gate was probably named after Aurangzeb's son, the Emperor Shah 'Alam Bahadur Shah, who died in Lahore in 1712. Rang Mahal gets its name from the great *haveli* of Mian Khan which was once there, built during the reign of Shah Jahan and destroyed during British times. Latif (1892: 230) writes that this *haveli* at one time was

> the highest house in the city, furnished with ten wells, numerous halls and arched chambers, supported by pillars of stone, reservoirs and fountains of water, underground chambers, balconies and upper storeys... The female apartments are now used as places for working the grinding mills, of which about two hundred, with four hundred houses, exist at this time.

For a while, attached to the *haveli* was a courthouse called the *Rang Mahal*, which was later used as a Mission School. That same area is now home to one of the largest wholesale bazaars in the country, Rang Mahal. The old mills and houses have given way to countless shops. Nearby, the gold dome of the Sonehri Masjid, built in 1753, overlooks Kashmiri Bazaar near its intersection with Rang Mahal, just near the woodworkers' bazaar.

On one side of Shah Alami Gate, heading towards Lohari Gate, is the most densely populated area of the Walled City, Wachowali Bazaar. Wachowali, along with nearby Gumti and Jaura Mori bazaars, was a largely Hindu area prior to Partition and remains home to many majestic temples and old British colonial buildings.

Just beyond the rubber sandal market off Wachowali Bazaar is an area populated mostly by *muhajirs*, Kucha Gulzari Wala. Men, here as elsewhere, are working and shopping in the bazaar. An occasional veiled woman makes her way in purchasing some household necessities. Around the corner, down an alleyway just past the only girls' school on this side of the Walled City, lives Chand Bibi, a widow stricken with tuberculosis, looking at least twenty years older than her age of thirty-five.

When entering the *kucha*, one sees that these buildings are higher than in most areas; they are four storeys each, instead of the usual three. Many remain from the Mughal era, though they now house a separate family on each floor instead of comprising a single large *haveli* as in the past. Most afternoons, women sit near the main window on each floor, looking out, watching the neighborhood below and occasionally talking with each other. Some are drinking tea, others are simply sitting, looking out at something that catches their attention, perhaps the young boys playing cricket below in the open spaces between the homes. The very existence of the *jharokas* in which they sit tells us that Hindus had constructed these homes.

After entering Chand Bibi's home on the ground floor, we walk up some steep steps to the next level. Until her death, Chand Bibi's mother-in-law had lived on the ground floor, but it now lies unoccupied while her family is trying to sell that portion. Chand Bibi enjoys standing on her balcony talking to a neighbor. She tells us that the neighbor's house was built "in the time of the Hindus" with a jutting-out scalloped *jharoka*. Two other women are sitting and talking together in a neighboring *jharoka*.

The entrance to Chand Bibi's home is covered and enclosed on three sides, somewhat like a veranda but not quite. A brass *hamam* used for storing water sits distinctively by the entrance, under a rope tied lengthwise to dry clothes.

We enter through the sitting room, the first of four rooms. It is clean, whitewashed, and well-lit although a bit run-down: a pile of clothes sits in its appointed place on top of a table in the corner, springs are nearly sticking out from the two sofa seats making them difficult to sit on, and the carpeting is worn in patches. Two cane stools, covered with yellow frilled tapestry, sit in the corner beside a new pedestal fan. A washing machine by the wall is covered tightly with its original packing, as if no one had ever used it nor was ever going to use it. The two wooden windows, painted brown, are curtained with a simple cloth. In the adjoining room, there is only one *charpai*, from which we can see the glow of the kerosene stove reflected on a steel box in the next room, the kitchen, which has only sparse utensils.

The architecture changes dramatically only a very short walk beyond Gulzari Wala. Fires in 1947 had virtually destroyed all the old buildings here. The newer box-like structures reveal nothing of the inner lives of residents from the streets. Durdana lives in such a building in Kucha Palarkal, where her husband runs a plastic factory on the ground floor. She and her family live and work on the middle floor, while four factory workers live on the top floor. The family's residence, sectioned off into two parts, contains a desert cooler, a nice bed and sofa set, and a tape deck.

Further towards Lohari Gate, just past the end of Wachowali Bazaar, is another bazaar, Jaura Mori. It once housed the famous Andhi Haveli with its wide, spacious courtyards and halls supported by pillars which was destroyed (supposedly) during the British period. One of the neighborhoods off Jaura Mori is Kucha Natha Mal, where Amina and her family live in two rooms. People joke and say that this *kucha*, one street long, was named after the bridal nose rings that used to be made here.

Amina and her husband had originally lived in Suter Mandi (closer to Lohari Gate) with some relatives after they migrated to Lahore from East Punjab in 1947. They left Suter Mandi in the mid-1950s when another relative of her husband's had the house in which they had lived allotted to him. Neither Amina's husband, his father nor his brother had any property allotted to them. She is glad that they had not lied and said her father-in-law owned land in India (he did not) because she thinks they would surely have been caught. They rented a house nearby (to this current house) for about three years while they arranged for this house to be built.

As poor as she is, Amina gives food to beggars whenever possible. She tells us that more beggars come for *sadqaat* on Tuesdays, Thursdays and Saturdays than on other days, but she sees no special reason for this; perhaps they go to another area on other days?

Another small *kucha* off Bazaar Jaura Mori is Kucha Sheikan. There, Bilqis and her family live in a small house. The cement walls are blue, a sort of whitewash which poor people use, though this is wearing off. There is a fan, one *charpai* and one stool in the entrance room, along with a big steel storage box. There are two rooms and a courtyard on this floor, plus two rooms upstairs. Outside of one door is a horse, as a tonga driver lives next door. Bilqis' family makes shoes, and while there are other families in this area which also make shoes, most are on the other side of the Walled City, near Kashmiri Gate.

Kucha Sheikan is just before the next gate, Lohari Gate, where I resided. The great Muslim Mosque with its green-beaconed minaret sits at the gate's entrance, overlooking the flower stalls and chemist shops. More people seem to buy food from the shami kebab, seekh kebab and nihari stands than from the Nemat Kedah Hotel just nearby. Men relax in front of their key and lock shops flanked by the masonry archway which clearly demarcates that you are taking a step *inside* an area different from the one you are leaving. Rickshaws and tongas rarely enter the gate, though horse-drawn goods carts often hurl themselves through it.

This is the gate where *lohars*, ironworkers, once resided. However, except for an occasional craftsman who makes metal bedframes, the ironworkers seem to have moved closer to Shah Alami Gate and Rang Mahal in recent years. The cultural richness inside this gate, known for excellent cuisine, is difficult to describe. A rotund overseer *occasionally* stirs his large vat of milk gently boiling, occasionally scooping out portions for customers to take home. Shops are often cared for by young boys seeming older than their ages. The men's bath is nearby, where political gossip is often exchanged. The bazaar is never empty, and everyone seems to know each other. When an "outsider" -- anyone not from Lohari Gate -- comes to make a purchase, the interaction is different, and heated bargaining may take place. Amongst insiders prices are understood, for families have an economic interdependence of sorts with each other.

Just through the gate, on the left, is Gali Sirki Bandan, traditionally the street of the bamboo blind makers. A few of these craftsmen still remain at the beginning of the *gali*, though the remainder is dominated by cardboard box makers. On a warm day, the smell of the glue mixing with the odor of the nearby moat (a part which was not filled in) combined with animal and children's refuse cannot go unnoticed. However, few people become distracted by this as they are busy going about their own business. Women, wives of tonga drivers, bus conductors and shopkeepers, wash clothes usually from *hamams* as water only intermittently runs from taps, and then hang the clothes out to dry on rooftops. The washerman at the end of the *gali* doubles as a general handyman, ready to fix anything that goes wrong in a home. From a second floor, a woman calls across to her neighbor on the third and they have a conversation about the sweets another neighbor has sent to them both because she was "saved" when she fell from her roof a week back. The son of a woman down the *gali* was not so fortunate when he fell from a third storey window, and his mother is now praying for another son to take his place. An occasional tailoring shop breaks the monotony of cardboard box makers, though the light is so dim in the narrow *gali* that it is a wonder the men can see at all. The television at the cold drinks stand is the meeting place when a cricket match is in progress; at night, an occasional woman surrounded by her family may even watch for a while.

In this environment, with a density of 80.55 persons per acre (51,552 per square kilometer; LDA, 1980: 108), everyone notes everything about each other's actions and everyone knew exactly where the foreign woman was living. Therefore, I decided it would be awkward and probably futile to conduct interviews in my immediate surroundings, which is why there are no interviews from Lohari Gate.[25]

In most accounts of the Walled City the next gate, Mori, is often not considered a gate: rather, it is the route by which refuse used to be removed and is often simply referred to as the old drain. However, the dirt entrance today has become an early morning fish mongers market and has taken away some of Lohari Gate's summertime breakfast clientele seeking delicious *chana/kulcha*. The area melds Lohari and Bhati gates' sub-cultures, though it has little historical identity of its own.

Bhati Gate is the most infamous of the Walled City entrances. It is reputed to be a tough area, housing gambling halls and drug dealers, and residents whose toughness equals its reputation. However, in all the time I spent by this western gate named for the Rajput *qaum* said to have populated this quarter in the past, I saw no evidence of this.

Just outside of Bhati Gate is the shrine to Hazrat Data Ganj Baksh, considered the greatest saint of Lahore and popularly referred to as Data Saheb. He is said to have arrived in Lahore in 1039 from Ghazni with the army of Masud, the son and successor of Mahmud. After Data Saheb's death in 1072, he was buried close to a mosque which he himself had built (Latif, 1892: 179). Data Sahab is a highly respected scholar and saint throughout the subcontinent. Salim Chishti, the saint of Ajmere, is said to have spent forty days at the tomb, and wrote a couplet in which he praised him as being "the bestower of treasure" -- *Ganj Bakhsh*: "The bestower of treasure in both worlds, reflector of the splendor of God, an accomplished spiritual guide for the learned and a guide for the ignorant" (Latif, 1892: 180). Later, the Emperor Akbar built a marble entranceway to the mausoleum which is always brimming over with people. A new, white mosque, just constructed, is said to be one of the largest mosques in Pakistan.

There is a separate section only for women which is extremely popular. Data Saheb is clearly the preferred *pir* whom most women of the Walled City periodically go to visit. They speak of him as if he is still alive, they go and talk with him, and they go there to talk with one another.

Just south of Data Saheb is a Shi'a Imam Bara, which houses reproductions of the tombs of Imam Hassan and Imam Hussain. Nearby lies the underground tomb of Gama Shah, the shrine that Shi'a women of the Walled City state they visit most frequently.

Bhati Gate is second to Mochi Gate as a political rallying point; processions begun here often terminate at Mochi Gate. Hawkers sell various foodstuffs on the entryway outside of the moat, crossing which one enters through the simple stylized gate. Just inside, a police station is on the right, a school on the left, and a lively crowded food bazaar ahead. Further down is a Mughal-era mosque built during the time of Shah Jahan, west of the Tehsil Court in Tibbi Bazaar. Making a left turn down a small path, we arrive in a very poor area, Noor Muhalla. Its inhabitants are poorly educated and speak little Urdu. Ironically, this impoverished *kucha* has incredibly beautiful old buildings in it. Towards the end of the *kucha*, Maryam lives with her family in one dark room, dusty and unhygienic, with a tiny area beside the room for cooking. The room hasn't been cleaned or whitewashed for a long time. The only ventilation is via the front door, covered by a curtain. There is a wooden bed covered by a slight mattress and a mattress-less metal bed. Beneath the wooden bed is an old wooden box, a wooden cart for carrying small things, and a small metal table, which is falling apart. There is one light bulb in the room, suspended from a beam.

Now in her late thirties, Maryam was young when her father died. She has five sisters; she said that her one brother died when he was about six from a pain in his ear. Maryam was sent briefly to study the Qur'an, but after learning to read two or three *saparahs* (verses from the Qur'an), her mother stopped her from going.

> We didn't have a good life. My memories aren't good. In my parents' house, I had no father, no brother, no good memories. There was no happy

day in my childhood. I can't remember any. My mother did her best to marry me off honorably.

She and her husband of twenty-two years have lived in this rented home for the last four years with their two sons and four daughters. Her husband earns about nine hundred and fifty rupees a month; she earns fifty.

Maryam has no expectations for her future. Only her family and her neighbors are important to her, and they all just try to survive on a day-to-day basis. While we went a number of times to speak with Maryam, we were unable to record her story in any detail. Either due to poor health, no education, or being distracted and talking about tangential matters, Maryam was unable to articulate the major details of her life to us, and was only able to talk about things in the present. From our meetings with other women in similar socioeconomic positions, Maryam's inability to tell her life story seems to be representative. They do not conceive of a lifestyle other than the one they have, and in living in the present they try to forget the painful past and not think of what the future holds.

Moving further into the center of the Walled City in the direction of the next gate is another area of high density, Syad Mithha Bazaar. In the middle of the bazaar lies the tomb of Syad Mithha, known for his piety, devotion and knowledge, who died in 1262 (Latif, 1892: 229). This area was home to about 3,500 households in 1980, with a population of nearly 23,000 and a density of 61.4 persons per acre, most of whom are quite poor (LDA, 1980: 108). In the direction of Tehsil Bazaar, just before the videotape shop which rents out the latest Hindi and Punjabi films, there is a white mosque on the left, the mosque of the five *pirs*. A thin cement platform arches over the open, flowing drain which must be crossed to reach the neighborhood behind it.

Itrat's house, just a short way up Gali Panch Pir, has two separate entrances to the outside. It's a high step-up into the house through the brightly painted green door of the main entrance. There are three rooms off this inner courtyard, but hardly any furniture in any of the rooms. There is some plastic, resembling wood, covering half of the floor in the room where Itrat makes artificial jewelry. The other half is simple concrete. There is whitewash on the walls, though it is wearing off on the bottom part near the floor. On a hook hangs a black *burqa*. Simple chairs are brought in for us to sit upon.

The second room houses a bed and some storage boxes, and is across from a small, unfinished area for cooking. A part of the upstairs roof is used for feasts whenever there is the social necessity; the other section is a shoemaking workshop, covered by a tin roof and accessed by the male workers via a separate, outside stairway. There is another room in the compound which used to be inhabited by a young man, his wife and his mother when he was sick and could not work. At that time, all the residents had to share one toilet and one bathing area. To smooth out the unavoidable interactions, the two families used kinship terms when addressing each other though in fact they were unrelated.

Just a bit ahead on the left, we reach the final entrance to the Walled City, Taxali Gate. The narrow unpaved streets here resemble those found in provincial Pakistani cities, bereft of modern trafficways or many formal shops. Most people are of the opinion that Taxali Gate takes its name from the mint, the *taxaal*, which was in this area during the Mughal rule. Today, Taxali Gate is known best for Lady Wellingdon hospital, where many Walled City women have their babies delivered. Nearby lives a popular female *pir*, whose home is visited daily by women seeking comfort and solutions to various problems they face. Upon arrival and removal of shoes, the women sit waiting in two lines in front of her. Each separately prays, moving a bit closer to the *pirni* as someone finishes her turn. One woman is there because her husband is unable to find a job; another is worried about infertility; a third is having too many arguments with her husband. When the latter's turn comes, she places a pile of roses purchased near Data Saheb's tomb in front of the *pirni*. The *pirni* says a prayer, runs her hands through the flowers, and finds cut glass amongst the roses. She declares someone has placed a curse on the woman, and that she must place a *taviz* (amulet) under her husband's pillow so as to break it. The woman is relieved with this knowledge, for she can now envision a better future with her husband.

Just further inside Taxali Gate, past the police station, is Kucha Sheikhupurian, well known for delectable food such as joints and cooked chickpeas. As we reach Paja's joint shop, we have come full circle around the Walled City, for this is where Hira Mandi begins.

While we can get our spatial bearings from the above description of life within the walls of the old city, we must step inside the homes of the women resident there to get a fuller sense of daily life. Therefore, we now turn to women's life experiences within their homes, which house the most important and formidable social institution affecting women in the Walled City, the family.

Notes

1. This is a systemized program for cutting back on electrical usage throughout the country. The government argues that as Pakistan is a poor country with limited resources, electricity must be rationed, especially during seasons of excessive usage.

2. As the majority of sweepers are Christians, the Lahore Municipal Corporation, their employer, has given them Sundays as their day off instead of Fridays.

3. Population densities for cities other than Lahore are based on data in UNDP, 1990:160-161.

4. *Encyclopaedia Britannica* Volume 13, 14th Edition, London: 1929.

5. The LDA has found residency patterns to be similar. In 1979, (LDA, 1979: 36) they assessed that 63.7% of households lived in 1-2 rooms, and 79.8% in 1-3 rooms.

6. Such buildings accounted for 63.5% of dwelling units surveyed in 1979 (LDA, 1979: 8). In 1979, 94.2% of all Walled City residences had dry latrines; this figure had decreased to 72.2% by 1984 apparently due to LDA/World Bank efforts to improve sanitation.

7. It seems there is a bit of historical controversy regarding the exact years of Mahmud's gaining control over Lahore, installing Malik Ayaz in charge, and Malik Ayaz's completion of the city's repopulation. This is based on the account provided by Kamil Khan Mumtaz (n.d.: 2).

8. Abdul Fazl, as quoted in Research Society of Pakistan (1976: 325).

9. In 1739, Nadir Shah encouraged Lahore's Mughal Governor, Zakariya Khan, to suppress the Sikhs, which essentially began the succession of battles between the Muslim army in Lahore and the Sikh armies in Amritsar and elsewhere in the Punjab.

10. The first official British census of Lahore in 1855 showed it had a population of 94,143.

11. Thornton (1850) and Goulding (1924) recall only a few Europeans living within the walls, and usually inside of important historic structures.

12. Fictive kinship relationships based on a common region of origin, the shared experience of a refugee camp, or residential proximity in a common *kucha* have often been cemented through marriages.

The 1981 District Census of Lahore (Population Census Organisation, 1984:74) reports that the Walled City's population was 190,000 in 1981. A World Bank/Lahore Development Authority (1980:22) study estimated its population would be 277,000 in 1986. More recent figures remain unavailable.

13. For example, Delhi Gate was repaired and repainted to its supposedly original color in 1990.

14. Additional kinds of European/American architectural adaptations have been introduced elsewhere in Lahore since Partition, including apartment complexes and multi-family bungalows. However, as the design of space and accommodation in the Walled City invariably pre-dates partition, any comparison with these newer forms of housing is irrelevant for our purposes.

15. Population Census Organisation, 1984: 74, Table 26. Females were 88,498; males were 101,478; for a total of 189,976. Census Ward 85 figures have not been included as the ward skirts the Walled City. Nearly a century earlier, in 1891, women comprised 41.9 percent of the population within the municipal limits of Lahore (Latif, 1982:'254, based on 1891 census).

16. The Lahore Development Authority (1979:35) found that about 70 percent of homes in the Walled City are owned by the occupants.

17. Samuel Noe's unpublished dissertation "Understanding the Islamic City" (University of Cincinnati, March 1978) provides a comprehensive discussion of the many characteristics of the Walled City of Lahore which make aspects of it the embodiment of a traditional Islamic city.

18. An LDA study (1979:42) found that "80 percent of the dwelling units in the Walled City are very old and [the] period of their construction can be traced during Moghul and Sikh regime[s]." PEPAC (1987:18) found that 38.2 percent of the buildings were between 40-100 years old and 16.6 percent were over 100 years, resulting in 54.8 percent of buildings in 1987 predating Partition. In contrast, less than 23 percent of urban housing units in Lahore District in 1981 pre-dated Partition (Population Census Organisation, 1984:11, Table III).

19. The LDA, in conjunction with PEPAC Ltd., conducted eight studies of problems confronting the Walled City and developed a strategic framework for a comprehensive conservation plan which is being supported by the World Bank. Refer to World Bank/LDA (1980) for further details on the first stage of the upgrading project and to PEPAC (1987) for the various alternatives that they have suggested for institutional development.

20. The second section not interviewed, between Lohari and Mori Gates, is discussed below. For a more complete description of Hira Mandi, refer to Irshad, 1986: 144-151. Tandon (1967) has an interesting description of traditional prostitution practices.

21. Men travel around the Walled City either on bicycles or with donkeys buying scrap metal and used newspapers. The former is sold to remelting mills in Badamibagh while the latter is sold for various types of purposes (all of which can be regarded as a form of paper recycling).

22. He was a saint from Gazrun, in Persia, who settled in Lahore during the time of the Tughlak dynasty. The mosque was built on the site of the tomb.

23. 89.5 percent of floor space in this *kucha* is used for residential purposes (LDA, 1980:119). The second pilot area selected is Muhalla Molliani, inside Lohari Gate in the direction of Wachowali bazaar.

24. Latif (1982:86) claims that the name is the corruption of *moti*, a pearl, and that the gate was named after Moti Ram, an officer of Akbar who resided here at the time. However, residents had never heard this story.

25. The LDA has conducted a household survey of this area in connection with sanitation upgrading. Refer to LDA, 1982.

2

Women, Families and Households

The most significant identification which women in the Walled City make is as members of families. While ties to their natal families remain important to most women, it is their status within their husband's household that has major implications for their lives. In trying to understand women's position within the family, we questioned our representative sample of Walled City women about their childhood experiences: where they came from, how long they had lived in Lahore, what growing up was like, and the dreams they had as children. For those who are married, we asked them how the marriage had been arranged, how it occurred, what their fears and hopes had been, details about their dowries and *haq mehr* (promissory gift from in-laws), and about their relations with their *susural* (in-laws). This elaboration of intrahousehold dynamics often refers to women's idealized position in Pakistani culture, yet very often we see that real life experiences are very different from stereotyped expectations.

Our random sample survey enabled us to interview women at all stages of life.[1] The women of the Walled City tend to have very vivid memories of their lives in their parents' homes, and remember very specific details of their weddings. Life histories recounted after marriage seem to be less detailed, and focus around the activities of children and in-laws.

Before commencing with women's accounts of their lives within their families, it is useful to note certain characteristics regarding education opportunities and marriage, both of which affect women's place and perceptions. The former gives us insight into an important aspect of a woman's childhood as well as the kind of preparation she received for being actively involved in the grown-up world outside of her family, while the latter tells us much about where she is today, how she views her place in society and the impact she might have on events as they unfold around her.

We found that 59 percent of the women we interviewed have had some kind of formal education; 28 percent studied beyond the primary level.[2] Seven of the "uneducated" women were, however, taught to read the Qur'an at home.

Of those who had formal education, only 4 percent actually withdrew from school because of economic pressures. Instead, concerns regarding a woman's participation in activities outside of the home as being a threat to her *izzat* caused nearly two-thirds to have to leave school. 16 percent consider their achieving puberty as the main reason for quitting, 25 percent because of marriage (either it occurred or her prospective in-laws didn't want her to study further), and 20 percent stopped because of "other family pressures." Interestingly, just over a third stopped because of "other pressures:" presumably, the greatest pressure here would be lack of appropriate girls' schools. There is no school for females beyond class ten (matric)[3] within the Walled City.[4]

We found three important characteristics related to women and marriage. The first challenges the common assumption that an overwhelming majority of adult women are married, and those who are not are either too young or widowed. 1981 census figures claim that in Lahore district, only about eight percent of women fifteen years and older were either widowed or divorced (Population Census Organisation, 1984: 18, Table V). However, we found that while 75 percent were married or had once been married, only 64 percent were currently married, thereby leaving eleven percent of the women to have to fend for themselves.[5] Second, most women are married within their *biradari*, so they view themselves as having some relationship to their in-laws through some sort of biological tie (however distant) as well as through marriage. More than half of the married women were closely related to their husband before their marriage. Third, polygamous marriages are rare in this working class area, as only two of the women's husbands had married other wives contemporaneously. Women, then, feel secure in the marriage bond, but remain fearful of what the future holds for them in the event of the death of a husband. While most expect that their husband's family will care for them -- as per the dictates of tradition -- many also recognize that resources are scarce and male relatives must be concerned with caring for their own families.

Women's Accounts of Family Life

Given this background, we now turn to the women's own accounts of their lives within their families. Their stories, prompted by questions, have been translated and edited into standard English. Here, as in the following chapters, we present the women in the order they have been introduced in Chapter 1. These accounts of growing up, daily routines, marriage circumstances and current dreams provide a context in which we can understand women's accepted roles and perceived norms, particularly as they affect economic activities and visions of power in the following chapters.

Laila

Laila was born about seventeen years ago in the house in which she still lives in Chuna Mandi. All of her siblings were also born here, in the main room. Her family is originally from Amritsar, speak Punjabi and are Rajputs. Her father has three older brothers and an older sister. Laila always uses exact denotative kinship terminology (as did all the women we met), thereby underscoring the importance of kinship relations and of the web of relations in which each woman lives.

> My *dada* is from Amritsar, though he moved to Tejgar, this side of Jallo Park, before Partition. He is my mother's *khala's* distant relative. My mother married into Tejgar, then they came here.
>
> My father works for WAPDA (Water and Power Development Authority) on McLeod Road, near the Walled City. He has been installing meters for the last ten years. He earns twelve hundred rupees per month. Before that, he worked in a sherbet/tea hotel. It was just a simple thing, on the roadside. It was someone else's. He's only studied until class five, but can read and write well.

The ages of her siblings are conjectures, as no one really knows how old they are:

> My oldest sister is twenty-two. She was married when she was 13-14 to our *khalazad bhai*. She only has two years' education, and now has a seven year-old daughter. My next sister is twenty. She's not engaged yet, as she has had an appendix problem.
>
> Next is my sister who is eighteen. She was married five years ago outside of our *biradari*, though with a Rajput. She was married outside because her husband and his family saw her at my eldest sister's wedding and became interested in her. They then found out about us, and talked to my *taya* and to my mother. My parents went to see the boy. Of course, my sister never met her husband before her marriage.
>
> After me, is my brother who is fourteen. He is learning to be a mechanic in a shop near my father's WAPDA office. He studied until fifth class. He always ran away from school as he didn't like it. My next brother, who is twelve, wants to be a doctor, and the youngest, ten, wants to join the army.
>
> I used to study in Anjuman Khudamuddin Banaat Girls Public School, inside Sheranwala Gate. It goes until tenth class and classes are in Urdu-medium, though English is taught as a class. It's a small school with ten rooms for some three hundred girls. Most of the girls studying there are

very young. It's a school for poor people; it's free, with no fees. It was initially only for Islamic education. Girls are taught the Qur'an and the basics of the religion. However, despite the school being free, not too many people want to send their daughters there to study because they want them to attend an English-medium school. So many girls start there, and then later study elsewhere.

My best schoolfriend is Ayesha. We studied together until we completed our matric degree, tenth class. We used to go to the bazaar buying soda, etc., when we were young, but we can't do that anymore. We still do meet together a few times a week and can talk about everything. She's been sick with typhoid, so I often go there to see how she is. Ayesha wants to study further, but I don't think she will.

I haven't been married yet because my family first has to save some money. My education has not affected whether I'm married or not. It just depends on my parents' wishes as to when I'll be married.

Every day, my mother gets up to pray and read the Qur'an. We awaken to the *azan* or we hear our neighbors -- they're all our relatives -- who live in this former Hindu *haveli*. We're awake by 5 a.m.

In the winter, while Laila is attending school, her daily routine is one common to many school-age girls in Lahore:

5 a.m.: wakes up, prays for about fifteen minutes (two *rakats*). Then reads one *saparah* in the Qur'an, which takes about a half hour.

We, my mother and my sister, each read the Qur'an, separately, though we sit together. Sometimes my father joins us, though he usually has to rush off to work. My two brothers go to the mosque by Sheranwala in the morning, then have breakfast at home before going to school.

6 a.m.: cleans the house: this takes about an hour.

My mother makes the breakfast, my sister washes the dishes. I sweep the house and fold the sheets, put them away, and put away the dishes and the pots. My mother and sister wash the clothes. It hurts my hands (said in jest, laughing) -- after marriage, I'll get a machine!

7 a.m.: eats breakfast, usually tea and a *paratha*, which takes about fifteen minutes.

Sometimes we have eggs: we have two female chickens in our house which we keep under the bed in a wicker basket. When they get big, we eat them, we never sell them. When a guest comes, we'll eat one.

7:15 a.m.: departs for school.

I go to school by bus. It costs twenty-five *pice* with a student card, otherwise it would cost one rupee. I go with my *tayazad behan*. If one of us is sick, my brother goes with us until Bhati Gate in a van, and then we continue on alone to the school, Institute College, which is by the Secretariat. It's a three-year program, but I am only enrolled in the two-year diploma course for sewing and cutting.

7:45 à.m.: must arrive by then at the school.

8 a.m.: school starts. There are three periods, of two hours each.

From eight until ten, we do machine embroidery. From ten until twelve, we learn cutting with sewing. Our recess is from twelve until one. An old woman works at a canteen there, selling *nan, chole,* chicken pieces, gum, and soda bottles while a man sells spicy fruit salad by the road. I usually spend about two rupees for lunch. From one until three we do knitting.

3:30 p.m.: arrives home.

I usually take a public van back, as it's more convenient for coming home. The bus is too crowded and has a lot of college boys. The van costs one rupee; they don't care for student cards.

3:30 - 6 p.m.: takes a nap.

6 - 8 p.m.: "I do my school homework, and some *salma sitara* (fancy embroidery) work if I have the time. My sister does the *salma sitara* work all day long."

8-9 p.m.: watches television with her family. "When the news comes on television, we shut it and eat dinner together. We sit on the floor in the kitchen."

9-10 p.m.: dinner takes one hour.

We eat less rice and *dal* (lentils) than we do in the summertime. We'll eat more *sag* (curried spinach or mustard leaves), and especially *sag* with meat and cornflour *rotis* for a treat. We eat carrots, potatoes, cauliflower, peas and the like; we have mostly vegetables with a little meat. We don't eat very much chicken. We might buy it from the bazaar or kill our own, but only for guests. We mostly eat beef (poor peoples' meat, the cheapest meat in Lahore). We eat some lamb too, but less.

10 p.m.: cleans up and goes to bed.

Everyone sleeps except me and my sister. We spend about a half hour washing the dishes and then we go to sleep. My parents sleep in the kitchen on *charpais* (string beds). My sister and I share a *charpai*; my fourteen-year-old brother sleeps alone on the other one, and my two brothers sleep on a third one.

During the hot summer, Laila no longer attends school, and her routine is rather different as her embroidery work becomes central to her activities:

6 a.m.: Breakfast is a *kulcha* (baked flat bread) and *lassi*, made from yogurt, and a *kulcha*, and sometimes *chole* which my brother brings from the bazaar. My three brothers usually eat *halva/puri*. I only have it occasionally, like on a Friday. It's not filling enough for me.

8 a.m. - noon: "I do *salma sitara* work at home with my sister. I practice the sewing I learned in school too."

noon - 3 p.m.: sleeps during the heat of the day.

3 - 3:30 p.m.: eats lunch, usually *roti* with vegetables, sometimes with a little bit of beef.

3:30- 7 p.m.: does *salma sitara* embroidery work.

7 - 9 p.m.: watches television with her family.

9 - 10 p.m.: dinner.

10 p.m.: cleans dishes, then sleeps in front of the house. "Everyone here sleeps in front of their own house as we're all relatives. Some people also sleep upstairs."

At this point in her life, Laila has no independent status. When and if she studies or not, marries or not, even eats or not, is all decided by her parents. When a woman marries, as seen in many of the following accounts, she begins to play a more central role within the family, although the limitations placed on her making independent decisions remain.

Gulzar Begum

While we were sitting with her in her two-room home inside Delhi Gate, she was knitting a child's sweater. She says that this is what she does for "relaxation." Gulzar Begum was born in the Walled City, and is now a widow in her forties. She is a Rajput, Sunni, speaks Punjabi, and is completely illiterate.

As she was recounting her childhood, she said that there were four sisters and three brothers in her family. She is the youngest of the sisters, and has one younger brother who is still alive. Her two eldest brothers have died. She was about fifteen when her mother died. She was married five years later, about twenty-seven years ago. Her father died two years ago.

She spent her childhood in Mozang Jehnaza, a working class area about a ten minute walk from the Bhati Gate entrance to the Walled City:

> My house had two rooms, like this house, one behind and one in front. It looks just like this house. My father told me that I should continue studying, but I could not, because my mother had died when I was young. In the old days, girls didn't get permission to go out and study.

This last comment is interesting in the light of the fact that her son does not allow her daughter to study now.[6]

> I had very good food in my parents' house. My father brought vegetables and all, and I cooked them and served them, after my mother died. I never cooked before my mother died, and didn't know how to cook then. I was the youngest girl, the *ladoo* (sweet) of the house. My married sister would visit us and stay for sixty days. Each married sister came, one by one, for two months at a time.

When we question her about her childhood dreams and aspirations, she always responds by saying, "None, I had none."

She provides a very detailed account of the events leading up to her marriage:

> My husband was from my *biradari*, a distant relative. My sister who lives nearby arranged the marriage. I was twenty when I was married. I had been engaged for five years, just after my mother's death. My in-laws wanted it for that long. At that time, my husband was a shoe salesman in Kashmiri Bazaar.
>
> My husband was hard-working, good, respectable, handsome, and from our *biradari*. He was my sister's husband's *khalazad bhai*.
>
> My sister told me about my engagement. I was a motherless child, how could I feel? My father had loved me very much; he loved me so much he only wanted to eat my cooking.
>
> At the engagement, they gave me two suits of clothes, a pair of shoes, bangles, and make-up: fat, wet lipstick, powder, nail polish and some combs.

My sister, brother and father sat with my mother-in-law, *jaith* and *jaithanis* to set the marriage date. My husband was twenty-five when we were married. The wedding lasted six days. Four days were for applying oil and *mehndi* (henna). They went twice to each home. One day was for the *baraat* and one for the *valima*.

Of course I remember everything in my dowry. It was one sofa, two chairs, one *palang* (western-style bed), a dressing table -- it's broken now -- and china and copper cookware. I've given it all to my daughters for their weddings. For cooking and water storage, there was also a steel *hamam*, a clay *hamam*, a big cooking pot, and one *matka ghara* (clay pot for cold water storage). I had cloth to make twenty-five suits (*shalwar kamizes*), four pairs of shoes, and an entire gold set: forehead *tikka*, ring, earrings, and a necklace, but no bangles. But the gold that was in my dowry was sold for medicine -- my husband was sick for fourteen years. The rest of my dowry I've given to my daughters.

We gave a gold ring at my engagement to my *susural*, and two or three suits at my marriage. My *susural* gave me four gold bangles, a whole gold set -- necklace, earrings and a ring -- and twenty-one suits.

The *haq mehr* was nothing, just thirty-two rupees, as in the *shari'a*. In those times, thirty-two rupees was okay, but nowadays, people demand more. There hasn't been any *haq mehr* for my daughters. They were married to close relatives, so we just went by the *shari'a*, of thirty-two rupees.

The traditions from those days to now haven't changed. Only the things have changed. The lipstick used to be in a golden box, now it comes in a stick. The texture of cloth remains the same, "*china pathi*." Now they get an embroidered shawl at engagements and give out *kishmish* (almonds, pistachios, raisins, etc.).

She appears content with the way her life after her marriage has turned out. However, she was unable to focus on details of her life together with her husband, who died ten years ago. Instead, her in-laws are predominant in her life after marriage:

I've lived very well with my in-laws for twenty-seven years. We get along well because it's from both sides. We had a tragedy here twenty-two years ago, when my *jaithani's* son got lost and never came back.

Her mother-in-law, who appeared one day in pretty white clothes with a geometric print, performed *hajj* last year. Her father-in-law had died during World War II. Her in-laws have lived in this house over a 100 years. Everyone says that her husband's *dada* had been a 125 years old when he died.

Of her two *jaiths*, one died last year. The one who is still alive has played a very important role in her family. He and his family live at

Chawk Wasanpura near Delhi Gate. She says that, from her heart, she feels that her own brother has had more influence on her life than her *jaith*. But if her brother wanted a *rishta* for her daughter and her *jaith* wanted another one, then the final decision is hers and her *jaith's*; generally, she defers to her *jaith*: "The difference is that when you're in your parents' home, there are no worries or anxieties. But now I have children of my own and a house to take care of."

She is overweight and her teeth are bent. She uses black hair color on her hair, as do many older Pakistanis.

> I used to wear flowers when I went out. Now, my children do, but I don't since my husband died. Since then I don't wear flowers, bangles, or put *mehndi* on my hands. My life is all upside-down since then.

She is wearing large, gold, rough earrings. Her sixteen-year-old daughter is also overweight. In her conversations with me, both she and her daughter used a lot of fictive kinship terms to describe people not closely related, such as *khala* (mother's sister) for female neighbors and *susr* (father-in-law) for her father-in-law's brother.

She wakes up at 5 a.m. every day. She then prays, makes breakfast, and cleans her house within an hour. Then she begins her work stringing flowers and shelling almonds. In her free time, she crochets *dupattas*. Then she sleeps at night.

Farida

Farida, a hairdresser living inside Delhi Gate, was born inside the Walled City near the water tank and Gumti Bazaar. She boasts that Mian Salahuddin, a well-known politician, "fights" from that area. She speaks Punjabi, is a Sunni Rajput, and is in her late twenties. She lives in her one-room home with her husband, who has recently become a drug addict, and their son.

> My parents have been living in their home for the last twenty-eight years. My brothers and sisters are still living there. I have five sisters and five brothers. My parents are selfish. My mother and father don't take care of their own children. My father is younger than my mother, by 2-4 years. My father sells *nan/chana* from a stand.
>
> All my sisters were married off at 13-14 years. My parents didn't bother if the boys were good or bad; they just married them off within the *biradari*. If someone came to their home and said "here's a man," they were just married off within a week. No engagement.
>
> My eldest sister lives in Faisalabad, the next eldest is in Gujranwala, and

my third sister is married to a famous *pehlwan's* nephew. Then there is my brother who drives a rickshaw. He is married to our *phuphizad behan* and has one son and one daughter. His wife doesn't work.

My next brother, who is thirty, still isn't married. He makes shoes. Then there is my sister who died, my other sister who is twenty-six, and then there is me. I also have three younger brothers: the older one went to Saudi Arabia (to work) a year ago, and the younger two do *salma sitara* work in a factory in Shadbagh.

None of her brothers or sisters nor her parents were educated or taught any skills. She studied in a school for about four years though remains virtually illiterate as she can only write a bit of Urdu. She had expected she would marry her cousin, but her father preferred a more conservative family:

My mother's *taya's* daughter had six sons, and my mother had six daughters. I called her "*khala*" as my mother had no sister. This *khala*, before she died, wanted me to be married to one of her sons. Everyone knew about it, but I was very innocent about things then. My *khala's* family had an open *mahaul* (social atmosphere). My *khala* was liberal. She wanted me to come visit the house and Humayun, her son, should visit our house. But there were many restrictions in my house. Once my *khala's* family became interested in the marriage, they wanted a picture of me. My family members would not give the picture to them and refused their marriage proposal. That was my wish, to marry Humayun. We only had a one-room house, and he would occasionally come, but I never spoke to him. My father didn't like Humayun's visits.

Humayun is now a businessman, and is married to the daughter of his *mammu's* (mother's brother's) son, an army major. Farida said that his marriage pended for three years as he was hoping to marry Farida instead. She was with her mother one day and saw him on a motorcycle. Humayun spoke with her mother and asked her how Farida was (in front of her). He said to her mother, "You haven't done good; she's not happy." Her mother said, "This is her luck."

This wish to marry Humayun must have started from a young age, as Farida was married to her husband when she was fourteen. Seven or eight months before her marriage, her future in-laws came to look at her and her parents went to see their home, where they still live. Farida never saw her husband until her wedding day.

My husband is from my elder sister's in-laws' family. He is a distant relative. In my dowry there were fourteen suits, a nose ring, forehead *tikka*, and earrings. There were two beds, four chairs, a table, a dressing table and a showcase, as well as copper and steel cookware, glasses and plates for six, three steel boxes (for storage), two suitcases, and two sets of full bedding: blankets, bedspreads and mats.

My *susural* gave me fourteen suits, one gold set with a necklace, ring, two bangles, and dangling earrings as well as make-up and three pairs of shoes. The *haq mehr* was 2,000 rupees.

My husband has six sisters and four brothers. He had seven sisters, then the fourth sister died. One brother died soon after, then another brother four or five years later, then his mother died. He has three sisters who are older than he is. His family has owned this house over 100 years.

My real mother-in-law died after having three daughters and two sons. Then my father-in-law remarried, and had three daughters and two more sons. My father-in-law died four years ago. His wife lives on the ground floor, I live on the second, my *chachi* and her family on the third, and *dadi* on the very top floor.

I have awful problems with my husband. I believe that before our wedding, my husband had a sexual relationship with his stepmother. My parents had heard about it, that he wasn't good. But my mother said, "Once you spit, you don't lick it up." I was young and didn't know what marriage was like. He would stay outside all night long, roaming around, often with other women. He's a useless person.

Now, my husband is a drug addict. He doesn't use heroin, he uses mandrax. He eats pills, and he'll die like a dog. If I leave him, he'll go back to his stepmother and will become better again. With her, he used to take drugs only occasionally. He hates me, and gets annoyed in my presence.

Farida claims to be on very bad terms with her mother-in-law, who wants her to leave the house. This would come as no surprise since Farida probably tells everyone that her mother-in-law is sleeping with her husband, one of the most vitriolic accusations a woman can make in this cultural context. She feels that her in-laws want her to leave so they could then arrange for her husband to be remarried. However, upon further questioning, it seems that finances -- and particularly her desire to have some input into how they are spent -- is the real irritant in the relationship.

My husband was the sole earner in his family, and gave all his money to his parents and gave me nothing. There was a lot of trouble in the house. We would fight for not having this or that. So I made up my mind to cook separately, but the fights were still there.

Desiring to make financial choices in a conservative and poor household goes against the accepted norms; the symbolism of the action of cooking separately must not go unnoticed. This is one of the few acceptable ways in which women can gain an element of freedom in this context.

Jamila

Jamila's husband, her *tayazad bhai*, left her four years ago after nineteen years of marriage. She is now about forty-five years old, and has been running her own trading business for about seventeen years. She has three sons and one daughter, who is married. Her youngest son sleeps in the house with her while the other two sons sleep on the roof. Her daughter's *nund* (husband's sister) -- her *chacha's* daughter -- lives next door. Jamila was born in the Walled City and has never lived elsewhere. Her family is originally from Lahore and she speaks Punjabi as her native language. She is a Sunni from the Rajput *qaum*. She went to school for about six years, and although she can read Urdu she is weak at writing it.

She had three brothers. Fourteen years ago, one fell from a four-storey house while fasting during Ramadan. He had been told by a doctor not to fast and to take his medicine. Jamila tells us that he died two days later, after hearing the *azan* (call to prayer). Her mother died 2-4 years after her brother had died. She had a heart attack on a Friday. Jamila has two surviving brothers and a sister. One brother works in Kuwait while the other sells shoes in Kashmiri bazaar. Her father is still alive and has retired from working in the railway department.

Interestingly, despite being a strong woman herself, when she describes the people in her family she never mentions anything about what the other women in her family do. In effect, while she has broken away from conventional female roles, she does not construct her own moral universe in such a way as to conceive of defining other women by what they do; instead, she still defines them by their marital status, how many children they have and how pious they are.

Jamila says that her husband's family had been against their marriage as they wanted him to marry into a rich family, but he had loved her even though he was good looking and she was not. He did not care what his family said. He never complained about anything.

> My husband had been happy with me for a while. We had a daughter and two sons. Four or five years of my life were wonderful. My husband was a very nice man. He didn't tell me what to do or not to do, things like *purdah*.

When she married him, her husband owned a cotton cloth shop. However, she claims he was addicted to films and started spending all his time and money on them. He started skipping work two or three times in every four or five days, and then eventually sold off the cloth shop. Jamila remained uncomfortable with her husband's laziness and addiction to movies and often complained to him about it, but says that this made no difference in his attitude.

About seventeen years ago, one of her sons died because they did not have enough money to buy the necessary medicines. At that time, she decided that she had to earn money and started buying and selling cloth. She recognizes that it was her dislike of her husband's unwillingness to work that caused the problems between them.

He left her nearly four years ago, though they remain legally married. Her husband now lives with one of his two sisters outside the Walled City and Jamila sees him once or twice a year. He earns about thirty rupees a day working at a cloth shop, but doesn't give her any money to help support the family. She thinks that he feels that since their two oldest boys are nearly grown up he no longer has to support her or the children anymore, although he does help support his sister. Her husband recently came to see their youngest son when he was ill with typhoid. Jamila was very disappointed that her husband only gave the boy twenty rupees, after not seeing him for three years.

With her husband absent, there is no male family member on whom Jamila is dependent nor to whom she must answer for her activities. As her sons become older, they are becoming more economically self-sufficient, but they have yet to interfere with her role -- and her outright power -- in her household.

Hasina

Hasina is very proud of being a Kakazaiya, although she defines the status of her *qaum* by what the men do ("they have factories, political power, etc."), not by what the women do. Instead, she defines Kakazaiya women by their physical appearances, that they wear bangles from wrist to elbows, their jewelry sets match the color of their clothes, and before attending a marriage ceremony most go to the beauty parlor to get their hair done.

Hasina was born in Kareem Park, near the Minar-e-Pakistan, into a Sunni family. She studied until eighth class and lived in Kareem Park until she was married at age sixteen, about eleven years ago. She feels the reason her schooling was so meager is that people used to have a poor opinion of education which is why they didn't send their daughters to school. "Now we send our daughters to school."

Her *dada* was born in Bhati Gate; her family has always been from Lahore and speak Punjabi. She remembers him as being very hard-

working and spending most of his free time with the boys in the family
-- not with the girls at all. She would see him at night but hardly spent
any time with him; she feels he loved the boys much more.

The house in Kareem Park was very big, about one *kanal*. She lived
there with her parents, *dada* and *dadi*, *chacha*, *chachi*, their three sons and
one daughter, her *phuphi* (father's sister) and her sick husband, their four
daughters and two sons. There were also three or four families who were
renters who lived in a separate section of the house.

Her family used to own a lot of land in Kareem Park. Her brothers
now have land in Shahdara (on the outskirts of Lahore), near Rana Town.
Her father had sold off the Kareem Park land for different weddings and
related expenses. No land was put into either her or her four sisters'
names; only her three brothers inherited land. Instead, land was sold to
pay for the girls' dowries and for the food expenses at the weddings.

> My father died a long time ago, before my marriage. He took care of us, he
> was an aristocrat and had a lot of respect. He had a big name, owned land,
> a house, buffalos, and helped poor people. He had sixty acres of land. He
> was often in the house, and spoke sweetly with me. He used to spend time
> with me, and played with all of us. He was very affectionate. But he never
> got the opportunity to do anything especially good for me as he had a heart
> attack and died suddenly. I was 14-15 years old when he died. My
> engagement had already happened. The worst thing he ever did was
> engage me to this man.
>
> My childhood dreams? I had no wishes or ambitions as a child. I had a
> good life. I studied until eighth class. There's no benefit from having great
> expectations.
>
> I was to have married my *phuphizad bhai* -- he's a Captain now -- but I
> wasn't educated enough. He married a doctor.

By Walled City standards, her dowry was very extravagant. It
consisted of fifty suits, two beds, a sofa, six chairs, a dining table and
showcase, a dressing table and a wardrobe, twelve sets of bedding, two
big steel storage boxes, three or four small boxes, two suitcases, a china
dining set, a Singer hand sewing machine, a lamp, a copper *hamam*, a clay
hamam, and six large cooking pots. The jewelry included one four-strand
necklace, a large pair of dangling gold earrings, four gold bangles, a ring,
and a nose ring. Her family gave twenty suits to her *susural*, as well as
watches to her husband and her father-in-law.

> But in my dowry there was no refrigerator or TV, so my in-laws say we
> gave nothing. After ten years, we still have not had to buy a single thing
> for the house.

She feels, however, that her *susural* gave her "nothing," as the only thing she kept was two rings. She was shocked that the rest of the jewelry -- six bangles, a small *tikka* for the forehead, a small nose ring, a small necklace, and small earrings -- was taken back three days later!

> I took off the jewelry after the *valima*, went to see my mother, came back, and the jewelry was gone. They told me that they've kept it in the bank. They also gave me eighteen suits, and then took eight back, the thick ones, with real *salma sitara* work on them. They had agreed to a *haq mehr* of 10,000 rupees, but went back on their word at the last minute and we signed a *haq mehr* for only 5,000.

Her *susural* had borrowed the jewelry from someone else, had presented it to her in front of everyone at the marriage, and then silently took it back and returned it to the real owners three days later. His parents even took back the *charpai* on which he used to sleep as a bachelor, and told him that the bed brought with Hasina's dowry was now his.

She says she has not enjoyed a good life with her husband, who works in Sohrab cycle factory near Gulberg. She is afraid of him and constantly says how hot-tempered he is. She questions his honesty and even his academic qualifications:

> He did his B.A.; the whole family says that my husband has a B.A., that's how I know he has it. He speaks English well. We were living with his parents until recently, when his brother told us to move out.
>
> My in-laws are originally from this *kucha*. They are the weakest in their family, but they don't realize it. Now their position is better. I don't know how they are with their other daughters-in-law.
>
> There is no man like my husband in my own family. After I was first married, I was scared of him....I had never seen a man like him...whenever I met him, I got scared of him, because his face was so scary. It haunted me....I didn't like the way he behaved or talked because no one in my family talks or behaves like him. My husband doesn't fight with men; he only fights with me. He is very wild.
>
> He fights more than any other Kakazaiya man. Most Kakazaiya men don't mind drinking or gambling, but my husband doesn't do either. In front of other men, he doesn't even talk. My mother-in-law spoiled my husband, and also his *chachis* spoiled him. He will fight with me over every little matter: if the flame on the stove isn't high enough, he'll curse me. He's been like this since childhood. My two *nunds* knew this, but no one told us. He sometimes curses his own mother, with such filthy words you can't listen to them. He's this kind of man that he'll remove my *dupatta* and my shoes and tell me to get out. (This is a traditional way of shaming a woman.)

In the beginning, he used to complain that I'm not beautiful and that I haven't brought much dowry: no buffalo, no television, no refrigerator. His expectation was that his in-laws would give him land, grain, etc., but they couldn't and they didn't.

I became pregnant after fifteen days of marriage. I was sixteen years old. When I was seven months pregnant with my first son, he beat me on my left forehead with a stick and I needed stitches. I was throwing up blood. I was in the hospital and all the doctors were saying it was very dangerous. People told me to "make a case" and report it to the police, but I didn't. When I was expecting my first child, my husband told me that if it's a girl he would divorce me. He had the divorce papers ready and he would have gone through with it. There are eight copies of each *nikahnama*: four are with my family, and four are with his family. When he used to threaten me, I took all eight papers into my possession. Then God blessed me with three sons, one after another. Then, a daughter came.

He's grabbed the baby's feeder, my arm, and bolted the door. Many times, he's pushed us into the street. When I got sick during last Ramadan, he pushed me out. He doesn't fast, he doesn't pray. He's stopped me from reading the Qur'an to do something for him, saying that it's the command of God for a woman to serve her family. He's stopped me from praying, though I read the Qur'an when he is not around. I think that I have been unlucky. There are many decent men in the world and many happily married women.

When I have left here, I have gone to my mother. I don't tell the whole story to my mother. I stay a week or a month. I send a message to my mother-in-law, who comes to my mother's house and then I tell her the whole story. My mother-in-law knows what kind of man my husband is.

Interestingly, Hasina associates her husband's harsh attitude towards her with his lack of piety. Her mother-in-law acts as the go-between, trying to patch up their marital problems and occasionally scolding her son. I questioned Hasina about her unhappiness and problems with her husband, as she does have four children:

Time after time, he beats me, but as sex is concerned, we continue to have relations. I am willing because it is necessary for me to stay in this house. I have to kill my feelings. If I try to stop him, he starts shouting, making noise and disturbing the entire neighborhood, so it becomes a question of *izzat* for me to obey my husband.

I don't think he sees other women because he's not very rich and he can't go without money to other ladies. The girls follow behind rich men. My in-laws have a lot of respect for me, but not for him.

I have no close girlfriends. My best childhood friend is Kausar. She is still not married, and I sometimes meet her at my mother's house. I can't call her here. After she saw what happened to me after marriage, she hasn't gotten married!

My mother doesn't have enough time to do anything special for me. She has so many responsibilities, with the house and the fields. The worst thing was that she married me to this Yazid.[7]

Bakr Eid is approaching, but we won't buy a goat or a lamb. No one in the neighborhood will give us meat, as we don't give them any. My mother-in-law hasn't bought any goat yet to sacrifice. We'll go to my mother's for *Eid*.

Shaking her head, Hasina reaches into her bra and takes out some money, a common way Punjabi women store valuables. She says she wishes she could do something about their financial problems, but doesn't know what to do.

Kanize

Kanize, the only Shi'a woman who told us her story, was born near Chowk Nawab Saheb, lying between Akbari and Mochi gates. Her family had a one-room rented house at the time that was owned by her father's sister. Both of her parents' families were originally from Amritsar and are Punjabi speakers. She believes her father was about three or four years old at Partition when his family came to Lahore.

Her mother died of stomach cancer when Kanize was about sixteen, eleven years ago. Kanize has no memories of her old house because "my mother died there." They moved to their own house, here, five years ago.

She has two brothers and two sisters (she is the third sister). She is the oldest and is about twenty-seven. Her married brother is twenty-four. She says that his marriage, which happened three years ago, was the only happy occasion in her life.

Kanize says that she studied for a few years at the Patran Haveli school near Akbari Gate, but told us that she was never happy at school. Her younger sister and brothers studied to about sixth class. Kanize instead just wanted to play all the time. When she used to come back home, she would tell her parents that the teachers beat the students, but it wasn't true. She said that when she was about eight, she finally convinced her parents to take her out of school. While this is her remembrance of the situation, a more likely possibility (rather than parents listening to an eight-year old wanting to drop out of school) is that her mother really needed her to help with the younger children. After her mother died, Kanize virtually has become the mother of the family. In response to this observation, she replied, "It's okay; time passes."

She cannot read, though she can write her name. She ascertains that she has no skills. In her "free time" -- when she is not making *samosas* for her father and brothers to sell in the bazaar -- she makes *handi* (hot curries), *roti* and washes the dishes.

Kanize's position in her home falls into a traditional context. As her mother is absent and there is no other older female to care for the daily needs of her home, she has become the surrogate mother. We met other older women in the Walled City who had once fulfilled a role like hers and remain a dependent of a married brother; presumably Kanize faces a similar fate.

Erum

Erum feels more comfortable talking with us in English than in Urdu as she teaches in English all day long. Now in her late thirties, she moved from Mughalpura to the Walled City in 1971 when she was married. The house in which she lives is owned by her *susural*, who have resided in it for over a hundred years. She lives in three rooms with Erum's husband, mother-in-law and four daughters. They are Sunni, of the Chughtai qaum, and Punjabi speakers.

Neither her *dada* or *nana* were highly educated (not beyond matric), but were very well off. Her *dada* had worked in Simla, where her late father was born. After her father completed his primary education in Simla, he studied for his matric in Lahore and then took some more courses. He became a foreman in the government railway carriage and wagon shops in Mughalpura.

Her mother was uneducated and was married when she was eighteen. After Erum's *nani* died, her *nana* didn't bother about his daughter or her education. Therefore, Erum's father spoke English while her mother did not.

Erum was born when her mother was nineteen or twenty. She is the oldest of six sisters and three brothers. Her *dada* and her father had many educated, English-speaking friends from Simla, and some foreign friends who influenced her father to educate all of his children. Erum, therefore, credits her father for her successful, happy life.

The house in Mughalpura where she grew up was very large. She remembers one room in that house being as large as four of the rooms in her present home. There were servant quarters, big lawns, a big area, and a garage where they kept some bull dogs, a motorcycle and a bicycle. The Government Railways department provided the house to her father. When he took early retirement, he moved to his own house in Gulberg. Her mother still lives in the front portion with Erum's two unmarried brothers and one unmarried sister (who is twenty-three or twenty-four; she had studied at Lady Griffen School in the Railway Colony area). The back portion is on rent.

Erum's primary education was at the European English-medium St. Andrews school on the Grand Trunk Road.[8] There was no co-education at that time. She studied there until third or fourth standard, then joined Kinnaird College where they had European teachers: Miss Nixon, Miss Wilson, etc. During those days, the girls also had to study the Bible at such schools. She received her B.A. from Kinnaird College, and then did her teacher training at Marian Training College in a well known girls' school in Lahore. In all, she studied for fifteen years and is fluent in both Urdu and English.

Some of her relatives -- her *chachi* objecting the most -- had opposed her studying after she completed her matric degree as they saw no need for Erum to study further. Erum's *chachi* and her three children were living with them at the time as her *chacha* was sick. However, Erum's father did not let her *chachi* interfere with her studies. The father proclaimed that *he* was the one to decide the matter, and it was fine with him for her to study if that was her wish. In fact, her next younger sister only did her Intermediate Degree, then sat at home until she was married.

Erum remembers her childhood as a lovely time with no responsibilities.

> I just had to study and play about. I especially liked badminton. I dreamed of a happy life and a happy house, that my husband shouldn't assert his way all the time.

Her father was nervous because hers was the first marriage that he was arranging. He wanted a respectable boy even if he was not rich. She recounts that her family received a lot of proposals as soon as she came of age because hers was a good family and she was well educated. While there were offers from other richer, well-qualified boys from abroad, she thinks her family was generally suspicious of these proposals. The family didn't know what the boys were like, whether they drank or went around with women, or if they had other problems.

Her marriage was arranged on her *mammu's* recommendation. She had "full faith" in her *mammu* because she knew he would check out her prospective husband's family well.

Her husband is from her *biradari*, although not a close relative.

> I was not closely related to my husband. It was only my *mammu* who knew him and his family. The engagement lasted nine months. Most people, including my husband, think that I did not see his face before our marriage. However, my *mammu* thought that I should see him, so one time when he came to our house for a visit, I peeked from behind a curtain.

Her husband's father was known to be a very good man, a very fine gentleman. She had not previously known anyone from her husband's family, although she came to know her *nund* a bit as her *nund* tried to be friendly with her. Erum felt shy when her *nund* came with saris and bangles before *Eid* and made a big fuss that she should wear them, even though the holiday had not yet arrived.

After her marriage, Erum moved into this house near Mochi Gate. Her father-in-law, who died long ago, had bought this house where her husband was born. Her mother-in-law owns it now and lives on the ground floor level. Erum doesn't know her neighbors well, although her mother-in-law and husband do. "We don't go to their houses really, only go now and then for deaths and marriages."

Her mother-in-law occasionally visits her son and his family who live upstairs too, but eats most of her meals and watches television with Erum's family. The other brother used to live downstairs with his family, but moved out some years ago.

Erum's first child was born in her parents' home. She took leave from teaching only two days before the delivery despite that her father had encouraged her to take leave earlier.

> The first child has to be born at the mother's place. It is customary to stay in the house forty days after the birth. But I took only one month maternity leave. After my daughter was born, people in the family said that I must now have a son. That is so narrow-minded! After the birth, my father wanted me to quit my job. The same thing happened after the birth of my second child. My in-laws didn't particularly like me working. My husband supported me, though. Also, since we had daughters, we realized that we needed more money. All of our daughters were educated at the school where I teach as I get a large reduction on fees because I teach there.

Her daily chores begin with making breakfast. In the winter, she makes quick breakfasts -- usually just bread and butter -- as they are in a rush in the mornings, though her husband prefers a heavy breakfast like french toast. In summer, they usually have *kulcha* and butter and eat fewer eggs, and sometimes have *halwa/puri* and porridge. When Erum returns from teaching, she prepares the evening meal. She is glad she can afford to hire a sweeper to clean the floors in her home, so she doesn't have to do that work too.

Chand Bibi

Chand Bibi's story is representative of women's experiences and changes which have arisen in their moral vocabulary due to poverty and other hardships. Very, very thin, with a mouth dyed red from *pan*, her husband of nineteen years died a year ago from "madness." While we were sitting there, Chand Bibi consumed three *pan* in two and a half hours. She said she had tuberculosis, and often coughed into the *chadar* (veil) she wears as a *dupatta* around her neck. During our first interview, she asked why I didn't speak better Urdu, and was surprised that people in the United States do not speak Urdu and that most do not even know of Urdu.

She told us that she had applied for *zakat*, as she is a widow, and had received 100 rupees monthly for a year until last *Bakr Eid*, when she was given 200 rupees. Since then, she has received nothing. She said that the chairman of the local zakat council, however, has recently built a new home for himself. Indeed, she strongly hinted that this was fraudulent.

She is a Sunni and is completely illiterate. Her family are Pathans from Bareilly in Uttar Pradesh, India, although she herself was born in Krishannager about forty years ago. Given her heritage as a *muhajir*, she still regards Urdu as her mother tongue and rarely speaks Punjab. Both of her parents were completely illiterate. Her mother had given birth to seven daughters; the youngest, Chand Bibi is the only survivor. Her mother had wanted a son but was a tuberculosis patient, became feverish and died when Chand Bibi was just about a year old.[9] She doesn't recall ever having seen her mother, and only heard this story from her *chachi* who raised her.

Her father and his brother (her *chacha*) came to Pakistan in 1947, followed six months later by her mother and her *chachi* after the men had arranged for a house. She does not know what her family had done in Bareilly other than they had lived there and that her father had worked as a *chaprassi* (peon) in the telephone office. In Lahore, her father became a tonga driver. Chand Bibi has vivid memories of him vomiting blood and dying from tuberculosis when she was six. Her *chacha*, who was working on the telephone lines at the GPO (General Post Office), took her to live with him and his wife who were now childless as their son and daughter had both died. The son died at about a year old: to put the child to sleep, the parents had given him opium, and they gave him too much and he died.

When remembering her childhood in Krishannager, she recalls there was no electricity; they used lanterns. Water was taken from a nearby tap. She never studied as her guardians feared for her safety: from traffic, from getting lost, from the outside world. A female neighbor also from Bareilly taught her how to read the Qur'an when she was between eight and eleven years old. Typically, after she woke up and prayed she would pour *ghee* over two slices of bread (sometimes over *parathas*) and eat them with tea. Then she would wash clothes, pray in the early afternoon and then, after she turned ten years old, she would prepare the evening meal. Her *chachi* did all the foodshopping at the bazaar.

However, after her *chacha* was promoted to be a superintendent at the GPO/telephone lines, his brain was destroyed when someone poisoned his rice pudding. After eating it, he slept for two days and had no idea what was happening to him. He lived in an insane asylum for four more years before he died.

When Chand Bibi was in her early teens, her *chachi* became a seamstress. She taught Chand Bibi how to hem for her. Because of this, despite their poverty, Chand Bibi had ample clothes growing up. She told us that she had about fifteen suits: some were for summer, some for winter, and a few fancy suits for weddings and other functions. While she learned how to sew, she didn't bother to learn how to cut fabric from her *chachi* because she was the *ghar ki ladli* (spoilt princess; gem of the house).

They lived in Krishannager until she was twenty, when they moved close to Shadbagh, near the Ravi River. She lived there two years until her marriage, when she was twenty-two.

Her childhood dreams revolved around getting a good marriage, particularly on marrying into a good family and having a good house. However, she couldn't recall a single special day in her childhood: "My life was so unhappy, so sad, there was no good day I remember."

Before her marriage, she went to Bareilly once with her *chachi* to visit her *mamani* and *mammu*, a furniture-maker. He had sent money for her and her *chachi* to visit them in India. Chand Bibi was also able to meet her future husband's sisters' families there. Her father-in-law had died in Bareilly from paralysis shortly after Pakistan's creation, and while her mother-in-law had followed her three sons to Lahore, her two married daughters had remained in India.

Whenever I asked Chand Bibi about her worst experiences in her life, she would start to talk about her marriage and how her husband lacked a hand and had weak eyesight. Her *chachi* had paid for the marriage which was arranged by a *wacholan* (matchmaker).

Her husband's sister had gone to the *wacholan* to see about finding a girl for him. Their family are also Pathans (but unrelated). There are no special meeting areas used by people from her area per se, although they meet at functions such as weddings and funerals. Chand Bibi said that, aside from those times, they really did not keep in touch with others from Bareilly and that there is way too much gossip if they meet too often. This is why families have to resort to having a *wacholan* seek out a bride or bridegroom. The *wacholan* who arranged her marriage was from Bareilly too and knew both families. However, Chand Bibi perceives the *wacholan* as having been her husband's family's *wacholan*.

Wacholans go from door-to-door, and by chance this woman came to know of me. I only met the *wacholan* after my marriage. People don't like it if you have a meeting with a *wacholan*. This one sold her house and left for Karachi two years ago.

The *wacholan* who arranged my marriage -- I only found out later, after the marriage -- didn't have a very good reputation. She had not told my family about his useless hand. Only tricky, clever women become *wacholans*. Nowadays, fewer women are *wacholans*.

My family went to my future husband's house twice; they came to see us twice; and then the wedding happened. I just sat in a corner. Fifteen days before my marriage, I came to know I was to be married. I had no engagement, only a *nikah* (marriage), it was very simple. But I was cheated: his age was old, he lacked a hand, and he lost his eyesight after one year. There was only the wedding ceremony; everything happened in one day.

Her dowry consisted of four *charpais*, a table (but no chairs) and some tiny stools, about fifty assorted pots, pans and dishes, some copper pots, a few boxes for clothes and bedding, eleven suits, a gold ring and a pair of gold earrings.

Her *chachi* requested that the *haq mehr* be 5,000 rupees. Her husband's *maulvi* said the *haq mehr* should be thirty-two rupees, as that is the amount stipulated in the Qur'an. His family said that 5,000 rupees was too much, but her *chachi* stuck to it and got it.

The night before my marriage, I was worried that my *chachi* would be all alone. I wept all night, I never slept. Five days earlier, I took off all my bangles, and wore yellow cotton clothes. My *chachi* had stitched them for me. The marriage was the last week in August, during the monsoon, so it was hot. It was just before Muharram.

I woke at 4 p.m., and wore a red *gherrara* with *gota* embroidery on it. My *susural* had sent it for me. They also sent a suit and a gold set: two gold bangles, a necklace, a pair of earrings and a ring. After eight months, they took the gold back. I think they gave it to my *dewarani* on her marriage.

What can I say about when I first saw my husband's face? I didn't feel afraid. What can a respectable woman say? The *wacholan* who arranged the marriage had pressured us into the marriage. My husband's age was about twenty years older than me. He died at about sixty years.

When he was small (two or three years old), he used to love yogurt, or so the story goes. One day, he saw some hot whitewash, and stuck his right hand in, thinking it was yogurt. Since then, his right hand was useless. He also had bad eyesight.

My *susural* were good. My mother-in-law told me that the gold that was given to me on my marriage was my *dewarani's*, so it had to be returned. "If your husband can afford it, you can have it later on." It was a question of *izzat* (respectability) that my *susural* requested the jewelry from my *dewarani*. There's an expression: don't cut off your nose in front of others.

I shifted to this house on the day of my marriage; I was sixteen or seventeen years old. Nineteen years have passed, that I've lived in this house.

While Chand Bibi claims to be about thirty-five, she looks as if she is in her late forties. Her artificial gold bangles somehow make her appear even weaker.

In this house, my *jaithani* lived in the room on the ground floor. My mother-in-law lived in this room (the room we were sitting in), I lived in the next room. My second *dewarani* lived in the room upstairs.

How does being a Hindustani woman from Bareilly make me different from the Punjabi women? Speech, and the way we live. My *dewarani* and *jaithani* are Punjabis; I speak Punjabi with them, and Urdu with my mother-in-law. We cook differently, and the taste is absolutely different. When we cook, Punjabis like it. We don't like their food. Punjabis cook sweet potatoes and make it sweet -- it's not good. For spicy meatballs, they use a machine to make it round, with some almonds and white cardamon, and cook it -- how awful! Punjabis also make *muli roti* (flat bread with radishes); it's not good. They become our disciples when they eat our ground beef curry.

I find too many Punjabis are mean and prejudiced against muhajirs. At first they try to be friendly, but they get under our skins. If a Hindustani corrects a Punjabi, the Punjabis greatly mind it. We don't mind it as much.

Chand Bibi is a wealth of information as to how marriages should be arranged, and shared many *wacholan* stories with us. She said that most people hold the impression that *wacholans* cheat, deceive, and overall are not good. However, *wacholans* are needed because it is difficult to find good marriage prospects, especially if there are many daughters. She told us that a *wacholan* had once told a girl's family that a boy was good. In fact, he was a drunkard and had strangled a child by the neck, in addition to being a divorcee and a cheat. Often, it happens that the girl's family tries to believe that the boy is good; if you believe so, then after a week or a month after marriage the girl comes to know that the boy isn't good.

A *wacholan* had arranged her cousin's marriage. The boy had seemed ideal: he worked in the Passport Office, earned 4,000 rupees per month, and had a B.A. But after seven months, he divorced her. He told her *she* wasn't good -- he accused her of not being a good wife, of having an affair. He restricted her to the house and wanted her to go out only with him. But the truth is that he had wanted to marry someone else and his parents would not allow it. At the time he left her, her cousin was pregnant; now the case for supporting the child has gone on for over three years in the courts.

Another *wacholan* had arranged a girl's marriage; the family had seen the boy, met the boy. On the wedding night, he took off his boots -- boots that must have cost 250 rupees -- and there was no foot in it! The girl went crying and screaming to her mother and father; the mother-in-law said there was nothing the girl could do now; her fate was sealed in her marriage.

Chand Bibi does not view the decision of her marriage as having been a question of desires or choices. She was ready to do whatever her aunt and uncle wanted her to do, and it never occurred to her that she had the option to agree or not.

Durdana

Her family are Sunni Sheikhs, originally from Delhi, though she was born in the Walled City. Now in her early thirties, she can speak Urdu well as it is her native language though she is completely illiterate. She has four sons and one daughter, and has lived with her husband in this house for the past eleven years.

All she knows about her natal family's background is that they had lived near the Red Fort in the old city of Delhi, had kept chickens in the house and had migrated to Lahore in 1947. She was born in Moti Bazaar, two *galis* over. She is the fourth child in a large family: she has two older brothers and an older sister, and five younger brothers and six younger sisters.

Her *dada* was the head of the family and everyone had to go along with his decisions. He made artificial jewelry in a small factory near the house, but did not own any other land. She remembers forty or fifty people working there, although she agreed that her perceptions of numbers from that time might be problematic. Her *dada* had a very short temper; Durdhana never attended school because her *dada* didn't want her to go. Eventually, he agreed that some of her younger sisters could receive some formal eduction but it was too late then for Durdhana. "I wanted very much to study -- I even got a beating, but *dada* said only bad females study."

While she never went to school, she did learn how to count. When she was young, she would sometimes go to the bazaar to fetch things, so she was allowed out at times. Between the ages of eight and ten she studied the Qur'an, learning from a lady in her neighborhood in the afternoons.

They lived in a three-storey building; one family on each floor. Their own living area was small and there were "too many people, too much cleaning up to do." As a child, she would play with dolls a lot. She made the dolls herself and would play hide and seek with *dupattas*. Everyone used to get angry with her because she played so much.

The best day in my childhood was my oldest brother's wedding day. After
the wedding, we caught sparrows on the rooftop by putting bait in a basket
and then covering the basket. My *bhabi*, who was from our *biradari*, was
fifteen or sixteen when she was married. I had a lot of fun with my *bhabi*.
Often, we used to set the birds free. A few times the sparrows died and we
buried them. We would say the *kalma* over the birds, and other prayers. My
father would get angry when he heard this. My brother hit both my *bhabi*
and myself when a bird died -- he was about eighteen then.

In those days, she used to dream that someday she would have a good
house, a good marriage and live in a "good society." She hoped that her
husband would be very rich and would have a very large house. Before
her wedding, there was no bad day at all that she can remember.

Everyone used to be happy when her *dada*, who prayed five times
daily, went to the mosque because they were scared of him and could
now relax. He died fifteen years ago from old age; her father died two
years later from tuberculosis. She says that her father was sick with
tuberculosis for about forty years, then it got worse, and he died.

About two years after Durdhana's elder sister was married at age
fourteen, her father decided it was time she was married. Her father said
that he wanted all his daughters married before he died. When Durdana
was eleven, she was engaged to her *khala's* son. The engagement was
broken three years later because her father became impatient to get her
married. He felt the boy was studying too much and he didn't want to
wait for the boy to complete his B.A. Another proposal was immediately
arranged with her *bhabi's mammu*; here, there was no real engagement,
just a verbal agreement. Durdana had menstruated three times before her
marriage, hence her father's urgency to want her marriage to take place
immediately, so she would not be at risk. She was married at age
thirteen, three to five years before her father's death.

Durdana doesn't remember the date of her marriage, but she knows
that it took place twenty-five days after *Bakr Eid*. The entire planning and
celebration lasted for eight days. On the first day, male members from
both families, plus the two mothers, met at her house to decide on the
wedding date. Durdana and her *bhabi* prepared the meal for everyone; it
consisted of special foods including rich curries, biryani, *lal roti*, sweet
rice, and fruit. On the second day, her future *susural* brought various
sweets which they distributed to all the close relatives of both parties.
Durdana notes that "nothing came from our own pocket."

On the third day, her entire family -- her mother, *bhabi* and the men
-- went door-to-door to relatives and close friends with invitation cards
for her marriage. No sweets or other things were distributed. The next
day, they concentrated on getting her dowry organized. On the fifth day,

her *susural* brought a yellow suit (which she was to wear until the actual ceremony), yellow paste made from turmeric and other spices, milk and oil with which she was massaged, and sweets for her friends.

On the sixth day, her family visited the boy's family with henna, oil and gifts. This was the final preparation before the *nikah*, which was held on the seventh day. On the final day, her *susural* held a small reception to which they invited their relatives to meet the new member of their family.

Her dowry included about 100 glasses, crockery, four sets of bedding, a large clay pot, a copper *hamam*, furniture (a bed, a stool, two chairs and one sofa), a table fan, fifteen suits, and one gold set consisting of a necklace, earrings and a ring.

Her family gave the groom a gold ring, a watch, one summer suit, two winter suits, two *shalwar kamizes* for summer, and one pair of western shoes. Her susural gave her a "red *gherrara sherara*" (meaning, the whole wedding suit, complete with embroidered *dupatta*), one sari, a sweater, cloth for *shalwar kamize* suits -- twenty-one suits in total -- and twenty *tolas* of gold. "All the jewelry was in my name." The *haq mehr* was 10,000 rupees.

In Durdana's family, wedding arrangements and celebrations sometimes last up to two months. She feels, however, that the dowry is never considered to be enough by one's *susural*. "Even if you give all the money in the world for your daughter, her in-laws will ask -- what did you give? -- implying that it is never enough..."

Her *khala*, whose son she didn't marry, was angry with her family for five years. But they all came together and reconciled with each other at her father's death. Her family then gave her younger sister to the boy's younger brother, which sealed good relations between the two families. Durdana expresses mixed feelings about her broken first engagement. "I wasn't so sensible yet when that happened, and I didn't understand what was going on, but this marriage is better for me." Presumably, she would say this as she remains married to her husband. It would look quite bad in this cultural context to have any regrets about what happened. The cousin she didn't marry ended up marrying an illiterate girl from within the family.

Following her marriage,

I first lived in *kucha* Badar Kali, in a house two *galis* over, for a month. My husband's family was given the house there as evacuee property. They bought another house there too. They had sold fruit and milk in Delhi. They began making plastic toys when they came here. We came to this house twelve years ago. Don't ask why we came, or I'll begin to cry. We first lived as renters next door for four years, paying sixty rupees monthly as rent. My big *jaithani* — the old house became hers. My small *jaithani* finally got her own house. Four years after we became separate households, the reconciliation came about at my *jaithani's* daughter's marriage.

Durdana's four sons and one daughter live with them in their small quarters. The only vehicle they have is a bicycle; she claims her husband is afraid of having a motorcycle, but given their economic condition it appears more likely that this is just an excuse she gives. In her view, her husband is quite pious: he never watches films and has performed *hajj* (pilgrimage) twice.

Amina

Amina, now in her mid-fifties, lives with three of her daughters, her one son, and her husband in a flat owned by her husband just off Jaura Mori Bazaar, a short walk from Wachowali. Her other five daughters are married. Hers is a Punjabi-speaking, Sunni, Rajput family. She moved to Pakistan when she was about fifteen years old during the height of the fighting after Partition. While completely illiterate, Amina has vivid memories of her childhood and commands a good analysis of the causes of events in her life.

She was born at her mother's house in Amritsar, before Partition. Her mother was 13-14 when she had been married, and gave birth to a total of five daughters and four sons. Three of Amina's brothers had died before she, the youngest child in her family, was born. Amina's eldest sister is about twenty-five years senior to her.

Her father had died when Amina was very young and she has no recollection of him. Her mother's health had been fine until her three sons and then her husband died. As her family did not own any land, they went to live with Amina's married brother, wife and daughter for a little while. However, when her brother became very sick with tuberculosis, a doctor in Delhi advised him to go to the mountains. He went with his family to Quetta, where, she says, he died one week after Pakistan's creation.

Amina and her mother then went to live with her mother's elder sister. She remembers the house had two rooms, a veranda, and basically had "a good standard of living" and was an "enough to eat and drink kind-of-house". They had cows and a male servant to look after the cattle and such work.

One of her *mammus* had died in his youth. He had become angry with the family and left for China.[10] Before he left, he had been married to a Pakistani woman. After some time, she went back to her own family. Amina doesn't know if she remarried. He married a Chinese woman though never brought her with him when he came back 2-4 times to visit. He used to send money to Amina's mother, but after his death, nothing came. His Chinese wife informed them in a letter of his death. While he was alive, they would hear news about his daughter, but since his death they don't know anything about what has happened to her.

Amina recalls that her mother had wanted to send her to school in Amritsar, though she never did and Amina does not know why. Instead, Amina used to spend most of her time playing, especially with dolls. She and her friends would play a game where they would toss 2-4 stones and a small ball in the air and they would have to pick up the stones and catch the ball before its second bounce. The girls played together, never with the boys. They made their own dolls by hand and would dress them up and have them get married. She realizes that, at the time, all of her dreams, goals and ideals revolved around her future marriage, and that this was expressed in play.

I'd play with my friends and dolls when we lived in my mother's house. My girlfriends and I would make dolls together and then we'd have them get married. After that, life was tough. If the parents are there, then it's a pleasant thing; without parents, life is difficult. When I was young, my brother and sisters loved me very much and bought me cloth and bangles. After my brother got sick and died and we went to my *khala's* house, life became more difficult. Later, my brother's wife, who is my *khalazad behan*, remarried and now lives in Shahdara. She is my youngest *khala's* daughter.

She doesn't think her family made the conscious decision that they wanted to come to Pakistan. They had virtually no other choice.

We were staying with my sister and her husband in Delhi when the disturbances broke out. The government told us to leave our houses and shift to camps which were quite far off. It would have been very dangerous if we had stayed in our homes. It was hard to get food in the camps. Only one man, my *mammu*, was with us, as my sister's husband continued to go to his office in the Red Fort.

When they were in the camps, they were informed that Pakistan had come into being. When the decision was made that there would be two countries, the Indian government asked them to leave for Pakistan at once. Her sister was pregnant at that time. "We didn't do anything in the camp, just sat around. Helicopters brought us food there. We only stayed a short time in the camp, a week or a month."

She had come to Pakistan with her elder sister, elder sister's husband, their two boys, two girls, mother-in-law and *nund*.

We arranged to take a train to Pakistan, but were detained for 2-4 days in
the train on the way. We faced a lot of problems. People were beheaded,
young girls were caught and raped by Sikhs. The train which had left Delhi
for Amritsar before ours met with a tragedy. It left a few hours earlier; we
were supposed to be on that train, but couldn't get a place so we had to
wait for the next train. Everyone on that train was killed; not a single
person lived. There was so much blood, so much blood, it was just like the
River Ravi. It was a sea of blood, all over the luggage, everywhere. We
didn't eat for three days. My sister gave birth to a baby girl in a latrine. It
was very difficult.

Amina cannot remember the day or the date when they arrived in
Pakistan. The government had made an announcement that they should
be informed if any relatives were missing in India. Her *mammu's* wife,
newly-wed, had been taken away by Sikhs during the journey to
Pakistan. Her two brothers were killed as the Sikhs took her off. Amina
recalls that the Pakistan army had camps by the border from which they
would leave for India and ransack Punjabi villages. This is how they
found and brought back her *mamani*. Her *mammu* had been crying over
her, over his *izzat* and his wife. They had her *mamani* say the *kalma* again,
as she had lived with Hindus and Sikhs. Her *mamani* went on to live a
regular life; her children are now married. However, some of the young
girls committed suicide after they lost their *izzat*.

After they arrived in Pakistan, she and her elder sister's family stayed
with relatives for a week -- or maybe longer -- on Mohny Road, near the
back side of Data Saheb. They then shifted to an allotted house in
Wachowali Bazaar arranged for by her brother-in-law. Many Hindus and
Sikhs had lived in that area, so now many homes were vacant.

I lived in Wachowali for two years before my marriage, at about age fifteen.
Since then, I have never lived outside the Walled City. I was happy to be
with my relatives. We thought we would get back everything as long as we
were alive and together. My brother-in-law was a double M.A. In India, he
had been employed as a guard in the Red Fort; in Lahore, he was employed
at the Lahore Fort.

Amina always has much praise for this brother-in-law, who she
admires as a "very qualified man." At one point, she told us he had been
an "ambassador," although this was probably used more by way of
admiration than with any sort of objective validity. What is underscored
is how subjective the term "very qualified" can be.

Of her own natal family, her eldest sister died fifteen years ago, and
all of her children live in Kuwait. Her second eldest sister, the one with
whom they came to Pakistan and whose husband is her *khalazad bhai* and

very respectable, lives in Karachi with her son. Amina's third sister lives in Sheikhupura and her fourth sister lives in Shadbagh, both areas on the outskirts of Lahore.

Two years' after the creation of Pakistan, Amina was married. Her second sister's mother-in-law, who is also her *khala*, arranged the *rishta*. While her husband is not actually a relative, he is in her *khala's* daughter's *susural*, being the son of the father-in-law's *mammu*.

Amina only heard about her engagement after people in her house started talking about it.

> The engagement happened, and then the *nikah* was six months later. I never met my husband before. He was about twenty-five, I was about fifteen. He was tall, handsome, in good health. But it was a *mammuli-si-shadi* (very plain wedding). My husband walked from Wachowali to Sutermandi Bazaar. When I left with the *baraat*, I was brought back on a tonga in which no horse was used; the men just pulled it. Because I had no brother, no father, my dowry was small: one set of gold earrings, 4-5 suits of clothes, plates and glasses for six, two cooking pots, and some bedding. There were no *charpais*, no stools, no bangles, no necklace. My *susural* gave me two gold rings, a gold clip, five suits, a *burqa*, 1-2 pairs of shoes and a *paranda* with which to braid my hair. There weren't any bangles. They gave us a *charpai* so we would not have to sleep on the floor, although I didn't own it.

Her husband's mother had previously died leaving her with no mother-in-law to either look after her or to argue with her. She and her husband lived with his elder brother, a tailor, and she had good relations with her *jaithani*, his wife. Amina's husband was a police constable in Kasur at that time. They were living in Sutermandi, near the sweet stalls, inside Lohari Gate. The building had three floors: she lived on the bottom; above her was her *khala's* relative; on the top was her *jaith* and his family. The third brother had moved to Multan (two of his sons have since married two of her daughters). After six months, her *jaith* said that they should live apart, with separate finances.

> My mother used to bring meats and vegetables, with her money. She would sometimes make *handi* (hot curry) for me. I was sixteen when my first daughter was born. I was afraid and naive when my daughter was born, a year after my marriage. We were happy as she was the first child. We gave out *ladoos* (sweets) to neighbors and close relatives. I had my daughter at home, with the help of my *jaithani*, mother and *khala's* daughter. There were no nurses, no Lady Health Visitors. Now Pakistan has progressed.

The next child came after three years. She became a bit worried after the second daughter because she now had too many responsibilities. The next child was a son, but he died at birth, and she became very sick with fever. "I cried a lot after getting six daughters – the next four were daughters! I prayed day in and day out for a son, and finally had one."

Amina's life, like so many of the women in the Walled City, has been more strongly affected by the forces of fate than by her own initiative or actions. When she was younger and desired something for her life, she was powerless to affect it and turned to prayer. Now that she is older, she finds she enjoys an enhanced degree of power within her household and especially over the lives of her daughters.

Bilqis

Bilqis, now in her late forties, lives with her husband, two daughters, four sons, and the four daughters of her *jaith* in a four-room house which her husband owns. She has lived here for the past seven years. The entire family is engaged in making shoes. They are Jats and speak Punjabi as their mother language. Bilqis was born in Amritsar and was nearly ten when she came to Pakistan.

> When I was in Amritsar at the age of five or six, I most remember that people used to threaten us that American aircraft would bombard the city, and we would be killed anytime. We were also threatened a lot with blackouts then.

Bilqis is not sure which war was going on at the time; she is most likely recalling events which occurred during the Second World War. She remembers that her family was able to buy dry goods from a government-run depot. To purchase cloth, they would first have to show their ration card and then, only after verification, they could buy it. They had to get the ration card from one place and then get the cloth from another, a lengthy procedure. Edible basics such as flour and sugar were also rationed.

Before she came to Pakistan, she had been admitted into a girls' school, but only studied for about a year. She says that the teachers used to beat the children with sticks and she would run away.

> Other memories of Amritsar? We used to see our Hindu neighbors. I remembers seeing the *chamars* (leatherworkers, untouchables) from far off. I used to meet with my *mammu, taya* and other relatives there. There were no restrictions on me in Amritsar. The *mahaul* (social environment) was much better than in this old city.

But when questioned about her childhood aspirations from Amritsar, Bilqis replies,

Mera koi khwab nehi. (I had no dreams.) I don't ever miss Amritsar. I've forgotten about it. When I was ten years old, the war between India and Pakistan began. I came to Pakistan with my mother. My father had been killed in Amritsar. At the Amritsar station, I saw so many people killed.

When they first arrived in Pakistan, they lived near Syad Mithha Bazaar, in Hakimawala Katra (inside Bhati Gate), the neighborhood where Itrat and her family reside. It is a fairly long walk from where Bilqis now lives in Kucha Sheikan, off Jaura Mori Bazaar, a short walk from Wachowali Bazaar and Shah Alami Gate.

It was exactly like this place, but this place is more restrictive. When my daughter goes out, people stare at her for no reason. Some people stayed in camps, but we didn't, we stayed in some Hindu's house in Syad Mithha. I came with my mother and brother. We came to know through other people that these houses are empty, so we went and took one. That house had not been allotted to us.

In Amritsar they had lived in a three-storey house, owned by her father, in the Old City. Her family made a claim for that house, and received a house in Wachowali as a replacement. Her four brothers still live in Wachowali.

All the refugees had settled in that area (Wachowali Bazaar), as that property had been owned by Hindus. Wachowali is near Shah Alami Gate, on the side by Sua bazaar, the gold bazaar. My brother still lives in that house. When we first came to Lahore, life was better than it is now.

She has two sisters and four brothers. Her brothers were educated, though neither she nor her sisters were. One brother completed his matric exam in Amritsar; the other two went up to class five or six. The one who did his matric from Amritsar went to London to work. He worked with machines in some sort of factory.

When my brother was in London, we had his *nikah* over the telephone. The entire family was in the Mumtaz Mahel Hotel in Shah Alami when the *nikah* was held. I never visited him in London. He has come back to Pakistan now after living there fifteen or sixteen years. He's been here about 2-4 years now. He has four girls and two boys. His house is better than most, in the same *gali* as mine. He rents his own shop. He is an iron-worker. But I don't meet with him, I don't go to his house, because when he was in England and used to come to visit Pakistan, he didn't invite us as he should have done with his elder sister.

In all likelihood, she and her family probably expected gifts which her

brother couldn't afford to bring. In the Walled City, there are many
adherents of the myth that whenever someone works outside the country
they become fabulously rich.

Bilqis was married when she was sixteen or seventeen. Her mother's
brother arranged her marriage.

> My *mammu* proposed a man for me, and then the marriage took place. My
> husband is not related to us. My *mammu* proposed him because my
> husband had lived near to them in Amritsar and my *mammu* knew him. He
> was now a neighbor in Lahore and I knew him very well before the
> marriage. He had been engaged in his *khala's* house first. The girl was
> uneducated and short, so he refused.

The above is curious as an excuse: Bilqis is also uneducated and not
very tall. She says that she didn't expect to marry him because he was
engaged somewhere else. Did her marriage happen by chance? "I don't
know. A girl has no choice in this country, and my mother said yes."

Her engagement took place in her house. She was told about it two
weeks earlier. The *nikah* took place a year later, when she was seventeen.

Her dowry consisted of "a small amount of things". It included
cookware and dinnerware (service for six), eleven suits, a large, decorated
charpai, one stool, one suitcase, and some jewelry (a ring, a nose ring, and
one set of earrings). "There were no chairs, bangles, or necklace. There
was no *haq mehr* either. The custom does exist in my family, but I did not
have any."

Her father-in-law now owns three houses. He had sold off the
replacement property he was given by the Pakistani government for
300,000 rupees, which was divided among his three sons (one of whom
is her husband) and they each bought separate houses. They had to pay
120,000 rupees for the house they live in now.

In the course of the following three years, I returned to visit all these
women in the Walled City. Only Bilqis' household circumstances changed
dramatically: her husband died during the summer of 1988. However,
except for his absence, nothing else seemed very different. The family
lived in the same house and everyone still helped out making shoes. She
feels that the reason why her life has not changed appreciably since her
husband's death is because her family remains together and she has sons.

Itrat

Itrat is in her late thirties and is from a Pathan family. She lives in *gali*
Panch Pir (off Bazaar Syad Mithha inside Bhati Gate) with her husband
-- who is her *khalazad bhai* -- and their two sons, four daughters and a

nephew and a niece. Another married daughter lives nearby. While Itrat is completely illiterate, she possesses a deep awareness that poverty has played a major role in the events of her life. As she achieves higher status within her family and household as her sons become older, she is trying to exert greater influence to overcome poverty's obstacles, such as by working herself and educating her daughters.

Itrat was born in Moti Bazaar, near Masti Gate, two years before Partition. She is unsure where her father is from, and says that he never spoke about having any relatives. Her father had gone to India and married her mother, who was from Delhi. Her mother used to talk in Urdu with everyone because that was her native language, so they spoke Urdu at home.

When I was young, I spent most of my time in my house, playing with dolls and my friends. I got the dolls from the bazaar, for a quarter or half of a rupee. Sometimes, even for one rupee! My family didn't have any money for studying, and they didn't think of studying. No one in my family studied.

My father and mother were both illiterate. My father did *salma sitara* work in a small workshop on the ground floor where we lived upstairs. The property had belonged to Hindus — we just moved in there. I don't know how, but the house was put into my father's name.

My sister was the oldest in our family, then my brother, then my other sister, then me. I used to wake up at 5 a.m. and help clean the house and prepare the food. When I was five or six years old there were no restrictions on me. But when I grew up, there were a lot of restrictions. I couldn't go here, I couldn't go there. All the time, my parents kept track of me. I couldn't go anywhere alone, and had to respect what they said.

My menses began two years before my marriage, when I was about twelve. I felt strange when they began; it was something new and bizarre. I wasn't so clever then, and really didn't understand what was happening to me. I was very innocent about life. Poor people, they don't have any knowledge about these things.

There was no special happy day or sad day in my childhood. Children have no awareness...what can they know? For *Eid*, we would usually get one or two new suits. We did have good food: good meat, nice desserts like *sivayan* (roasted vermicelli in milk), good *handi*, and roasted meat. We would eat roasted meat at least once a week, sometimes more, as it wasn't so expensive then. We usually had *dal* and vegetables. On a special day, we would have chicken. I liked everything; I didn't have any special preferences. Because of poverty, I had to be happy with everything I had. Poor people have no life.

As a child, I didn't have the sense to ponder things. I had no awareness of any dreams, hopes or wishes.

Two months before her marriage occurred, she came to know that it was about to take place. There was no engagement.

My sister told me that soon I was to marry my *khalazad bhai*. I was indifferent about marrying him. I knew him, but I had no emotion, not happy, not sad, not angry. It made no difference to me if he was a relative or not. I had no girlfriends to discuss it with and I couldn't talk with my sisters as they were older. There was no one around at all to talk to, whatsoever.

My husband is ten years older than me. He has three brothers and one sister. His family has lived in this house since Partition; the house is now in his name.

The wedding lasted five days for everything, from putting the henna on my hands at the *mehndi* to my *susural's* reception. My family gave out invitations a few days before the *mehndi* ceremony. There was a lot of singing at the *mehndi*. About a week before, they applied special yellow paste to my arms, legs and body so my skin would be light and clear. I wore no make-up, and just washed my face and teeth, that was all. I wore yellow clothes the entire week before. That week, I wore fresh flowers for earrings and bangles, but it was like I was in prison, I couldn't go outside at all.

Her dowry consisted of five suits, one bed (no other furniture) and miscellaneous cookware, whatever her family could get. She points out that there were no stools, no tables, "nothing" because they were so poor.

Her *susural* gave her a pair of dangling earrings, a pendant necklace, a *tikka* for her hair, three rings (but no nose ring), a half kilogram of silver, eleven suits and a pair of silver anklets. The *haq mehr* was agreed to be 2,000 rupees.

Her life after marriage closely resembled her life in her parents' home due to their poverty.

There was no difference after I was married. My life didn't change at all because I had the same housework to do, the same restrictions. My husband could not provide me with good clothes. I had better food at my mother's house. My *susural* cooked the food to their own taste, and I didn't care for it. I had a good relationship with my mother-in-law, who was also my *khala*. My *khala* was older, and when I became annoyed with her I just kept quiet.

Life was very hard for me after my marriage. My father died, then my mother, then my sister, my brother, and my other sister, then my sister's daughter died of a brain hemorrhage. I now have no brothers or sisters. My brother went to Ireland, had a heart problem and died there. His son lives with his mother in Gujjar Gali in Syad Mithha. My brother had dealt in diamonds and his son is also a goldsmith. My eldest sister died eight years ago; the second eldest died eleven years ago. One of these sisters was Shamsa's mother. My elder sister's husband still makes goatskin hats and hides in Moti Bazaar.

Itrat's father died when she was fourteen. She had been married a year earlier, when she was thirteen. "A year after my marriage, I had my first daughter. The first three were daughters, then two sons, then two more daughters." Her mother died a year after her father, when Itrat was fifteen. However, the timeline of events in her life remains extremely unclear, as she provides various accounts ("she died when I was fifteen," and "she died six or seven years ago"), underscoring the fluidity of time to women.

While Itrat emphasizes that her husband is a good, understanding man, she doesn't express much happiness about her life. She cannot recall what was the best day in her life since she was married.

There hasn't been any, so I can't tell you. When my children were born, we were very happy. There are too few girls in my susural, so everyone was equally happy at the birth of the girls as the boys. Most of my daughters will probably marry within the family. If money is there, there's happiness. Without enough money, there's nothing. No happiness, no life.

Itrat had been close to her late sister, whose son and daughter she is now raising. She feels it is important that her niece, Shamsa, be married off to a good family. Itrat still starts to cry when she thinks of her sister. When we were visiting one day, Itrat had gone with Shamsa's brother to meet her prospective susural, and we had a long talk with Shamsa about the arrangements for her upcoming marriage. Everyone else told us that Shamsa is about twenty-five; she herself agreed that she's probably twenty-one or twenty-two. Her mother was a Pathan, although her father is a Sheikh. The *rishta* is from outside their family, with another Pathan family. The bridegroom works in the weather bureau in Sialkot; I presume he is an office worker there. Itrat had never met the boy before the wedding arrangements were underway. The boy has no parents, so the newly married couple will live off the Upper Mall with his married sister and her family. Her husband does not work, although one of the family's sons makes steel bangles, another is a welder and the third is a motor mechanic.

Only close relatives (and we) were invited to the wedding. Not a single unrelated person came from the neighborhood. The house did not have a festive look; indeed, most people just looked anxious, waiting for the *baraat* to arrive, occasionally singing and laughing. The house was decorated with multi-colored electric bulbs, although there wasn't any electricity as there happened to be a power outage at the time.

The *baraat's* procession arrived at 6:45 in the evening. A car had driven the bridegroom as close to the entrance to Panch Pir as possible, and then he walked the rest of the way (he didn't come on horseback, the still-preferred mode in the Walled City if affordable, as cars are usually not). The groom's family shot off firecrackers and small rockets to signal his arrival. When they entered Itrat's house, her relatives offered floral garlands to the guests. Some cousins delighted the guests with Punjabi folk songs sung to the beat of a drum. There was no gossiping, laughing or chatting once the *susural* arrived. People became much more serious; the laughing among themselves stopped.

The dowry was not laid out for formal display as is common at weddings in wealthier families, so we went inside a smaller room to look at it. There were a few suits, some china, pottery, copper and utensils. Shamsa told us that the furniture -- a bed, stool, table and showcase -- had been sent to her *susural's* house on a tonga earlier that morning.

The food, here as in other weddings, was identical and delicious: *lal roti*, chicken curry, rice and yogurt. For dessert, there was *kheer* in disposable clay bowls.

A few weeks later, we visited Shamsa in her new home on the Upper Mall. She seemed very comfortable and happy with her *susural*, and blended in so well that it appeared she had lived there for years already.

Now that we've placed women in their households, we want to look at their lives in more detail. We find that these women's lives are indeed very full as they balance kinship, labor and religious obligations, and that the women now have great hopes for their futures. However, it seems that the kinds of obstacles which have prevented their empowerment in the past still serve to limit them in the present, although women are learning how to maneuver around them.

Notes

1. The age breakdown of the women respondents in our random sample survey is as follows: seven women between the ages of sixteen and nineteen years, thirty-four women between twenty and twenty-nine years, twenty-six women between thirty and thirty-nine years, twenty-five women between forty and forty-nine years, and eight women between fifty and fifty-nine years.

2. 45 percent of urban women age fifteen and older in Lahore District are literate (Population Census Organisation, 1984: 21). The urban female literacy rate for the whole of Pakistan is 37 percent (World Bank, 1989: 39).

3. After ten years of education, students in Pakistan receive a matric degree, styled on the British system of education.

4. In early 1991, I was informed by someone in the government that such a school is open or is just opening in the Walled City. I was unable to verify that information, and none of my informants within the Walled City had heard of this school.

5. Of these eleven women, one was separated from her husband, two were divorced and eight were widowed.

6. This issue and others pertaining to mothers' relationships with their daughters is covered in Chapter Four.

7. While it is Shi'as who generally associate Yazid with all that is evil about humanity, many Sunnis do so as well. Yazid's forces killed the grandson of the Prophet, Hussain, on the battlefield of Karbala, Iraq.

8. St. Andrews is now a government-run school, and is Urdu-medium.

9. This may or may not be true. It is very possible, given her class, that her mother ran off and either Chand Bibi was never told this or she refuses to disclose it.

10. He probably went to Hong Kong, as it was much easier for Indians to travel there during the British Raj than to go to mainland China.

3

Women and Their Work

Women's productive contributions in many Third World economies remain dismally underreported and miscalculated, particularly in those areas such as Pakistan where women tend not to work in the formal sector.[1] Lourdes Beneria (1982: 127) warns that

> Studies on women based on conventional labor force statistics must use a great degree of caution in their analysis of and inferences about women's work. The danger of tautological conclusions is obvious: if active labor is defined primarily in relation to the market, and if production and labor not *clearly exchanged* [emphasis mine] in the market tend to be grossly underestimated, then the positive relationship often found between women's activity rates and some index of economic development is clearly circular thinking...yet numerous studies on women's labor force participation continue to ignore the problem.

In general, discourse on options for women's employment in Muslim countries revolves around the issue of whether or not women should work for remuneration, instead of recognizing the existence of the work in which they are already engaged. As the monetarization of economies under colonialism was primarily channeled through men, women were confined -- at least ideologically -- to the domestic sphere. As poorer Muslim women are often physically veiled, so too are their productive contributions "veiled" in popular assessments and official documentation. When new technologies are introduced in areas such as Pakistan where work roles are complementary, they are usually directed towards men's activities (Rogers, 1980; Barnes-McConnell & Lodwick, 1982). The result of this tendency is a strengthening of the commonly held assumption that women sit at home solely engaged in food preparation, childcare and domestic maintenance; the reality is that in addition to all this, women are often engaged in labor for remuneration as well. However, the implications of overlooking women's labor are directly related to issues of women's empowerment economically, socially and politically.

The problem is particularly relevant to conditions in contemporary Pakistan. For example, official unemployment rates are comparatively low, averaging about 3.5 percent. One of the reasons cited for this by the government of Pakistan has been "the low rate of female participation in the labor force" (Planning Commission, 1978: 173). In the 1981 Lahore district census, 26.4 percent of persons over age ten are considered to be either working or looking for work; 48.2 percent of males and only 2.6 percent of females. Merely 3.6 percent of urban women in Lahore District are included in this category. The Lahore Development Authority (1980: 124) recorded only one percent of production workers were women in a survey of industrial establishments conducted in selected areas of the Walled City. Such official assessments, however, obfuscate economic realities.

On the basis of the predominant fiction that most women do not labor outside of their domestic chores, there has been a hesitancy on the part of the government to adopt deliberate policies increasing women's employment options and to pass laws providing legal support for women's labor force participation. While true virtually everywhere, it is particularly important in poorer areas of Pakistan for a woman's status (as well as for that of her family) that her activities are popularly considered to be respectable. Historically, this has implied a prohibition on mixing freely with unrelated men and a marked sexual division of labor. No one would stop a woman from working in a field or from taking care of another woman's child if her labor was considered necessary and beneficial to her family. When a family came to identify with a higher class, any female member who had worked for others would generally withdraw from paid employment as soon as her contribution was no longer necessary for her family's basic needs. Therefore, concerns over traditional notions of propriety have not prevented women from working for pay; instead, they often simply prevented women and their families from admitting that they engage in such work.

The sexual division of labor in most Third World cities is marked by the majority of working women participating in marginal sectors of the economy, with relatively few working in the formal labor force[2]. Women here are confronted with an additional dilemma in that sociocultural mores virtually exclude them from many of the informal sector activities in which their counterparts engage in other countries such as selling roadside snacks or raw fruits and vegetables from pushcarts. Instead, women are primarily occupied as piece-rate workers in home-based cottage industry, but with a remarkable social "twist": they essentially do the exact same work which men do in the bazaar, but given sociocultural norms of women's limited mobility, their workplace is solely within the home and they therefore labor for significantly less remuneration.

Alejandro Portes et. al. (1989) have noted that while the existence of the informal sector is a response to a common core of social and economic realities, it is difficult to delineate a comprehensive set of propositions regarding how informal sectors are established and their effects throughout the world. In their view,

> variations in the form and effects of the informalization process are not random, but reflect the character of the specific social and economic order in which they occur. (Portes et. al., 1989: 298)

The World Bank (1989: 89) estimates that seventy percent of Pakistan's urban labor force is engaged in informal sector activities. Here, the informal sector predominantly consists of

> a large number of small-scale production and service activities that are individually or family owned and use indigenous inputs and labor-intensive, simple technology. It overlaps the small scale sub-sector, particularly household enterprises, and covers much of the "service" sector outside public service. The usually self-employed workers in this sector are engaged in activities ranging from hawking, street-vending, marketing, knife-sharpening, shoe-shining, and junk-collecting to selling fruits, vegetables, etc. Others find jobs as mechanics, blacksmiths, carpenters, small artisans, handicraft workers, potters, barbers and domestics.

Maria Mies discovered in her research on the laceworkers of Narsapur, India, that the social definition of women as housewives, particularly among the poorer classes, obscures the reality of their economic activity. In both Narsapur and the Walled City of Lahore, the informal sector work in which women engage has become virtually invisible, unrecognized by official statistics or by community leaders (who are predominantly men).

However, the situation in the two communities differs in that Mies (1982: 10) argues that in Narsapur, the "masculinization of all nonproduction jobs, especially of trade" has occurred, with the concomitant "total feminization of the production process." In the Walled City of Lahore, the informal sector is also an important part of the economy but it takes on a unique character. Here, while men similarly control nonproduction work, they share in the small-scale manufacturing and production process, as seen in Table 3.1. Nearly three-quarters were self-employed in 1980 (LDA, 1984: 11); men therefore enjoy a markedly greater degree of economic freedom than do women, who are dependent

TABLE 3.1: Type of Work Performed by Major Income Earners in the Walled City

Kind of Work	Respondents Thus Engaged (percent)
Selling in a shop and/or on the street*	30
In an office	13
In crafts	11
In a factory	7
As drivers	2
As domestics	2
In "other" work (generally making things such as boxes, incense, etc.)	33
Unemployed	2

Source: LDA, 1984

on a middleman.[3] Men and women make virtually the same goods; what differs is where they make them and the compensation they receive for their labors. Men work in small shops in the bazaar, where they can also congregate around nearby food stalls, barber stands and other places in the visible public sphere. Women in the Walled City -- unlike women entering the workforce elsewhere in Lahore -- generally only work in the private sphere of the home. They thereby maintain their respectability and that of their families by remaining solely within the walls of their own homes, though working for significantly less remuneration.[4]

When women's work is broadly categorized (Table 3.2), we find over half of the income-earning women employed in manufacturing within the home; nearly two-thirds of the total do some sort of work in their home. This differs from the location where the "major income earner" works; over half of the men work in their own work area, which is not inside the home.[5] But when we look more deeply into what the two different classification systems really mean in terms of what it is that men and women actually do, we find little difference. Men string *sehras* (a type of wreath used at marriages and saints' shrines) in a shop; women string them at home. Men make shoes in shops in the bazaar; women either make them at home or prepare component parts of the shoes at home. The fundamental difference, instead, lies in *where* they do their work, as women overwhelmingly remain inside the home.

However, there is nothing in women's ideals of remunerated work that would necessarily require this. When we asked the women who wanted to but were not currently earning an income about the type of work they

TABLE 3.2: Type of Work Performed by Working Women in the Walled City, by Broad Work Category

Type of Work	Respondents Thus Engaged (percent)	Subtotal (percent)
Piecework at home	45	
Family work	9	
Subtotal of home manufacturing		*54*
Other work within home	6	
Subtotal of labor within home		*61*
Teaching	18	
Work outside the home, not teaching	21	
Subtotal of working outside home		*39*

would prefer, over half did not identify employment that would require the task be done at home. The "anything" category in Figure 3.1 consists of work a woman would be able and allowed to do (and hence maintain her respectability); but after extensive questioning it became apparent that this labor need not be performed exclusively in the interior of one's home. This opens up possibilities for women to work in areas that unrelated and unknown men do not frequent, where it popularly could be perceived that a woman's respectability would not be compromised.

The vast majority of those who do earn an income do not work outside of their homes: the only exception to this are teachers and women living on their own, without a male to take responsibility for them. 17 percent of our respondents had themselves worked outside of their homes at some point in their lives; 29 percent of all households have had a close female relative work outside the home at some point. Conversely, 38 percent of families have had the experience of a woman engaging in remunerative work within the home.[6]

While women who work assert that their numbers have increased in recent years, there is good reason to believe that there have always been a sizeable number of poorer women who worked in their homes, making things. Indeed, more than half of the income-earning women had begun working within the last five years. Eighteen percent had been working between six and ten years while 28 percent had been working for more than ten years. Only three of the working women combine their efforts with their family's and hence have no distinguishable income of their own. But of all the women we interviewed, only 10 percent have any income which they set aside as separate from their larger family's

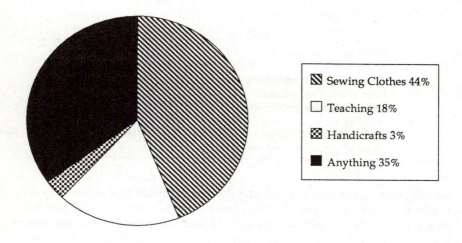

FIGURE 3.1. Type of Work Preferred by Currently Unemployed Women Who Want to Earn an Income

income. Quite a number of women do seem to be engaged in new types of work, although one aspect appears to remain the same: while their labor does open up opportunities to earn an income, this occurs under discriminatory and highly exploitative circumstances which offer little opportunity for mobility and questionably affects empowerment.

This dilemma reaches the extreme among women in the very poorest classes. For example, Maryam, the sickly, illiterate woman living inside of Bhati Gate whose life story we were never able to record viably, does whatever work she is able to find. Sometimes she glues shoe straps together, for which she earns two and a half rupees for every fifty shoe straps. As she doesn't get the shoe strap work often, she also stitches *panchas* for *shalwars* as this work is more readily obtainable. She works on the *panchas* with her sister, but sometimes they don't get work for six months. She would like more work to do, but it just isn't available.

As the experiences of women in the Walled City show, many women are either engaged in remunerative work, or would like to be. Of the women interviewed in our survey, 34 percent already do such work while 33 percent would like to work. Indeed, over two-thirds of the women are already earning or have skills which they perceive should enable them to earn an income (Table 3.3). Nearly three-quarters of the women who said they know an income-earning skill said

TABLE 3.3: Skills of Women in the Walled City[a]

Skill Type	Respondents With Skill (number)	Of All Having Skills (percent)
Embroidery only	4	9
Sewing clothes	26	55
Sewing other things	4	9
Total Sewing	34	72
Teaching	2	4
Shoemaking	1	2
Jewelry-making	1	2
Factory work	1	2
Handicrafts	3	6
Trading	1	2
Food preparation	1	2
Domestic	2	4
Hairdresser	--	0
Piecework	1	2

[a]Forty-seven women replied that they have some kind of income-generating skill. This chart depicts the percentage breakdown of those replying that they had a skill.

they learned it at home either from relatives or from neighbors while 19 percent said they learned their skills at a technical school. However, when we separate out the question of whether a woman engaged in remunerative labor is earning an income from her skill or not and simply ask if she *has* a skill, only 47 percent perceive that they do.[7] For example, Kanize, who has made *samosas* for as long as she can remember, and Farida, who is employed as a hairdresser, do not perceive they have food preparation or hairdressing skills, respectively. They and other women, in effect, do not perceive of what they do to earn an income as requiring a skill, a subtle way in which women undermine their own successes.

Of the one hundred women interviewed in our random sample survey, 33 percent said that they were presently earning an income. Table 3.4 shows the various occupations of employed women in the Walled City. Many women acknowledged the seriousness of the constraints they face to do work. Quite importantly, of the sixty-seven women who did not work, 51 percent (thirty-four) stated that they would work if they had the opportunity to do so. Of these, while 44 percent stated they would like to sew, 35 percent stated they would do "any work." In sum, 67 percent either work or say they would if they could.

The most prevalent work-related skill reported was sewing and/or embroidery, including *gota* and *salma sitara* embroidery which is used on suits for special functions such as weddings. This ability was known by nearly three-quarters of the women reporting to have skills, although only seven women reported deriving an income from sewing and three from embroidery. While there was some overlap of the two categories (seven women could both sew and embroider), no woman was earning from both skills.

All of the women earning an income in these two categories said that they work at home and are dependent on the largess of a middleman to deliver the raw materials and to pick up the finished goods. This makes them fearful of negotiating for more money since the middleman (who often sends his wife or a child to their home as his representative) can just stop coming at his whim, which would be disastrous for both the woman's respectability and her family's living standard. For example, Laila embroiders an average of four necklines daily and receives one rupee for each completed neckline. She earns eight rupees when a neckline includes intricate *salma sitara* embroidery. Working together with her sister, the two women can do an entire roll of fabric of eight to ten necklines (a *pulla*) in about three days, and jointly earn between sixty-four and eighty rupees ($3-4). At one point, Laila and her sister wanted to be paid better, but when they asked for an increase for their labor the middleman just stopped coming. Through the intercession of a neighbor he finally came back, but continued to pay them at the old rate.

TABLE 3.4: Women's Work in the Walled City

Occupation	Percent of All Women Who Work
Seamstress (clothes)	21
Seamstress (other)	9
Teacher	18
Shoemaker	6
Artificial jewelry maker	6
Factory worker	3
Handicraft maker	3
Trader	12
Food preparer	3
Domestic worker	9
Hairdresser	3
Pieceworker	6

The interior of a two-room home (housing six people) near Wachowali bazaar.

Preparing *samosas* for sale in Rang Mahal.

Parandas, used for braiding hair, on sale in Kashmiri bazaar. This is another item often made by women working at home.

A woman buying dry goods inside Bhati Gate.

Sehras on sale in Kashmiri bazaar.

A young girl cutting out pieces for shoes. Her aunt will paste the pieces onto the shoes that the male family members sell in the bazaar.

Boys helping assemble rubber mouthpieces on plastic horns.

Stringing flowers in Muhalla Namd Garan.

The next most popular "skill," reported by twelve percent of the women with skills, was having a good education. This skill could be used either to teach or to give private tuition lessons in one's home. All but one of the women who stated they have this skill are actually earning from it -- indeed, the only two women who leave the Walled City to work do so to teach in schools outside of it. As teachers, these women are relatively more independent than the seamstresses or embroiderers, but are equally subject to others' generosity when it comes to giving private tuition. The teachers told me that it was due to their high level of education that they are able to leave their *kuchas* and not draw criticism; many women -- not teachers -- did not find this such a respectable occupation, especially when leaving the *kucha* is involved. Indeed, while we found that 41 percent of the women in our sample had at least completed primary school, apparently most of these do not perceive of literacy as a marketable skill.

It should be noted that women do not have a monopoly on the kind of work I have been discussing. Men labor as tailors and embroiderers in small shops in the bazaar, teach school and give private tuition as well. An important difference, though, is that they are integrated into economic networks of solidarity and so need not be as subservient as the women to insure a steady income. Another important difference is that men often have the option of leaving the country to earn a better living. Nearly half (48 percent) of the families in our survey had some male family member who went abroad to work, fairly representative of the experiences of the poorer classes in Pakistan. Seventy percent of those who traveled abroad for employment went to the Gulf. This option, however, does not exist for a woman, except in the rare instances when she accompanies her husband abroad.

Sewing, embroidery, and teaching -- activities which are generally regarded as extensions of domestic tasks done at home -- are skills known by 41 percent of the respondents but are a source of income for only 16 percent of the total. These three kinds of tasks are popularly assumed to be the bulk of the work that women do, but only 48 percent of working women are so engaged. This raises a question: what kind of work are the other 52 percent of the women doing?

The remaining 52 percent of working women are predominantly engaged in small-scale manufacturing at home. In most instances, the women are again doing the same work as men: some glue straps to shoes, decorate *sehras*, assemble plastic toys, string flowers, prepare *samosas*, and so on. However, a common characteristic is that women earn appreciably less than men for the same task, usually less than seventy percent of what men earn for the same kind of full-time work.[8] In most instances, women have never been to the bazaar where their wares are sold. Kanize, preparing *samosas* in her home which are sold by her father and brothers in Rang Mahal bazaar, has never seen the family's *samosa* stand although it is a mere five-minute walk from their home. When questioned about the kind of work she does – despite her making *samosas* virtually from sunrise to sunset, only stopping to clean the house and prepare family meals -- she says that she does not work, and she has no income of her own.

Therefore, of all women working, 61 percent work within their homes, 18 percent work outside their homes as teachers, and 21 percent do other work outside of the home. Of the seven women in the latter category, three work within their *kucha* while four must leave it to work. Two women working within their *kucha* are domestics while the third decorates nameplates for bicycles in a nearby factory where all the other workers are also women. Of the women working outside their *kucha*, Farida is a hairdresser in a "women's only" section of a beauty parlor located outside the Walled City, another is a domestic, and two (both older women) are traders: Jamila buys and sells cloth free-lance, while the other woman sells vegetables in a bazaar. The four women not working as domestics are in their professions due to extenuating circumstances where there is no man to oversee their activities: Farida's husband is a drug addict; Jamila's husband abandoned her some years ago; the vegetable-seller is a widow; and the factory worker never married but instead raised her younger brother and now lives with him and his family. I met other unmarried and widowed women who were earning incomes, but as they remained integrated within their families (the former group with their natal families and the latter group with their in-laws, most often a *jaith*), they perceive that they are being supported by their families despite the reality of their own financial contributions.

Most women share the ideal that being either a teacher or a doctor is the best occupation a woman could possibly have. However, given the low literacy rate, they also pointed out to us that such ideals are generally unrealistic. Sales professions and bank tellers are automatically ruled out as having no *izzat* because they require women to mix with men without having gained the status derived from education, which being a doctor or teacher bring. Hasina voices a strong opinion on the importance of retaining respectability, *izzat*, at work.

Working in a bank is not good for a woman, as she has to work with men. We watch on television dramas that men take advantage of girls. It's not so bad but the girl doesn't keep her *izzat*. Regular people don't retain *izzat* like that. Even a nurse or a lady doctor isn't so good, as she looses *izzat* when she mixes with male doctors. I think hospitals are strange, and I'm embarrassed there. Isn't she embarrassed to mix with men? She sees them in an operation. It's best in her own private clinic. If a girl works separate from men, it's good work. But, in my opinion, it isn't that free. I've seen pregnant women wearing *dupattas,* and men saying remarks behind their backs. It all comes back to *purdah.*

Dais (mid-wives), sweepers and *wacholans* (matchmakers), while recognized as providing necessary services for women, are also deemed not to be respectable: attitudes to these occupations reflect the familiar "somebody's got to do it but not me or my daughters" syndrome. One woman told me that she would like to see her son become a "big officer," like a judge, doctor, pilot, or lawyer. When I asked her if she would like her daughters to be in these professions, she replied:

> We just don't have our women become such people, not in high positions. The future of my grandchildren depends on my daughter's in-laws. It will be difficult to convince them that the granddaughters should have a profession. Now, the grandson is a different story.

Chand Bibi, the widow who can barely support her four daughters by making artificial earrings, defines which professions are best for women by whether or not they must intermix with men at the workplace.

> A girl should be in school or college where there are no men. She shouldn't work in a post office or a railway. She shouldn't work anywhere where there are men. You can't predict what sort of men they are. They might be *sharif* (honorable), or else they might run off with a girl. There's no *izzat* as a bank teller, if four to six men are sitting with one girl. That's not respectable. A lady doctor is good, as long as she only attends to women.

From the last comment, we can see that not all women agree that even a lady doctor is an ideal profession. One commented, "They marry doctors of their own free will!" which seemed to her the end result of what happens when a woman loses all sense of respectability.

Given the kinds of social constraints under which these women live, such a perspective that women who work outside of their *kuchas* may end up marrying men of their own choice -- a fear, actually -- is widespread and, in the context of women's lives, makes a lot of sense. To begin with, women's actions are circumspect, and few wish to risk drawing additional attention to themselves by leaving the security of the *kucha* where all of their contact with others can be readily observed, monitored, and hence approved. Overcrowded living conditions themselves, therefore, become a form of social control. This, combined with a community-based orientation and the influence of Islamic notions of the demarcation of sexual space between men's and women's activities, leaves little room for women to justify leaving the *kucha*, especially on a regular basis.

Times and mores, however, are changing. We can see this reflected in the responses by more than three-quarters of the women interviewed as they would like to see their daughters work. The ideal of the domesticated woman no longer dominates their viewpoints, if it ever did.

Women's Lives and Their Labor

Women are eager to discuss the work which occupies much of their time and efforts. As so many of them generate an income from sewing or embroidery, it is most fitting that we first turn to Laila's story embroidering *salma sitara* designs on fancy suit pieces.

Laila: Salma Sitara Embroiderer

I have been doing *salma sitara* work for the last two years. It is special embroidery mostly used for wedding suits. It's *salma sitara* work when it is pearls set in embroidery. The most common is silver around pearls. I started off making *hars* (marriage garlands) and *sehras* for bridegrooms about seven years ago. My elder sisters have also done *salma sitara* work.

My eldest sister started doing this work with the help of a Hindustani woman from Delhi who was making *hars* and *sehras* for a shopkeeper. That Hindustani family left for Karachi a few years ago. She is a distant relative of ours. We don't mix with their family, though the women come to the marriages in my family. My sister went to her house to learn. We knew about her because her house is just in front of ours. My sister didn't spend very much time with that woman; she learned in a short period of time, about six months. It could have even been faster, but the woman taught her slowly. She didn't have to pay that woman anything to learn, but she also earned no money. After about six months, the woman said that my sister had learned it and that she could now do it in her own house. She came home so that she could earn money here. She then taught it to my next eldest sister before she got married (she was thirteen when she was married), who then taught it to the next and then taught it to me. We sisters learned fast from each other.

He (the man for whom they were doing the embroidery) had come a few times and told us that our work wasn't good enough and that we were taking too long. He just stopped giving us work and told us to improve our skills. We were making *hars* and doing *salma sitara* work then. After he said this we were just sitting idle. My father asked us to stop doing the work when this happened, that the man wasn't satisfied. But we wanted to work and we needed the money. We went to the Hindustani woman and spoke to her and asked her to persuade him to give us work again. That woman convinced him and he started giving us work again.

When that Hindustani woman who used to get us this work left for Karachi with her small son and husband to join her three married daughters -- all of whom were now in Karachi -- then another woman began to come, who we call *baji* (elder sister). Before the first woman had left, she told this other man that there are girls in our *kucha* who know this work, and he should have them do it for him. He just showed up one day after she had left for Karachi. He's also a Hindustani; we can tell from the way he talks. He uses strange words and he doesn't speak Punjabi. He's very old and must have been born in India. Most of his relatives are from Delhi. He showed us samples and we did them well. So after that, he began to send us the goods. He comes twice weekly to give us the raw materials and take away the finished things. We completed the work we had to do for him yesterday, but the man doesn't come again until tomorrow so we're sitting idle for two days.

We are paid one rupee for each *har* we make. We can do about four per day, so we make four rupees a day when we make *hars*. We sell our work to the middleman who then sells it to a shopkeeper. The shopkeeper then puts rupee notes on the *hars* we have made and sells them. For a *sehra*, we are paid three rupees. With great difficulty we can make two per day, and then we are paid six rupees. My sister makes the same amount as I do.

We get eight rupees for each neckline of *salma sitara* embroidery. We can also do *salma sitara* on velvet. In three days we can do an entire *pulla*, which has 8-10 necklines on it, for which the two of us receive sixty-four to eighty rupees. (This averages out to ten to fourteen rupees each, per day.) We sometimes can make one hundred sixty rupees in a week. Nowadays, we are mostly making necklines and cuffs and embroidery work for sleeves. My mother often drops the goods off at "*baji's*" house (which is where the man picks the goods up from, apparently). We give all our money to our mother after the man pays us and we ask her for money when we need it. Sometimes I keep some money, maybe ten rupees a month. I use it to buy things for school.

My father only earns twelve hundred rupees per month. He leaves the house at 8 a.m. and comes back anywhere between 3 p.m. and 10 p.m. Sometimes he comes home as late as 2 a.m. My father has a bicycle; no motorcycle. My father's salary can't cover everything: school fees, food, rent and other expenses. The four hundred rupees which my sister and I earn each month goes towards paying the daily expenses for the household. Our family does not have any savings.

I don't think working makes any difference, personally, in my life, though it makes life easier for my family. Everybody can buy more things. Last year, my father bought us a color television and a pedestal fan. I think my dowry will be better because I've been working: my parents will have more money. But there's no difference concerning agreeing to the marriage they will arrange. Both my parents will decide, but it's mostly up to my father. They'll ask my two elder brothers, but not the youngest, about the arrangements for my marriage. They'll ask my sister's opinion because she's older than me. Her opinion is equal to the opinion of my younger brother.

If there was an older brother in the family, then that would be the most valued, but there isn't.

My mother never did any work at all, never in her life. My best friend doesn't do *salma sitara* work or any other kind of work as her family earns enough. Her family knows that I do this work. I have embroidered a shirt for her and one for her sister. When I was making her shirt, I paid a lot of extra attention to it, more than usual.

Does my brother also do this work? No, he is studying and wants to be a doctor. I never thought of becoming a doctor. No, I like to sew. I am going to sewing school, the Institute College near the Secretariat, with my *taya's* daughter. Her brother has gone to Saudi Arabia to work.

I think the best work for a woman to do is sewing, because it's necessary. A girl should be literate so she can be responsible for herself in a good way. The best professions are a teacher, doctor and lawyer. The best professions for men? He should work in an office, like my father; he should be a bank manager; he should be a PIA (Pakistan International Airlines) officer so he can see the world.

Gulzar Begum: Flower Stringer

Gulzar Begum, now widowed, has been stringing flowers at home every day for the last twenty-five years. Her late husband used to sit in a shoe shop and sell shoes, though he did not make them. In those days, she did embroidery in her home, but her eyes are too weak now for that kind of work. Her daughters, until they were married, used to help her string the flowers. Only one daughter remains to help her now. To earn extra money, Gulzar Begum occasionally also shells almonds, which she doesn't enjoy as much.

She finds stringing flowers to be a pleasant social activity: flowers give off a wonderful fragrance, and she can talk with her friends and relatives while she works. It appears that stringing flowers often becomes a special communal time when women share information. Women from the neighborhood, friends who are now fictive relatives and other real and fictive kin drop by and string a few flowers. Royal Crown Cola bottles are sent for at once; at three rupees each, this can add up very quickly.

She and her daughter usually string between two and three kilograms of flowers per day, for which they are paid ten rupees per kilo. They use a large needle with string to make the necklaces. All materials also come from the middleman: needles, thread, flowers, cardboard, foil paper for the center of earrings, etc. They make about twenty necklaces from one kilo of flowers. Thursdays are the busiest days for garlands as this is the day women traditionally visit saints' shrines. There is no difference in the amount of work she gets throughout the year.

They don't have *motia* (a small white fragrant flower) in the winter; we only use roses then. If you throw a vial of *motia* over you, it will give you a good, sound sleep. I like *khushbu* (sweet smells, e.g., perfume, flowers) too much. Roses are the king; *motia* is the *wazir* (minister).

The *motia* is weighed by the kilo before it is given to them to string, unlike the daisy-type of flowers that have no smell which is just given in a large tub. Bholla, who gives them the flowers, is a neighbor.

His mother used to give them to us, then his father, then he himself after he grew up. He has gardens of his own in Sandha, past Mozang, and a shop where he sells the flowers, behind Saifullah's shrine near Masjid Wazir Khan. He has hired many people as gardeners who pluck the flowers and deliver them to his house, and then his children deliver the flowers to us.

I string the most flowers of all the women who work for him. The other women can't make as many as I do in a day; some only make five rupees, some three rupees. I can usually make two or three kilos. I get more work than other ladies. In the winter season, other ladies refuse the work because the flowers are cold and they don't want to touch them as it hurts their hands. Two of them (in two other houses) are wealthy enough. Whatever work they do in the summer, it's their own choice. The other women are as poor as we are, and they have to work in the wintertime as well.

I usually get paid after a month, but if it's necessary, I ask him for money. At first, I used to get paid once a week, but now he pays me after a month. My daughter keeps the record of how much flowers we use. For this reason, I sent her to school, so she could keep the records. Her elder sister used to keep the records before her. My daughters are all very sweet and helpful to me. They used to take their tuition in school, come back, and then help me. Before my other two daughters were married, they used to stitch *panchas* in the house. Now they don't work as their husbands are fine and there are no money problems.

They give us the other flowers just like this, in a tub. Either Bholla (the middleman) comes himself, or he sends his children. The flowers usually come between 11 a.m. and noon, and are certainly here by 1 p.m. He picks them up between 4-5 p.m., and certainly by 6 p.m. If he comes for the flowers and I'm not finished, I tell him to come back later, and he does.

Men also string flowers; Bholla also does this work. If someone dies, he strings a *chadar* (sheet) of flowers himself. He also makes *sehras*.

Five women in her *kucha* string flowers for Bholla, but many others string flowers for different shopkeepers. Her mother-in-law used to string flowers, and her *jaithani* and *nund* both still do. Her *jaithani* also knits cardigans -- for payment -- for other people.

When we walk in, her daughter is stringing flowers with a neighbor's daughter. She is also cutting out cardboard circles on top of which she has pasted colored foil paper, to use with *motia* flowers to make earrings. Her daughter says she has completed tenth grade and looks to be about sixteen, although Gulzar Begum had said she was eighteen. She said she feels like she has been doing this work since before she was born.

The flowers left in the tub will all be strung. There are some remaining sweet-smelling white *motia*, which are being used to make a four-string *har* with some of the other flowers. Her daughter says this will cost ten rupees in the bazaar. In response to my question asking how she feels about the fact that she will only earn twenty-five *paisa* (1/4 rupee) for it, she acknowledges, resignedly, "He's going to make the money, not me."

While they are stringing flowers, her daughter bites off the bottom of a flat, dark pink rose, spits it out, and continues to string the flowers. Has she ever cut herself with a needle while stringing flowers? "Yes, often, especially if I'm doing it in a hurry."

There seem to be so many strung flowers just in Gulzar Begum's house, that I question if Bholla will really sell all these flowers at his own shop. In reply, I am told that since today is Thursday, there's more of a rush than on any other day, and all of these will be sold by midnight. I'm left with the sense that Gulzar Begum and her daughter really have no idea if he sells flowers anywhere else or to anyone else, and how could they? Gulzar Begum knows where Bholla sits in the bazaar and believes that he only sells the flowers near Masjid Wazir Khan, but she doesn't know at all about the wholesale flower market outside Lohari Gate in which he must surely participate.

In addition to stringing flowers, Gulzar Begum occasionally stitches quilts, does embroidery, crochets *dupattas*, and knits. She does this work intermittently, only as often as local women in her *kucha* ask her to make things for them. She can also sew, but does not do it to earn money.

When she's finished with the flowers, she begins to clean and sort almonds for her *jaith's* dry fruit shop. He pays her about eight *annas* (half a rupee) per kilo. She makes thirty to forty rupees for preparing one sack. It usually takes four or five days to clean a sack; if she does it quickly, the work can take three days.

In total, Gulzar Begum earns about a thousand rupees per month but remains unable to have any savings. Her *jaith*, who has retired from more lucrative work making knives in his former shop in the bazaar, gives her an additional five hundred rupees monthly. It is interesting that she still considers her *jaith* to be the major income earner of her household although in fact she, herself, is.

Farida: Hairdresser

Farida, who is only twenty-four, is now the major income earner in her family. She earns about three hundred rupees per month, and has no savings. As she didn't want her in-laws to question why we were talking with her, she requested that we meet for her lengthiest interview at the beauty parlor where she works in Gulshan Ravi, about fifteen minutes away from the Walled City. She takes either a bus or a minibus to the shop. She walks through a front section (which is for men) to get to the small back room where she works, which is reserved only for women. Men come and go into the shop, but cannot be seen from the back room, nor can people in the back room be seen by them. However, this also means that for a woman to reach this section she must walk through the men's section. In the four hours we spent with her and her young son there, no women came into the shop at all.

This is the first proper job for me. I used to do sewing. People would give me clothes to stitch. I learned to knit from Mian Salahuddin's (a Walled City politician) daughter-in-law, after her marriage. I got sick from knitting. The doctor told me that I could get tuberculosis from breathing in all the wool particles. I did sewing for one or two years, and knitting for one or two years. I never actually learned cutting, though I picked it up. But I couldn't earn much from sewing. I worked mostly for different relatives, and they didn't pay me.

I first started hairdressing in Samra Beauty Parlor, in Kashmiri Bazaar, in front of the Sonehri Masjid. The owner is my brother's friend's sister-in-law. I told her the story of my marriage, and she gave me a chance. I learned there for about two months, and then worked there for about six months. I earned five rupees per day there. Sometimes they forgot to pay me, though. Whenever my relatives came there, I had to cut their hair for free.

My girlfriend who studied the Qur'an with me now lives near here, in Gulshan Ravi. I used to visit her here. Once, when I was passing by this shop, I came inside. I had wanted to learn more about make-up and styling. The man here (presumably senior hairstylist) said that we need a woman for the ladies' section, and that I could work here and learn as well. He teaches me, that a "fall" should be like this, etc. There is another lady who comes once in a while to do make-up.

The owner of this beauty parlor works in the railway office. He has hired people to work in the shop. I work at this beauty parlor, doing haircutting, make-up and threading on faces, arms and legs. We charge fifteen rupees for "half-cutting," which is cutting just the front part. (Her own hair is "half-cut": she has a long single braid in the back, but the front part is fashionably trimmed.) We charge six hundred rupees for make-up and hair-do for a bride, though I have never done this. Another woman comes when we request her to do that work. We charge forty rupees for threading (removing the hair) both arms. I have never threaded anyone's legs yet. We also charge thirty rupees for face threading; twenty rupees for waxing arms and legs, and ten rupees for a manicure.

I also keep the accounts for the shop. I earn ten rupees per day, whether anyone comes or not. The other men working here don't bother me. They respect me here. The day they don't respect me is the day I'll leave. There's a lock on this door; I lock it in the afternoon when I take a nap. I want to stay working here. The owner is good, but I'll have a problem when my son returns to school. I'm worried about what to do, but I haven't figured it out yet.

My husband doesn't care if I work, he tells me to do whatever I want. He doesn't know that I'm working here, although I have told him. My husband is useless. He's a mandrax addict. He used to sell new iron and steel drums at the Railway station. They are used for kerosene oil, cooking oil and silicate. He stopped that work seven years ago. He used to earn between five hundred and a thousand rupees per day, though he didn't do it every day. He would use all the money, then go back to work again. But now, he goes to Data Saheb and other places, and begs.

Farida sees herself as the sole income earner for both her own and her son's support. Work for her is a necessity, and she aspires to improve her socioeconomic position -- and hopefully, enhance her personal happiness -- through her own efforts and she perceives there is no one else who will do this for her.

Jamila: Cloth Trader

Jamila says she has loved clothes since she was young. Her father used to get four free railway passes every year, and her family would travel together to cities like Peshawar and Quetta. She remembers her mother buying her pretty clothes in such places. When Jamila s husband owned a cloth shop in Kashmiri Bazaar, she went with him to different places to buy various kinds of cloth. They often went to Swat and other areas in the northwest mountains and typically would buy cloth worth sixteen to twenty thousand rupees at a time. From this, she had gained a little experience.

Her husband sold his shop about seventeen years ago for about ten thousand rupees. They spent six thousand rupees in renovating their house, and he started a new business selling dal, rice, salt and dry goods with the remaining four thousand rupees. At about the same time, she started trading in cloth and clothes. She attributes the eventual turbulence in her marriage to the combination of his selling the shop, his lack of ambition and her frustrated reaction to the situation.

My husband and I loved each other so much. I never imagined this would happen. It happened because I would bother him to work or do some job. I wanted him to realize that I didn't want to sell cloth anymore. I have been doing this work now for seventeen years, since three or four years after my marriage. He would go to his dry goods shop for two days, then close it for a day. He didn't want to work.

She now runs her business by travelling to different places, buying clothes and related items like cloth and shawls, as well as goods such as plastic dinner sets and photographs of Imam Raza (popular among Shi'as). Basically, Jamila trades in any small consumer goods that she can purchase cheaply and sell at a reasonable profit. She usually travels to Quetta, Peshawar, Iran and India. She once went to Singapore when a family gave her 25,000 rupees with which to buy a television and a refrigerator for them. She also went to Kashgar in China once.

She took 25,000 rupees with her on her last trip to Iran. Of this, 10,000 rupees was a loan that one of her relatives secured for her from a money-lender at a thousand rupees per month interest. She also borrowed some of the money from shopkeepers who asked her to buy things for them. These loans were usually between three and four thousand rupees. She also took a number of small loans from others. She normally gives people who loan her money a gift (such as a polyester "japani" suit) when she returns.

On her trips, she normally just looks around for the first couple of days to get a feel of what is available and what "the good deals are." She then buys what she wants and carries it back with her to Lahore. She usually has to pay a customs officer something whenever she has to cross a border. In spite of all the expenses she incurs, she feels she manages to make a good profit as she can usually sell the goods at double the price she pays for them. She earns anywhere between 2,000 and 6,000 rupees over six months. She often sells a lot of what she buys in her *kucha* itself.

Her eldest son works in the restaurant of a good international chain hotel on Mall Road, where he earns about 850 rupees monthly. Her middle son, about twenty years old, accompanies Jamila and her youngest son of nine on her trips to buy cloth. When it has been necessary, she has traveled alone to Quetta and to India. In Quetta, she stays with her *chacha's* daughter; in India, she stays with family friends who live in the Old City of Delhi. In Iran, where she says she will never venture alone, she and her sons stay in hotels. She likes her sons to travel with her because she wants them to know what she does so they do not believe any rumors they might hear about her. Also, they are the only ones with whom it is socially acceptable for her to travel.

Hasina: Occasional Seamstress

Hasina knows how to sew; she learned how to stitch *shamizes* (*kamize* undergarments) from a neighbor before she was married. Six months ago, she bought a zig-zag sewing machine with the intention of earning some income with it, but as yet she does not. Other women in her family have a history of working -- she herself stitched *shamizes* in her home on a piece-work basis for two years before she was married -- so the precedent of women working in her family has already been established. Her cousin's wife has been attending patients in a hospital (presumably as a nurse) for the last fifteen years, and her *phuphizad behan* has been stitching ready-made clothes inside her home for over two years.

It seems that Hasina is in a frustrating position: she would like to earn some income, has the skills and even the machinery to do it, but because of poor communication between herself and her husband she is unable to take that first step and begin working to earn. She feels her husband, the Kakazaiya man who often fights with her and who works in a bicycle factory, wants her to remain dependent on him and undermines her attempts at being able to earn an income from sewing. She blames her poor relationship with her husband as the main reason why she doesn't work as he keeps interrupting her when she is trying to sew.

If I start to work, it would take up a lot of time for me to be introduced to people so that they can know that I can sew. In addition, I have so many other liabilities as a housewife. I have to devote some time to my mother-in-law, my three sons, my daughter and to my household chores.

First, I thought I'd do some work with my sewing machine, but the needle has broken, so how can I do any work? I had just put a new needle in it. My husband fought with me when the needle broke. He abused me, yelled at me and beat me. After some time, I'll bring a new needle, it's eight rupees. When I got the machine, it came with eight needles.

Twelve years ago, he worked as an accountant in WAPDA, and he was earning a thousand rupees per month. But his friend working there fought with him. My husband told him that either you leave or I leave: the friend was very smart and didn't leave, so my husband resigned. He was free, without work, for a while. He lived as a rich man's son. After Zia came to power, he reapplied for his old job. They said you yourself quit – had we fired you, we'd give it back. So they wouldn't give it back. The one who was with him, he now earns seven thousand rupees per month.

Now my husband works in a private firm, Sohrab Bicycles. His job isn't good, his salary is low. He used to make only three hundred rupees a month, but I really don't know how much he makes now. He gives me no pocket money and we have no savings. For my needs, my mother gives me money, and sometimes I borrow money from my mother-in-law but I can never give it back. My husband brings soap, ghee, and different kinds of dal from the Sohrab Bicycle factory store. He pays for it. Only factory workers can buy from there. I have never seen where he works. Other family members also work there, and outside men too. It doesn't look nice if I go there.

We are having many financial problems in these days. We can't even pay the rent of four hundred fifty rupees per month. We've been in debt for about three thousand rupees for the last three months. I'd like my husband to have his own shop, but I know he won't be able to run it because he hasn't the patience to sit all day long in a shop. Since his childhood, he's been like this.

Hasina sees earning an independent income, however, as only a small part of what is needed for her empowerment.

Kanize: Samosa Maker

From early morning every day, Kanize starts to prepare *samosas*. Her father and two brothers buy the ingredients daily: ten kilos of flour, garbanzo beans, two kilos of clarified butter (*ghee*), and potatoes. They use a variety of spices, including red pepper, coriander, garam masala, salt, and black pepper.

> That is the work that we do, and we have to give it more importance than housework. My brothers knead the flour. Then I shape the *samosas*, fill them, and close them. My two sisters and my *bhabi* help me.

People are walking by where she is sitting. They cut through the area, walking over where she is working. Flies sit on the potato mixture and on the *samosas*. She makes the *samosas* in this courtyard during the hot summer, and on colder days prepares them indoors in the house's only large room. In the courtyard, there is an old tire lying nearby, and a pair of shoes.

While sitting on her haunches, Kanize takes some kneaded flour in her hand and flattens it into cakes. She then turns each cake into a cylinder -- like a snow cone -- and fills it with the potato mixture after rubbing water on the *samosa* shell. The potato mixture is kept in a circle, surrounded by the as yet unfilled shells. A board which can hold about a hundred and fifty *samosas* sits next to her work area.

She makes the *samosas* from 7 a.m. until 1 p.m. Then she prepares lunch and has it ready in time for her father and brothers to eat when they arrive home. She serves them, washes the utensils they had used in the bazaar, and then she takes a nap. When her father and brothers return to the bazaar, she does the housework.

Kanize's father sells the *samosas* from a table -- not a shop -- in Rang
Mahal, the busy commercial area inside Shah Alami Gate. Her brothers
bring the *samosas* to the table from the house. She has never been to the
place where her father sits in the bazaar. Kanize does not consider that
her making *samosas* is work nor does she earn a separate income from her
labor. Her idea of work is the sewing that one of her cousins, a *phuphizad
behan*, has been doing in her home for the last eight years. Instead, Kanize
sees herself as simply helping her father and brothers who work,
although her contribution is certainly critical to her family's informal
sector activity of selling *samosas* and sweets on special order. She
estimates that her family's monthly income is about three thousand
rupees, though is not certain about it.

She especially likes to eat *samosas* in cold, cloudy weather. She takes
a great a deal of pride in her family's work.

> We make the *samosas* very tasty, neat and clean. We're very careful about
> it, and when people try our *samosas*, they always come back for them. In all,
> we make about fifty rupees profit per day. The materials cost about a
> hundred and fifty or two hundred rupees.

They also make small, sweet rotis to sell in the bazaar and *ladoos*
(sweets for celebrations) on special order for weddings. Only her father
makes the *ladoos*. After finishing them, he sits in the courtyard and wraps
each one in white tissue paper, then places them in a green tissue paper
covered basket to bring to the wedding. From a large tray of *ladoos*, they
make between ten and twenty rupees profit.

While Kanize rarely sees herself as acting in social contexts outside of
her family, she has very set ideas regarding acceptable and unacceptable
kinds of work for women. She regards the best professions for women to
be doctors and teachers even though she finds it inconceivable that she
could ever be either one. Moreover, no woman she has ever known well
is one either. She has mixed opinions regarding most other occupations,
such as a *dai* or a *wacholan*, even though she does know women who
work as these.

> A *dai* goes from house to house, so she knows what is going on in the
> neighborhood. Sometimes they have to consult with doctors in the hospital.
> My father would not want me to become a *dai*. It's also hard for us to do
> that job because we have no training. Even if I were to be trained, it would
> still be out of the question because it's not in our family's tradition. We are
> not permitted out of doors, so how could I go house-to-house? It's not
> respectable to do that.
>
> A *wacholan* has no respect. If she arranges a good match, both sides
> appreciate it. But if she doesn't, people curse her.

If it's necessary to work, and a girl gets her parents' permission, then I suppose it's O.K. to work in a bank or some office. But what sort of *izzat* is that? I don't know, that's the same problem with being a salesgirl.

In Kanize's family, there has been little attempt to break out of their condition of poverty. No one in her family has ever gone abroad to work, or even thought about going abroad. Her father told us that some of his friends had once tried to convince him to leave Lahore for Kuwait, but he felt it was too hard for him to leave his daughters alone.

Erum: Schoolteacher

Erum's work experience is much different from that of any of the other women we interviewed in the Walled City for two reasons: she works in the formal sector and receives a good, steady salary. She teaches at a girls' school that is popularly recognized as being one of the best in Lahore and that is still not nationalized. Girls study there from about age four or five until they are sixteen or seventeen.

Before she had started teaching, she had applied to be an air hostess with Pakistan International Airlines (PIA).

> I wanted to see the world and I wanted to earn money. I got through all their tests, but then some of my relatives objected. My father said that I had to ask my *mammu* for permission also. A cousin of mine was very angry; he said that the air hostesses have to stay alone overnight at hotels and "You don't know what happens." This scared me and I changed my mind and decided to become a teacher.

Since she had begun teaching a year before her marriage, it was fairly easy for her to continue to teach after it.

> In those days, an old man used to take me to the school. I would go by (motorized) rickshaw, and at the school I would take off my *burqa*, fold it up, and put it away in a drawer there. At the end of the day, I would put it back on and return home.
>
> Before my marriage, I thought that if anyone allowed me to continue, I would teach. If not, I would give it up. I had been frank about this in my job interview. My engagement was arranged three or four months after I had started to teach. But then, after my marriage, I had a girl, then another girl, and another. That fixed it in my mind that I should continue teaching, for the benefit of their schooling.

Erum's mother-in-law used to take care of her daughters while she worked. Erum often felt uncomfortable and rather guilty when her children were unwell and at times felt she should not work. Her mother-in-law also harassed her sometimes because Erum worked and couldn't always care for her children; her mother-in-law felt that caring for them was too much work for an old woman like herself to do. Her school has been flexible in facilitating the periodic adjustments her family has undergone.

> Once, my mother-in-law just refused to care for my daughters. People had talked into her ear, that why are you looking after your granddaughters? At that time I almost resigned, but my principal told me to think about it and they offered to give me leave until things blew over.
>
> I lived with my own mother for a while once when my mother-in-law refused to look after my daughters. My husband allowed me to do this, although he didn't shift there as well. It wasn't for too long, either.
>
> Despite these problems with my mother-in-law, I've continued to work because since we have daughters, you need more money for their dowry. With extra money, you can buy your children extra things. Also, we can get them well-educated without having to pay high fees.

Her school usually charges students three hundred rupees monthly in fees, though she pays only three hundred and fifty rupees for both of her daughters because she teaches there. With other expenses, like books, it comes to a bit over five hundred rupees monthly.

She copes with the rigors of a full-time job by cooking in the evenings, and then leaving the prepared food in the refrigerator for the next day. She has hired a woman, who herself is a great-grandmother, to spend about two hours a day cleaning her house.

In the spring before the summer holiday recess, she and her daughters leave their house at 6:30 a.m. and travel by a minibus to arrive by 7 a.m., when the school starts. School is over at 12:30 because it gets too hot to study during the afternoons. They usually take a motorized rickshaw back to their home, which makes the journey longer. If the school's special bus comes while they are waiting, they take it. The bus only costs one rupee per person while the rickshaw is about eight or nine rupees.

> I hate going in a tonga. In a car or a rickshaw, the brakes are in the driver's hands. But a horse cannot be controlled the same way. I have seen many accidents and many people laugh at me because I'm afraid. I was once in an accident in a tonga: my mother-in-law had fallen by the horse's foot, but she wasn't hurt badly.

Sometimes Erum expressed that she was happy that she works, and felt that she would have continued working even if she had a different kind of job such as working in a bank. However, on other occasions, she stated that teaching is the most respectable occupation for women, so it is questionable if she would have indeed kept working if she was employed in a more public position and location. She says that her husband would have been supportive of her working even if she was not a teacher because in her family, husbands are devoted to their wives and there are no pressure tactics.

She does not perceive any real difference in the amount of freedom she has compared to that of the other wives in her husband's family who do not work. In her mind, the only difference her working makes to her family is the extra income; it makes "no real difference" in her relationship with her husband. She feels that, more likely, she enjoys more freedoms than other women because she is better educated rather than because she earns her own income. This is impossible to substantiate, of course, as she has been working since before she was married; while it is meaningful to her that her working makes no difference, in actuality it most likely does.

In her *kucha*, most of the women are uneducated and do not work. Erum feels that they respect her as she is educated and is a teacher. She met most of these women when she first moved into this house seventeen years ago at the time of her marriage. She has occasionally helped their children with their studies, and has refused payment from them.

> I don't know many men in this *kucha*. Men here work in their own shops, with machines and some workers. Government jobs are considered to be good as they are secure jobs. You may get less pay but you can't get thrown out.

Her husband is forty-two or forty-three years old. He works as a foreman in the railway workshop. After completing his Intermediate Degree, he did a four-year course in engineering at the Polytechnic Institute, near the railway station.

> He works with big machines, making heavy things for trains, like wheels. He has an office there. He works six days a week, from 1 p.m. - 9 p.m. He looks after the children in the morning. That's why I've been able to continue my work. Otherwise, it would have been terribly difficult. Sometimes his schedule changes, but mostly, his duty has been like this.

Her income is about the same as her husband's, which combined is about five and a half thousand rupees monthly. Unlike most families in the Walled City, they have been able to build up some savings over the years, and hope to use the money to build a house in Gulberg, an upscale suburb of Lahore where they have already purchased some land.

Erum realizes that her family holds fairly progressive views about educating females and allowing them to work to earn an income, and that her work experiences are different from those of most other women. Yet she evinces a conservatism about how far women should participate in activities outside of the home.

> My sister has been filling and packing medicines in the Wyeth laboratories for the past six years. The conditions there are harsh, but women do not join unions at such places. I have some reservations about women protesting. They can go to jail and/or they may lose *izzat*. Women should leave things like politics to men. Only when special problems arise do they protest. Even then, they don't protest on roads. Women won't get permission to go out. They might if they are doctors or lawyers. But then, only to go in the neighborhood.

In other ways, too, her family has tried to improve its circumstances. Her youngest brother has gone to both Iraq and Kuwait to do construction work. He had completed his Intermediate Degree, but then his father died and he had to work. He was in Iraq when the war with Iran started. He only returned to Pakistan four years later when his company closed. He then went once again to Kuwait but returned to Lahore after becoming ill and homesick. Now he works in a paper-making factory inside the Walled City. Two of her husband's brothers also went to the Gulf area in search of work.

> Both my *jaiths* went to the Gulf to work. One went to Dubai and Saudi Arabia, the other went to Bahrain and Saudi Arabia. One *jaith* did his matric degree, the other did his Intermediate Degree and four years at Peshawar studying engineering in a technical school. Both improved their financial conditions a lot. Their children are getting well-educated. All the work is laborer-work. My *jaith* said to my husband that he wouldn't like that work. My *jaith* had worked at a chemical company in Lahore for three years, then left and went to Dubai. He worked on machines there, not in an office job. He became very experienced. His family went there for some time. In Saudi Arabia, he became a purchasing officer with a company, but his family was here. My husband helped look after them. My *jaith* came back after only nine or ten months, he missed his children so much. He did not even stay to do *hajj* while he was there. Now he does private business. He gets order, has someone make them, and then delivers the orders. Once, my husband wanted to go to the Gulf but he could not get good work. He was about to go abroad, somewhere in the Gulf; he had a visa and a plane ticket, and then we found out that if was a fraud. Money was given and all, but the men who went did not have jobs there.

Given her own privileged position, it is surprising to hear that she also has mixed feelings about certain professions for women. In reply to our question about the respectability of *wacholans* and stewardesses -- an occupation which she once desired for herself -- she answers:

> Both *wacholans* and PIA air hostesses do a good job, but the job is not good. Our culture does not like women staying among men. If you are poor, it's better to sew or do crafts in one's own home. You don't go from house-to-house, listening about everyone's relatives. However, *wacholans* definitely serve a purpose: two of my sisters' marriages were arranged by *wacholans*. However, poor women are *wacholans*; it is not such a respectable profession. When they do some service, we give money and clothes to them. You cannot look down upon sweepers and *wacholans* since you cannot live without them. Being a *wacholan* is not a new profession; people who want or need a *rishta* (marriage arrangement) outside their family use *wacholans*. I think those days are gone when they used to arrange marriages for fourteen-fifteen year olds. These days, the first question they ask is how well educated the girl is. The *wacholan* comes to the house, and asks if they need any *rishta*. One has already asked a few times about my daughters, but my daughters are still studying.

While Erum does not regard being a salesgirl as a respectable occupation, she does find being a lawyer, a doctor or a computer programmer in an office acceptable, probably because they each require a great deal of education. Not surprisingly, however, she states that "the best profession is teaching."

Chand Bibi: Seamstress and Artificial Jewelry Maker

When Chand Bibi lived with her *chachi*, before she was married, women used to come to their home and give them things to sew. Hence they sewed clothes for individuals, not for other tailors. She, along with countless other Pakistani women, can sew and do other aspects of tailoring but cannot cut patterns. Often, women are dependent on male tailors to do this. Chand Bibi says that she didn't learn cutting because she had been the *ladli* ("star of one's eyes"; spoiled daughter) in her aunt's home, always fawned over. Her aunt had said she would cut the patterns as long as she was alive, and therefore did not teach Chand Bibi this skill.

When Chand Bibi's husband was alive and in good health, he had been an incense salesman. Her *dewar* used to make the incense in their own small factory in the bazaar. As her *dewar* earned enough from his labors in the factory, her *dewarani* never had to make incense. However, Chand Bibi's husband did not earn as much, and she had to prepare incense in her house for him to sell for twelve or thirteen years.

> While making incense, I never did other work. On rare occasions, someone
> would come by and say "*Baji*, you can sew this; please do it for me." I
> would charge them for the work.

She says that she no longer embroiders or sews clothes because
tuberculosis has left her too weak to do many things. She had been
making artificial jewelry for a few years, but has recently stopped.

> I haven't made any artificial jewelry in over a month. My eyes were going
> bad from making the earrings under this light. For this reason, I am
> embroidering and putting lace on *dupattas* and crocheting necklines of
> *kamizes*. So now people come to me for this work. My neighbors know that
> I do this work. I can't work at night if I use black thread, though.

The room indeed appears dark, especially for close handwork. We
checked the wattage on the light bulb: while the bulb states it is 100
watts, it seems less power comes through it, only about 60 watts.

Women find out that she can sew and embroider (and it looks very
impressive) through informal networks, and they bring work to her. She
does not leave her house to seek work from anyone, despite her fairly
desperate poverty. Her customers bring her the necessary cloth and
thread, and pay her fifteen rupees for each *kamize*. It takes her one full
day to crochet the borders of a *kamize*.

Chand Bibi once again brings out her brass *pandan* to make herself a
pan. She opens the *pandan* and shows me the betel leaves, ground
tamarind, tobacco, *safed* (white powder), and *supari* (betel nut), each
stored in their separate compartments. She cracks the betel nut with a
nutcracker.

> If I don't eat my *pan*, I can't work. I try to work on something every day.
> I make a frock, a *kamize*, something. I make over a hundred rupees per
> week, if I can get the work. If I can't get enough work, I have less money.
> You can see I have three daughters here. I have to pay their school fees, for
> their clothes and all. If I can give them proper food, that's enough for me.

Chand Bibi was never quite sure about how much money she actually
earns from her labors. Numbers seem fluid to her, and at various times
she stated very different incomes. Given the piece-work rate she earns,
however, her income is probably a bit under five hundred rupees per
month, and I think she's accurate when she says she has no savings.

While she would like to work for some shopkeeper and hence get
regular work to do, she doesn't have any extra money to buy the goods
that she would need.

Shopkeepers expect you to come and find the work done first, and then pay you. I recently tried to get some work from them. I myself went to 2-4 shopkeepers in Rang Mahel to get more work. I didn't go to too many. I showed a *kamize* which I did to the shopkeepers, though I didn't show them any *dupattas* which I had crocheted. One shopkeeper gave me a sample *kamize*, to copy the neckline. He gave me some *tikan*, white cloth which is used for embroidery so it's stiff. It's used especially for collars, *panchas* (for *shalwars*) and sometimes necklines. I crocheted three neck-samples on the *tikan*. He paid me for the neck samples. He gave me the same rate for all, five rupees each. This is the same rate that I take from women who come here. He also gave me two *kamizes* to crochet. He paid eighteen rupees for each of the two *kamizes* and gave me eight rupees for the thread I used.

As mentioned earlier, Chand Bibi fears any profession for women where she has to mix with men. Interestingly, while she is angry with the *wacholan* who arranged her own marriage and with other *wacholans* who hurt the lives of other women she knows, she does not regard that profession to be as dishonorable as that of a bank teller, a salesgirl, or a lady doctor who treats male patients.

Being a *wacholan* can be respectable. There are so many girls waiting in their homes for suitors. A *wacholan* has to go from door-to-door, but she usually only talks with women. But I don't want to see my daughters as *wacholans*.

Her ideal for her daughters would be for them to sew or knit at home, or else teach in a girls' school. Indeed, there are role models who do such labor within the Walled City who can be emulated; she knows no woman who works in an office. The key issue to Chand Bibi is that interactions remain confined to other women and, for her, within the Walled City.

Durdana: Plastic Toy Assembler

Durdana's husband owns a small plastic toy molding factory on the ground floor of their building, from which a constant shrilly noise emerges as the molds are made. The room was always dark when I peeked inside it. Upstairs, in the living quarters, green and blue plastic horns are lined up on the floor and dominate the room. There are black rubber tips which Durdana attaches to the plastic horns. She has been helping to assemble plastic items ever since she was married. Given her good relations with her husband, she does not see this as a chore, and defers all matters relating to the business to him.

Before my marriage, my husband was doing this work. From the beginning,
I helped my husband with this work. Neither I nor my children get any
separate money, but he feeds me well and clothes me well. My life has been
fine.

   I work until 1 p.m., then rest. I do this work every day. We have four
workmen downstairs, doing the plastic molds. They all live upstairs. They
are from far away, from past Jehangir's tomb (past Shahdara), from a
village there called Kot Abdul Malik. We have no domestic servant -- the
children help me. The market is nearby where we sell the horns. It's Mumti
Market, in Shah Alami Bazaar.

Today they are assembling dark blue and pink horns.

We line them up, to put the finishing parts, the rubber for the mouth, on
the horns. We also make *chankaria*, it's like a rattle, something to shake. We
used to make plastic soap dishes and plastic crockery but we didn't get
much profit from that. We started the toys four years ago. My children and
I do the final assembly for the horns. We complete forty gross daily.

As Durdana's husband enters the room, he corrects her and says that
they manufacture ten or twelve gross daily, for a total of about fifteen
hundred pieces. Compared to his illiterate wife, he is well educated as he
has completed his matric degree. Durdana is unable to answer our
question regarding the price of a gross of plastic horns; her husband
informs us that the price is eighty-four rupees. Her daily totals are nearly
half of what she estimates as their weekly income.

We make a hundred to a hundred and fifty rupees daily, maybe a thousand
to twelve hundred weekly. Over a year, the monthly average is low, as we
don't work all the time. It's usually five thousand rupees when we do. This
isn't a lot, as everyone -- me, my children, my husband, the four workmen
-- we all do this work.

   We sell a lot at *Eid*. Afterwards, when the month of Muharram begins,
it will all be stopped. We can then eat and drink in comfort.

Durdana does not regard what she does as "work," and has no separate,
independent income, although she does have some separate savings that
she squirrels away. She maintains that family customs prevent women
from earning money. She does not perceive of any profession as being
respectable for a woman, not even a lady doctor: "That's still working,
and it's not good." She observes strict *purdah*, and believes in stringent
rules surrounding women's activities.

Amina: Sehra maker and seamstress

Amina and her daughters work in their home sewing *sehras* which are used at shrines and weddings. Her only son is an apprentice in a curtain shop outside of the Walled City while she refers to her husband as a "hawker." He calls passengers to get onto busses that are headed for either Faisalabad or Multan. After a bus fills up and leaves the stand, he begins calling passengers for the next one.

Their circumstances have not always been as difficult as they are today. Previously, her husband had been a police constable in Kasur, a provincial city not far from Lahore. He left the police after the birth of their first child and joined his brother as a tailor in a shop in Suter Mandi. In those days, she never helped him in his work.

When my husband left the police to become a tailor, I was a child, and didn't ever ask him why he left. There wasn't enough money in the police. My husband worked 2-3 years as a tailor. He didn't like sitting, so he left tailoring. He went to Badamibagh and became a conductor's helper on a government bus. He still does that today as a day laborer. He earns about eight hundred rupees per month. It's enough for *roti* (food), but for clothing and other things, we have to earn it.

A neighbor who I met one day -- who fights constantly with Amina, other neighbors and with her own family -- told us that Amina's husband is a beggar. Perhaps he is, or perhaps she said this either because she was angry with Amina or perceives that he is a beggar because it is financially necessary for Amina and her daughters to work to supplement his income.

Some years ago, after Amina had given birth to three children, she began to work as a seamstress. She never went to others' homes; as with the case of Chand Bibi, neighbors and their relatives came to her when they needed something sewn. She worked as a seamstress fifteen or sixteen years, professing to have only recently stopped after developing diabetes. Besides making private orders, she also used to sew bedsheets for shopkeepers. A man she refers to as *Bhai* (brother), though unrelated, used to give her the cloth and thread and later collect the finished bedsheet sets to sell to shopkeepers. He has since stopped doing this business and now works in a cement factory.

The financial problems in her family started about ten years ago when her husband had a pain in his knee. It became very swollen and he had to have an operation in Mayo Hospital.

He was in pain 2-3 months, in the hospital for one month, and two months recovery. My husband's friend, a former neighbor from Amritsar, suggested we make *sehras* for display at mosques, saints' shrines and weddings, as he was making them. He suggested this as a favor, to help us.

I've been doing this work for the last ten years, and in all that time the rate hasn't changed. He comes about once a week, though not at fixed times, to pick up the finished *sehras* and drop off more materials for us to make them. I don't know anyone else who is doing this work for him in their homes. All of my daughters have helped me with this work, although only three unmarried daughters remain at home to help me now.

They make nearly every part of the *sehra*. Only the ornate *gota* work is embroidered by someone else.

The four of them work all day long, every day, when they have the goods with which to make the *sehras*. They begin working on them in the mornings at about 8 a.m., after they make breakfast and clean the house. One day when I am visiting, they are working on *sehras* adorned with religious expressions in Arabic which are for use at mosques. One has an orange plastic "*Ya Muhammad*" while another one says "*Bismillah*." Amina is putting glue around the paper edges while one of her daughters pastes gold ribbon on it. They had earlier cut out cardboard shapes and pasted shiny gold paper on them, and had used thread to apply red velvet with gold *gota*-work to the gold-covered paper. Her second daughter dries the glue as the third daughter stitches a plastic phrase on more gold paper for other *sehras*. They receive one rupee per dozen *sehras* and usually make sixty to eighty dozen per week, for a combined income of about seven hundred rupees per month. After all this time, her family still has no savings.

If she had a choice, Amina would prefer to do other, more steady work in her home for which she could receive better payment. Sometimes they have to sit idle for a few days if they have completed their work but the man has not yet come. However, she does not know anyone who could get her involved in a new system so she is forced by circumstances to continue making *sehras*. In her entire life, she has never worked outside of her home; no woman in her family has ever worked outside of the home.

While the family confronts poverty daily, their *izzat* (respectability) remains very important. When I asked her daughters what they thought of women who work in their homes, making *sehras* as their mother does, they said vehemently, shaking their fingers, "No, no!" Amina looks at them, and wishes they had more options.

Education is good, but the environment of this area -- this *gali*, this neighborhood, isn't good for girls to go out. Labor is good; high education is good. People talk so much about women who go out, that it's impossible.

The best work for women? A *wacholan*, no, that's not work. Why should

a girl be a *wacholan*? There is no *izzat* in being a bank teller either. If she has
to work beside men, that's not good. A PIA stewardess has to mix with
men, so it's not good. Really, no work that a woman has to do outside the
house can be good.

With the latter comment, however, her daughters began to disagree. They
said that the only way a poor girl could see other parts of the world
would probably be as a stewardess. The eldest sister bemoaned the fact
that she had wanted her two younger sisters to become stewardesses, but
their grades had not been good enough. Amina retorts with a stern
glance at her daughter.

People think badly if a woman works at all. Whether she works as a lady
doctor, or a teacher, people still say that her mother and father eat from her
labor. The point is that whatever kind of work a girl does, if she has to
walk outside to do it, it doesn't look good for the family. A girl can work
inside of her home, and no one knows. I would not have given my
permission for my daughters to have become air hostesses even if their
marks were high enough. It's up to me before their engagement and their
marriage. After marriage, the husband also won't give his permission.

I returned to Amina's house on many occasions in the ensuing years.
In early 1991, I found that she and her daughters had finally given up
sewing *sehras* and instead were hemming curtains in their home. Their
change of circumstances is due to her son getting a job as a salesman in
Azim Market, the large wholesale cloth market near Rang Mahal. He now
provides them with the material people have ordered and brings the
curtains back to his shop when they are completed. That they are no
longer dependent on a middleman has made a dramatic improvement in
their financial position as they now earn between five hundred and six
hundred rupees weekly. This change, however, was not possible until her
son became old enough to work himself, and then was able to set himself
up as a virtual middleman for them.

Bilqis: Paster of Shoe Straps

In the courtyard of her home, Bilqis and others in her household help
make shoes that her husband sells in the bazaar. He also makes and sells
shoes out of a one-room shop in Wachowali bazaar which they refer to
as a "shoe factory." Bilqis' eldest daughter used to help them also before
her marriage five years ago, but has since been sewing clothes for others
in her own home.

They make the shoes in the courtyard and two downstairs rooms, and sleep in the two upstairs rooms. The room in which she and her daughter work together has a simple brick floor. They are putting paste on the bottom of shoe straps. Bilqis then places the straps in a circle, carefully, after pasting them. In the other room a niece, age six, puts gold foil over cardboard strips which one of Bilqis' sons then hammers into flat shoe straps. Another of her sons uses a metal die bought from the bazaar to pattern out heart designs for the shoe straps. Her other little niece, age five, is separating silver paper hearts to apply to the design on the straps. Some of the shoes they make are sold by Bilqis' husband, though most are sold by larger companies.

> When we do the work, one of my sons goes to the person who gives them this material and returns the finished goods. Sometimes he is paid in cash; other times, he tells my son to come back another time for the payment. The whole family gets the payment for the work.

Bilqis pastes shoe straps for three to four hours a day. The rest of the family works from early morning until 6 p.m. in the summer, and until 8 p.m. in the winter (when the children study). She receives no separate wage as all the money which the family earns is communal. Her family has a combined income of about four thousand rupees a month, from which they have managed to set aside some savings.

> Our work is not enough to open our own shop. We buy the materials and then sell the finished shoes. This order we're working on now, we will sell these ladies' shoes for twenty rupees a pair. We make sizes from 11-3 (11, 12, 13, 1, 2, 3). We spend twelve rupees per pair, so we get about eight rupees profit each.
>   We use golden foil on the bottom of straps, and on the sides of the top. They are covered with black, maroon or red velvet cloth. We use cardboard in the center for strength.
>   I only paste the straps to adhere them to the sole. We have fat straps and thin straps. When I was young I used to do sewing for the straps. But now they've changed the style. We don't do sewing, we just paste it to adhere to the sole.

As we are talking, Bilqis sticks her finger in the glue and applies it to the sides of the straps. Then she puts paste on the border of the undersoles. I am taken aback by the strong smell of the glue, and ask her if she has ever felt sick from it.

> At the very first there was a bad smell, but now I've gotten used to it. I've done it for ten years. In my childhood, I used to sew shoe straps for my

brothers. I got married when I was sixteen. At that time, my husband and his brothers were together and he ran the shoe factory in Wachowali. He used to have twenty or twenty-five people working for him. Later on, they separated their businesses due to some dispute. My mother-in-law played some role in the separation. My mother-in-law is still alive, and I now have good relations with her. She lives with her oldest son, near the primary school in the bazaar.

Bilqis' husband walks in and tosses some shoe soles (covered with gold foil with red velvet cloth on the border) on the floor. With the presence of her husband in the room, she now defers all questions about their business to him. He tells us about the growing problems that shoe manufacturing in the Walled City has had to confront since the 1971 civil war which resulted in an independent Bangladesh.

There are so many restrictions, and the goods that we used to send to Dhaka we don't send anymore, since it's been under India's control. Kabul is also closed. We work very, very hard, but it's only the big industrialists who make money out of it. They won't give us as much profit as they should. Sometimes, for instance, if the price is one rupee, they give twelve *annas* (75 percent). So all the money goes into their hands. We got a more reasonable profit when we could deal with Dhaka and Kabul. But now, in these days, we're not satisfied, because when we do our own work -- in the morning, when we go to the bazaar -- people who buy our goods aren't so willing to take them, and they give us less money.

Life was better here in the past than it is now. We had enough money for everything. Our business, making shoes, was good. We used to do business with Kabul and Dhaka. But now, the business has gone down because of the war with Bangladesh and the fighting in Afghanistan.

Bilqis, working alongside her husband and sons, commands a great deal of respect and power in her family, especially when compared to that held by other women in the Walled City. She says that she is primarily responsible for deciding what the family purchases, and her husband neither questions her decisions nor really asks where the money gets spent. She is supportive of the idea of women working and feels that whatever a woman has to do to earn an income is acceptable, whether it's being a *wacholan* or working in a shop or office. Of all work possibilities available to women, she feels that being a teacher is the most respectable.

When we returned in the end of 1988, Bilqis's family had undergone a major change: her husband had passed away a few months earlier. While the family still mourned his passing, they all agreed with her opinion that because they remain together as one economic unit -- and especially because she has adult sons -- the death of her husband has not appreciably changed her life. They were all sitting in the same courtyard, making plasticine pumps for women in a variety of bright, fashion colors such as pink, turquoise and yellow.

By this time, the government in Pakistan had also undergone a major change. It was still the "honeymoon" period for Benazir Bhutto's newly-elected PPP government, and she symbolized the hope for the future for many people in Pakistan.[9] Even then, for many working class people such as those residing in the Walled City, these hopes were tied to economic improvement. Bilqis' eldest son shared his views with us about Benazir's government. While they were avid supporters of Benazir and her government, the demand for shoes in the bazaar had decreased and hence the volume of work available for them had also decreased. If conditions didn't change within six months, he felt they would have to look elsewhere for answers. The events of October 1990 underscored that there was much foresight behind this comment.

When I returned in early 1991, I found their economic condition had improved enough that they were able to add on an additional upstairs room. But instead of the political enthusiasm present in 1988, Bilqis and her sons were resigned to what they perceived as their current political reality: whatever government may be in power will have little impact on their lives, for their class is never the ruling government's priority. While they worked ceaselessly to raise their family's standard of living, they felt that the real variable in making a difference in their lives has thus far been pure luck.

Itrat: Artificial Jewelry Maker

Itrat has been making artificial jewelry in her home ever since her family started facing financial problems some six or seven years ago. Her husband used to supply shops with leaves which were used as plates for *halva/puri* or as trays for wrapping other food. However, after polyethylene bags were introduced into the market, there was no longer any demand for the leaves and he had to shut his business down.

Her *bhabi* was making jewelry at home at the time. Itrat thought that she could do it too, so her *bhabi* sent the woman who supplies her with her materials to see Itrat. The woman's husband owns an artificial jewelry shop in Anarkali, the largest commercial market in Lahore just opposite Lohari Gate, running past Mayo Hospital nearly all the way to Mall Road. His wife meets with the women who make the earrings and necklaces, and either she or one of her children comes to deliver the material and pick up the jewelry.

Only the man doesn't come to our house because it's not right. We have no relationship to him. I am a *purdah*-observing woman. On a few occasions, I have had to send one of my children to get the materials. Whenever it comes, I try to finish it that very day, by the evening. But sometimes I have to sit around waiting for work, because they don't send anything.

Itrat is sitting and working on the floor, near a low table on which there lies nearly-completed artificial earrings. The earrings have red beads hanging down from artificial gold. They are remarkably similar to the gaudy real jewelry Pakistani women prefer to wear.

She usually completes a dozen pairs a day because it's a lot of work for each earring and there's a lot of housework that she must do as well. She receives about twenty or twenty-five rupees for a dozen pairs of this type, which sell for thirty-five rupees each pair in the bazaar.[10] Hence, only five percent of the retail price is paid for labor.

I make earrings and necklaces. Sometimes I get earrings to make, sometimes necklaces. I do whatever comes; mostly earrings come. In a day, I make one or two dozen earrings. I earn one or two rupees per pair, or between twelve and twenty-four rupees per dozen. Sometimes, he returns the earrings to me if they're not right. Just today two pairs were returned; they were not the same length and I must fix them.

A whole set consists of a choker, earrings and a large necklace. I earn fifteen rupees for each necklace. In the bazaar, they sell for two hundred or two hundred fifty rupees. I would like to have more of this work to do. All the sets don't have the same price. Sometimes I get fifteen rupees, sometimes less. Usually, I can make five sets in a day. Then, I can earn seventy-five rupees daily. My usual weekly income is about a hundred to a hundred twenty-five rupees because I mostly am given earrings to make.

A very large necklace has six strands of pearls, with eight gold twists connecting them. I make this on special order. It's going outside, maybe to Iran, Iraq or England. I don't know for sure where it goes. It goes to Karachi and then is sent outside. The same man gives me this work to do. We came to know it's a special order because he said so, and he asked us to do it quickly. Three people have to work on it, and it takes one or two hours each. The gold twists are made in a factory. The person who takes them from us applies colored glass in the center of the twists.

I have no other skills. I can sew a little for my children. That's all. I give the expensive cloth to a tailor to stitch. The other clothes I stitch myself.

Itrat had never imagined, when she was younger, that she would have to work. No woman in her family had ever worked, and her husband's business with the leaves was doing well when she married him. But his income now is quite meager.

combines it with the amount that her husband earns, and credits the total to his efforts. We know she works and earns money but she herself will not state that she helps to support her family and that her husband cannot support them on his own.

We began this chapter by looking into the kinds of work opportunities that are both accessible and acceptable to women in the Walled City. We then delved into the actual work experiences themselves, elaborating on the work women actually perform and the barriers which they perceive constrain them from enjoying better working conditions or greater remuneration. When a woman works, this act inevitably does more than only give her an income: questions of empowerment in other spheres of life naturally arise. Whether in response to questions of respectability, health matters (physical and psychological) or other related issues regarding power in their lives and in the lives of their children (especially their daughters), women in the Walled City have developed informal networks and practical strategies by which they survive, and it is, therefore, to these that we now turn.

Notes

1. For further elaboration refer to Boserup (1970), Charlton (1984: 39-44) and Beneria (1982). Waring (1988) argues that a deeper problem lies in the overall weakness of what national accounts systems value which perpetuates the institutionalization of census collection worldwide to make women's lives invisible. See especially Waring, 1988: 93-117.

2. This, however, is changing in those areas which have focussed on export-oriented manufacturing and are integrating large numbers of women into working in established factories, many of which are owned by transnational corporations.

3. They also found that the major income earners are overwhelmingly (97%) engaged in full-time work, and they found no one holding two jobs (LDA, 1984: 11).

4. Ann Duncan (World Bank, 1989: 29-36) provides an overview of women in the urban economy in Pakistan. This is based in part on a study conducted by A. Sathar and S. Kazi in 1988 for the Pakistan Institute of Development Economics on female employment in Karachi. Sathar and Kazi estimate that 68.5 percent of women are employed in Karachi's informal sector; 52.6 percent of all employed women were engaged in home-based work of some sort (World Bank, 1989: 90-94). We must bear in mind that sociocultural demographics differ greatly between Karachi and Lahore, and between other areas in Lahore and the Walled City.

5. The LDA (1984) surveyed where the major income earner from households in the Walled City works. It assessed that 52 percent work in their own work area, separate from their home; 20 percent work for a private firm; 13 percent work in government offices; 3 percent work in someone else's private household; 2 percent work in their own house; and 10 percent work elsewhere.

6. Please refer to Table A.2 (in Appendix) for characteristics of women in families who have had the experience of a woman working either within or outside of the home.

7. Some women do earn an income, but claim not to have the skills to do so, most often in teaching and food preparation.

8. This category includes husbands and fathers, the major male income earners noted in the survey. Table A.1 (in Appendix) contrasts the percentages of women's earned income with those of men's.

9. The effects of the symbolism of Benazir Bhutto's victory for women in Pakistan are addressed in the following chapter. See also Anita M. Weiss "Benazir Bhutto and the Future of Women in Pakistan" *Asian Survey* 30, No. 5, May 1990, pp. 433-445.

10. When I returned three and a half years later, she was receiving the exact same rate for her labor.

4

Survival Strategies and Images of Power

Two important dimensions of power affect the lives of women in the Walled City: the extent to which they can make significant life decisions for themselves, and the extent to which they can do something -- act -- independently. The former consists of issues such as whether a woman is consulted regarding who she will marry or what might be included in her dowry. The latter includes being able to follow through on getting an education, gaining access to healthcare or seeking employment. An integral part of both dimensions includes the choices that women are making concerning activities and participation in social networks outside of their extended kin groups, as well as more abstract issues such as how a woman remains respectable in these changing times or what vision she may hold of freedom. This results from what Mernissi (1987: xvii) refers to as the renegotiation of new authority boundaries, thresholds, and limits, which culminates in a subtle change in the abstract perception of what a woman is. By exploring how traditional means of power and social control have been replaced by new orientations towards women's roles, what are the prisms through which women now view these dimensions of power in their lives?

The meaning of women's power is slowly being redefined both here and throughout the Muslim world. Nadia Hijab argues that instead of viewing power solely in terms of access to formal political and economic structures, a more viable option especially concerning women is to look at informal networks and whether or not they support women's interests both within the family and in the larger society. Hijab (1988: 140) writes that

Power is the extent to which a person or group can exercise control over their situation; in the case of women, the extent to which they can influence factors related to their situation in order to serve clearly defined personal (or family, or community) interests.

Carla Makhlouf (1979) contends that one of the major ways in which North Yemeni women wield power is in their access to and control over information. However, this is under circumstances where the women's world is clearly demarcated from the men's world such as exists in many Arab areas. In the Walled City where that demarcation is not as clear, information subsides as being a critical variable and is instead replaced by strategies which women use to overcome existing constraints and restrictions. Power, therefore, cannot be conceived solely in terms of women exercising control over other women as their destinies are intrinsically tied up with the actions and decisions of the men in their lives. Power is constantly being negotiated and renegotiated, through notions of respect, rights, obligations and requirements.

Before we can understand the ways in which women gain -- or try to gain -- access to power affecting "factors related to their situation," we must recognize existing constraints and restrictions on women's actions. The extent to which they are involved in making simple decisions such as daily food purchases shows that while women's mobility is certainly restricted, there is scope for decision-making within the home. Nearly three-quarters of the women in our survey have some sort of input into deciding what should be bought for their family's daily needs, although less than a quarter of them actually go outside to buy the goods themselves. However, although about half of their significant males (husband, son, father, brother, father-in-law) do the daily shopping in the bazaar, only eight percent of these men have input into deciding what to buy.

The extent to which women are involved in daily decision-making within the family appears to be based on objective circumstances which are not generalizable. In some instances, women are consulted and their suggestions or wishes are considered while in more traditionally orthodox households, male members' wills tend to remain more determinate. Age is not necessarily a significant factor, as some families take daughters' suggestions into consideration while in others even wives are not asked for their input.

Who is actually responsible for making the decision to purchase major items (e.g., television, fan, refrigerator) is not as clear. Men make such decisions solely by themselves in nineteen percent of the households. The women in our survey -- by themselves or with input from others -- have been involved in only thirty percent of the decisions. Sometimes children can be influential, such as Itrat's children who urged their father to buy an iron last year, but everyone in the family claims that the actual decision was her husband's. Other decisions have been made by parents, in-laws and in tandem with significant males' male relations when the input of the women surveyed has been omitted.

Health, Healing, and Visions of Freedom

An important aspect of decision-making power surfaces when we look to see how women respond to their healthcare needs. We recall Erum's story of how, in an earlier era, her mother-in-law could not leave her home to buy medicine for a son, and hence the child died. Today, there are many conventional and informal healthcare choices available from which women can choose.

When inquiring how often the surveyed women had become sick in the preceding year, 47 percent reported 2-3 times: this is that same category of "a bit, but not too much." 16 percent reported having a chronic illness. We were rather surprised to find that western-style allopathic medicine and medical practitioners are the preferred choice of women in the Walled City in response to an illness or injury. We had expected more women would rely on the opinion of a *hakim* (*unani* practitioner) or a *pir*, whose services have been traditional options in the Punjab. 92 percent of households reported having seen a medical doctor in the past year, while only six percent consulted a *hakim* and no one went to a *pir* for an illness or injury. 74 percent had used the facilities at a hospital, though only 10 percent did so for emergency medical care.

We can, therefore, see a clear preference by the women we met in the Walled City for allopathic medicine and medical practitioners. However, in their accounts, women's experiences with conventional medical options have not usually been very positive. The majority of women knew about medical resources which existed; what was problematic for many was access to them, either to just be seen by a doctor or to pay for the care. Early childhood health care was the one area we found to be working fairly successfully. Government-employed Lady Health Visitors (LHVs) visit homes periodically to ensure the necessary immunizations have occurred. The Lahore Development Authority (1984: 7) reports that 84.4 percent of children in the Walled City have received immunizations against major diseases.

It should also be mentioned that women here do not see childbirth as a "medical problem" per se; few even considered the option of having a child in a hospital as births generally occur in the home. Birth control options are sometimes regarded as a medical issue, and sometimes regarded as a religious one. For example, when we were spoke with a group of women at Bhati Gate about available options for controlling birth, four of the women's views virtually span the range of opinions:

Woman #1: I use nothing for birth control. After some time, children just come.

Woman #2: I use the coil. Sometimes it hurts, but it seems to help.

Woman #3: I go to Pir Makki Sher Shah Wali, behind the mosque. I believe in *pirs* and *taviz* (amulets), but not in women who do *jaddu* (magic). I go on Thursdays.

Woman #4: I want to have an operation to stop having children. I'm hoping to have it in Jalaldin Hospital, near Mori Gate. I'm not educated; how can I know what that medicine is, that they want to give me to stop having children? It's written in English. My husband wants me to have dozens of children...but General Zia (the government) isn't giving me any land to feed my family. I'm determined to have that operation.

Smaller hospitals such as Jalaldin, which appear more like clinics, are the most frequently visited. Other popular small hospitals include Javaki Devi Ladies Hospital, Ittifaq Hospital, Chitta Hospital, and Safia Haneef Trust. A number of women use the health clinics at the many mosques which provide them, most notably at Data Saheb, Muslim Mosque at Lohari Gate, and the Agha Khan facility inside Shah Alami Gate.

The most popular government-run hospital frequented is Mayo Hospital, the multi-purpose facility convenient to many parts of the Walled City which was built by the British. On any given day, tongas overwhelm the intersection beside the hospital. Other popular working class-oriented hospitals include Lady Wellingdon (by Taxali Gate, within the Walled City) and Gunga Ram (off Mall Road, a fifteen-minute tonga ride). A few women, particularly the ones from wealthier families, have also visited the "top" hospitals of Lahore, including Services, Fatima Memorial, United Christian and Sheikh Zayed, all quite far away from the Walled City on the other side of Lahore.

But conventional medical options make up only a part of women's healing needs. We cannot overlook psychological needs, especially in this environment in which most women wield little power to substantively affect their own lives or even to be able to physically travel somewhere at will. Family, friends and religious leaders or shrines provide vital emotional support and underscore the importance of both fictive kinship and religiosity in women's survival strategies. As we can see in Table 4.1, two-thirds of the women interviewed visit *pirs* or shrines at least once or twice a year. Women also frequent *pirnis*, female *pirs*, when they are confronted with problems such as infertility, domestic strife and illness. The *pirni*, in providing *taviz* or specific prayers to women, enables a woman to become an active agent in affecting her fate, at least psychologically.

TABLE 4.1: Who Is Visited and How Often by Women
in the Walled City

Relatives:

-- 15% go to see relatives at least once a week;

-- 27% see relatives occasionally (once or twice a month);

-- 48% visit relatives very occasionally (once or twice a
   year);

-- 10% never go to visit relatives

Neighbors:

-- 29% visit with neighbors daily; they have become fictive kin.

-- 43% never visit neighbors; they have not become fictive kin.

Friends:

-- 8% see friends at least once a week;

-- 71% never go back to visit friends (presumably they will see each
   other at functions, however).

Maulvis:

-- 90% never go to visit a *maulvi*;

-- 8% will go once or twice a year.

Living Pirs and Saints' Mazars (shrines):

-- 64% visit *pirs* or shrines once or twice a year, usually to Data
   Saheb, but also to Syad Suf, Meera Saheb in Masjid Wazir Khan,
   Gama Shah, Pir Makki, and Bibian Pak Daman;

-- 5% go at least once a week;

-- 27% never go to visit a *pir* or shrine.

Religiosity becomes evident when we look at what time women
usually awaken. While eighty percent of the women reporting that they

wake up before 6 a.m. implies that they have a long work day, in the Walled City it has an additional meaning which becomes evident in the life history accounts. Most women are awakened by the *azan*, the morning call to prayer. This is a quiet moment that a woman has all to herself, and many have remarked that saying morning prayers is a calming, important time.

The basis on which decisions are made and the extent to which women are involved in carrying them out contributes to another aspect of changes in decision-making power, notably perceptions of respectable activities for women and the visions they hold of freedom. In this area where social control by virtue of high density remains a formidable power, the key points which surface are that a woman can engage in virtually any kind of activity provided that she remains under the watchful eye of the community, and she does not mix with men. Women have not become "free agents" (nor do they wish to become such) but instead are responding as responsible decision-makers to changing economic, social and political conditions. Erum sees changes in public power relations as being responsible for empowering women in the private sphere.

> In the past, husbands were very strict... (and) they would listen to their mother over their wife. My mother-in-law and her *bhabis* couldn't do anything, not even send for medicine on their own. Now it's different; I and my *bhabis* are freer to do what we want...we (now) go to buy everything: clothes, shoes, etc. We just don't go to the bazaar for food.

She credits the combination of television, politics and education for enabling her daughters to be able to go out of their home when they have a purpose to do so.

Freedom is intimately linked to power and is associated with such issues as being able to study, being able to dress in the latest fashions, controlling one's fertility by the use of contraceptives, and overall mobility. The issue, however, that elicited the most passionate responses concerned the most potent symbol of Muslim women's freedom (or lack thereof): the veil.

Almost all women in the Walled City -- 96 percent -- observe some sort of *purdah*. There are numerous characteristics that we can associate with following *purdah*. Table A.3 (in Appendix) provides comparisons of various characteristics of women who observe *purdah* by wearing a veil with a *nikab*, wearing a veil without a *nikab* and those who observe *purdah* by keeping separate from men. Table 4.2 provides a breakdown of three types of *purdah* observed: the most strict, when a woman never leaves her home alone; the moderated form, in which she can go out alone but

TABLE 4.2: Type of Purdah Practiced by Women in the Walled City,
of Those Observing Purdah

Type of Purdah	Percent
Never leave house alone	49
Wear a veil	49
Avert eyes from men	2

wears a veil when doing so; and the least strict but also the least practiced, when a woman does not wear a veil but she averts her eyes from men. Puberty appears to be a watershed for beginning *purdah* (82 percent of the women began *purdah* at that time), although the first time many of the women ever had to wear a formal *burqa* was on her wedding day or shortly thereafter. Many women initially found wearing the tailored *burqa* upsetting, although as new brides they knew they could not go against the wishes of their *susural* and hence had no alternative. Of those who wear a veil, 83 percent use a *nikab*, which can cover their face to provide greater anonymity. Amina, after bearing nine children, was finally able to set aside her *burqa* for the more comfortable *chadar*; 2-4 years ago she finally set her *chadar* aside after the onset of diabetes. In fact, a suspiciously large number of women stated that they had given up wearing the veil because they had become diabetic.

Hasina, the Kakazaiya woman frustrated by her husband's attempts to stop her from sewing to earn an income, sees a big difference in the degree of freedom a woman possesses if she can remove her *burqa* and replace it with a *chadar*. However, Gulzar Begum, the widow who strings flowers, feels that there is a marked difference in respect (*izzat*) accorded to a *burqa*-clad woman over one wearing only a *chadar*. The men in her family (of whom she is afraid) would be angry if she stopped wearing her *burqa*, despite her advanced age. A third woman who had previously never left her home without her black *burqa* complete with *nikab* instead occasionally takes a *chadar* or a large scarf-like *dupatta* now. She doubts that her daughters, when grown, will have to wear a veil, and that a *dupatta* will suffice completely in ten years. While some women resisted giving up the *burqa* or *chadar* because doing so implies that she is old, others felt that the *chadar* is going far enough in terms of empowering women with freedom. Only one woman ventured beyond such conventional portrayals when she stated that ultimate freedom for Pakistani women would be when a woman could have "a sexual relationship with another man". This viewpoint, however, extends beyond the parameters which most women would even consider when they discuss the notion of social freedom for women.

Personal power, however, is consistently seen as separate from deciding on marriage: no woman who I interviewed had any say in who she married, and no woman advocated her daughter having any say in her marriage either. Erum, the teacher who has a fairly progressive attitude and is committed to educating her daughters well, feels that the cultural norm of the prospective bride and groom not knowing each other until marriage should be preserved: "Nowadays, girls and boys are brought in front of each other and sometimes are allowed to talk. Sometimes this is not good, because the girl or boy may say the other is too dark, short, has small eyes, too fat, etc."

The implication here is that a male as well as a female lose respectability if they have any input into judging the qualities of their prospective spouse. While women may have some influence over *someone else's* marriage, they remain virtually powerless in terms of their own. As a means of accepting this aspect of her fate, Amina, who used to sew *sehras* and now hems curtains, comments that "If I could have gotten a better husband, my life would have been better, but that was out of my control."

That arranged marriages continue to be accepted as the norm is no surprise in this collective-oriented culture. Far from their cultural center, Pakistanis often continue to maintain that the overriding needs of the family unit take precedence over all else. For example, in her study of Pakistanis in Britain, Verity Khan (1976: 100) notes that in the larger society no one is an individual agent acting on his or her own behalf, but exists only in relation to family and kin. However, a disparity exists between the degree to which most men and most women are locked into the complex system of familial duties and obligations, as the former are often able to garner support for their proposed activities. If we find this to be the case among those who have moved away, who have undergone significant sociocultural and economic upheaval, we can expect and do find these values even stronger within the Walled City.

However, in the past, women were married shortly after they began menstruating, generally by age sixteen. The trend now is to marry off daughters in their early twenties. While social pressures apparently remain potent in deciding upon marriage options, women are increasingly trying to provide their daughters with survival alternatives.

Some women regard education as that alternative, such as Farida, the hairdresser whose husband is a recent drug addict: "If I was educated, I could be making a thousand to twelve hundred rupees per month (instead of three hundred). I would work in a factory, or be a teacher, or give tuition."

Many women complain that relatives (usually male) object to their educating their daughters and they have often had to withdraw girls from school because of this. Cost is also a constraint, as Itrat, the artificial jewelry maker, points out:

> I want to send my daughters to school. Education is helpful, but poverty stands in the way. We have no money to pay for fees and books, for our children to study. My relatives protested when my daughter went to school, but it was really poverty that stood in her way.

Chand Bibi, the widow who enjoys eating *pan*, earns a meager living. However, what little extra she earns beyond subsistence goes for paying her four daughters' school fees and tutoring costs, over two hundred rupees ($10) per month. On her own initiative, she had begun sending them for private tuition in the afternoons after her eldest daughter failed twice and she became afraid the girls' school was not adequate.

Women also consider skill improvements for their daughters as a survival alternative. Daughters usually learn these by working beside their mothers at home, stitching *sehras*, embroidering shirts, stringing flowers. I am not arguing that education or skills are the bulwark; what came through in the life stories is that these daughters perceive their right to earn money if they wish to do so as a given, whereas their mothers were only able to work because it was perceived as a necessity. The days of a woman being married and simply resigning herself to her fate are waning, although how she chooses to respond remains somewhat ambiguous.

The solutions she sees to change in her life lie in her daughters' futures. Marriage is not the avenue which will enable them to have a better life than she has had; she expects her daughters to become qualified and work someday. With "God's will," her second daughter will become a doctor and her third a schoolteacher. Despite her poverty, respectability remains an important criteria through which she makes moral judgments. However, other than providing for her daughters' education, her fatalism -- trusting in God's will -- in a sense prevents a more dynamic response to her predicament of poverty and ill health. She sees the social world changing and is trying to prepare her daughters for that new world, though she does not see herself as an active participant in it.

While Chand Bibi's fatalism and subsequent conservatism was echoed by many others, it was not a universal orientation. It seemed to be common to women at the lowest economic levels; once subsistence needs were met, questions of personal power and freedom began to surface. Fatalism is usually a factor only in enabling women to *accept* harshness and difficulties in their lives, though was rarely referred to in how decisions are made or hopes for the future. Women whose husbands and/or sons are able to support them generally appear more complacent than those whose circumstances are not so. However, it must be recalled that the number of women without male support is expanding rapidly for several reasons:

* the breakdown of extended families causes male relatives who in past times may have felt an obligation to the woman and her family now to not perceive that obligation as they see themselves as only being distantly related;
* the trend for male members to work abroad results in women learning how to fend for themselves and taking more responsibility for their public affairs;
* the growing problem of drug addiction in this working class area is having an impact in that husbands, brothers, sons and cousins may abdicate traditional responsibilities.

Poverty and illiteracy also serve as constraints to women's greater participation in the economy. Educational opportunities are limited. There are many elementary schools for girls within the Walled City but there are no secondary girls' schools. Many women told me they would have liked to have continued studying but were unable to travel alone to a high school outside, and no male in their family was available to accompany them. Further, while there are many private and public sewing schools, there is no technical school for girls within the Walled City where they can learn industry-related skills other than sewing.

Skill-oriented schools such as the Sir Sikander Hayat Vocational School, Dergha-e-Batool Vocational School, Anjaman-Khadam ul-Muslameen School, and countless private ones in women's homes, while teaching a range of crafts, focus on sewing. Their popularity seems to have increased substantially in recent years. Traditionally, most women could sew simple *shalwar kamizes* for their families, though an increasing number are seeing this skill, as discussed earlier, as an important survival strategy offering the potential of an income. Government-run schools, such as the Zenana Dastakari School at Mori Gate, are very low cost and virtually anyone can afford the fees. Officially titled "Industrial Home, Lahore Municipal Committee, inside Lohari," it charges a one-time admission of two rupees, and then only two rupees per month to take classes in sewing, embroidery, knitting, handwork, glasswork, and painting. However, due to over-crowding, most of the girls we spoke to said they spend most of their time at the school waiting to use a sewing machine or to get the attention of one of the three teachers. The girls are not allowed to bring their own sewing machines to the school.

The overcrowding at the government-run schools has led to a

proliferation of mosque-run and privately owned sewing schools within the Walled City. The Muslim Mosque, at the entrance to Lohari Gate, runs the Anjaman-Khadam ul-Muslameen School, housed next to its small hospital. The Auqaf Department of the government, which oversees property owned by religious groups, essentially administers the school, opened in 1960. Girls, having completed a few years of formal studies, generally come for about six months and are charged 30 rupees ($1.25) monthly for sewing and embroidery classes and 40 rupees ($1.75) monthly for knitting classes, though orphans (a woman who has no father) pay half price. The school has two periods: 7:30 a.m. - 9:45 a.m., and 10 a.m. - 12:30 p.m. Most of the students live within the Walled City, and come to the school because other girls -- sisters, cousins and former classfellows -- told them it has a good reputation.

Sewing schools run in a woman's private home often cost the most, but the student gets more personalized attention, access to a sewing machine (or permission to bring her own) and have more flexible hours as they remain open virtually all day long. We visited such a school in Kucha Hussain Shah just behind Masjid Wazir Khan. The students, most of whom are in their late teens and come from areas by Shah Alami and Delhi Gates, refer to their teacher as *"Baji"* (older sister). She told us that she does not allow any girls from her own *biradari* to study with her as her own daughters will marry within it and she doesn't want those relatives to know what she is doing. Of her four daughters and three sons, two daughters are already married. While she talks with us, it seems that all the girls are calling for her attention at once: one to cut a pattern out of newspaper, another to check the sleeve for a little boy's shirt. In the winter, she has about ten or twelve students; it is double during the summer. The one-room classroom is the entirety of her home: she and her family sleep in the room during the winter (when it is too cold to sleep on the roof), and there is a small room off the side for a kitchen. There is an interesting informal network among the students here, for most either attend Baji's school with a relative, or a relative had studied with Baji some years back. Baji charges about 80 rupees ($3.25) monthly, but the school is open all day long. The students tell us that they believe they can learn sewing faster with Baji than at the government or mosque schools. Some would like to earn an income from their sewing in the future, but most have no idea how they would begin doing such work.

Virtually all women with whom we spoke in the Walled City identify prevailing social values as being the most powerful constraint on women's economic activities. It is not only the question of a woman leaving her *kucha* and thereby bringing her morality into question, but the larger issue of a woman earning an income and feeding the men in her family from that income that comes to the fore. Women are not opposed to doing this; they are just concerned about other people knowing about it. As Amina sums up the situation:

> People think badly if a woman works at all. Whether she works as a lady doctor or a teacher people still say that her mother or father eat from her labor. The point is that whatever kind of work a girl does, if she has to walk outside to do it, it doesn't look good for the family. A girl can work inside her home and no one knows...

Hasina is skilled as a seamstress, but her husband does not allow her to take in work because of questions of *izzat*. She feels that if a woman has to work (*majboori*) then work is not freedom, but if she works because she likes it (*shawk*), then it is. To her, freedom essentially consists of three things: being able to study; being able to dress in the latest fashion; and being able to take off the *burqa* and put on a *chadar*. Most of the women I interviewed agreed, at least with the last point.

Women's Ways of Surviving

Strategies of action and responses to power are cultural products (Swidler, 1986: 284). This becomes evident in the accounts of the women of the Walled City in response to questions relating to how they maintain their health, observe purdah, hear about news, and the strategies which they have derived for their and their children's empowerment, especially their daughters'.

Laila

Since Laila's family lives in an old, converted *haveli*, she has daily interactions with her relatives who also inhabit it. She visits Data Saheb's shrine at least once a month, although is only able to visit girlfriends with whom she used to study in school every other month. This will probably not change after she completes the technical sewing classes she is taking, as she will then spend a large part of her time doing her *salma sitara* embroidery, as she currently does during her summer vacations.

As the youngest woman who shared her life history with us, Laila has been a recipient of the Pakistan government's success over the past two decades in providing basic medical care in urban areas. She knows that she had her first inoculations when she was a year old, and had injections against measles and smallpox a few years later.

At first, a man came door-to-door from the hospital and informed people about the inoculations and its procedure. I went with my mother, and the next time with my eldest sister. They knew about me from my birth certificate. It is the responsibility of the midwife to inform the government that such and such a child, girl or boy, was born in this house. My parents got my birth certificate a few days later, for ten rupees.

We also had some injections in school, but we mostly get them outside the school. By Masjid Wazir Khan, there's a place to go for free injections.

As her life reflects changes which have occurred in access to healthcare, it also reflects changing views on *purdah*, how women are connected to news information and networks, and how they are taking initiatives to change those aspects of their future which is possible to affect.

When I go to school, I wear a *dupatta*. I don't wear a *chadar*, and I'm actually not in *purdah*. My mother wears a fashionable brown *burqa*, with a *nikab*. My older sister also only wears a *dupatta*. After marriage, our custom is to wear a *burqa*. However, if given a choice, I don't want to wear one.

I hear about news on television, and through people. As when a bomb went off in the Railway station, there was a boy from here who was there at the time. He told us. Then yesterday, they found a bomb at Masti Gate. My brother told us about it when he came back from tuition. There are no secrets here.

The best day in my life was the day that I passed my matric exam. I didn't go on to study for an Intermediate Degree as I preferred to go to sewing school. I am currently enrolled there in a two-year program. I went to my school even during Ramadan. We had four days holiday for *Eid*, then we went for five days to get work for the summertime. Then our holidays began. For example, I'll make a sweater over the summer. In the fall, I'll give it to them, they'll hold it until I graduate, and then they'll return everything to me. The girls have their boxes in the school, and as they make the things, they put it there for their dowry. One can put together an entire dowry this way.

I began in February. There is a fifty rupee entrance fee; the rest is free. There are fifteen girls in each class. There are two first-year classes and two second-year classes. There are two periods, with a recess for eating and drinking.

My life is very different from my mother's as my mother didn't work like my sister and I do. My mother was freer than I am because I spend most of my time at home doing *salma sitara* embroidery. The *mahaul* (social environment) of the city also isn't so good, so we can't go out so easily. In her times, women didn't do such work in their homes.

Laila's mother confirmed this, that when she was younger few women worked in their homes. She said "In those days, people lived happier lives. My father was like a rich elite in his village -- we could eat well. That's why I didn't have to do any work or chores." But while she is saying that her life was happier and easier than those of her daughters', she is also saying that poor women in the past led more fuller and freer lives than do poor women today.

Returning to Laila, when we asked her to differentiate if she wants to work or if she *has* to work, she responds: "I *have* to work. But after all this, my contributing to my family's income will make no difference with my marriage. I'll still have no say in it." As her mother was sitting with us at the time, she looked constrained when asked how she felt that she'd have no say as to who she would marry, and she just smiled shyly. At least she's thinking that she would like to have a say in it. This is a significant difference here between her and many of the other women with whom we have talked. Perhaps this is due to her younger age; perhaps it is "the times."

Gulzar Begum

Gulzar Begum is not pre-occupied with medical problems, as were some of the other older women whom we interviewed. Her late husband apparently had suffered from asthma. She is unaware of any other medical cause for his death, so links it to asthma in some way.

My husband got sick after our marriage, with asthma. He had an appendix problem; the operation wasn't a success. It hurt his intestines, and that switched to asthma. He had asthma for 7-8 years before he died.

Religion, though, is an important preoccupation with many members of her family. We were unable to tape record our interviews with Gulzar Begum because she thought her twenty year old son, who is very religious, would not approve.

He is a *hafiz-e-Qur'an* (someone who has memorized the whole of the Qur'an). He doesn't believe in these things, that women should go to mosques and hear *maulvis* and other things. In Ramadan, he leads the *taravian* (8 p.m.) prayers in the mosque. I just have to ask him permission for such things. He believes that his mother and sister shouldn't be seen by other men.

My *jaith* is very religious; my son was brought up there. They are very *purdah*-observing. My *jaith's* sons have done their B.A.; the girls have done their matric. The girls begin to observe *purdah* at age fifteen. My *jaith* always guides us: this thing you have to do, etc. This is ever since my husband's death. My husband wasn't as strict as my *jaith*. He was more liberal, which is a major difference.

Her late husband did not try to control her actions as much as her *jaith* does, who is much more strict. She and her children are scared of him as he is a very short-tempered man and they are afraid of being verbally abused by him. He is the eldest in the family, and they feel they must respect what he says. Most importantly, they will need his help to arrange marriages in the future.

Gulzar Begum, who strings flowers which are sold near *pirs'* shrines, visits those of Syad Suf and Meera Saheb in Masjid Wazir Khan monthly, which are in the vicinity of her home. Whenever she goes out, she always wears a *burqa* and uses its *nikab*. She began observing *purdah* when she was twenty. She considers that it was her brother who put her into *purdah*, and she remains in *purdah* now "for my respectability." However, if she were to stop wearing a *burqa* (although she is in her late forties), her *jaith* would be very angry.

She prefers to wear a *burqa* over a *chadar* and feels that the difference between them is that a *burqa* gives more respect. "In a *chadar*, your body can be watched by everyone; they can't watch it in a *burqa*."

There are other things that she does that she believes commands respect. For example, as a widow, she can apply to the government for *zakat* funds, as Chand Bibi has done. However, her family sees it as demeaning, so she has not sought them: "I never applied to receive *zakat*. My son doesn't allow me to apply for it. He doesn't like it."

Another important indicator of respectability, to Gulzar Begum, are the restrictions that she, her *jaith* and her son have placed on her daughters' movements:

> They should stay home, not go to see films in the cinema, not go for picnics, etc. When their father was alive, they saw Shalamar Gardens, Minar-e-Pakistan, and other places, but they don't do these kinds of things anymore. If they want to go somewhere now, they have to talk to their *taya* (her *jaith*) first, and only if they can persuade him can they go somewhere.

She hears about news from informal networks between women, and gossip plays a particularly important role: "Women come by. If one knows something, everyone will soon. The woman who was in my doorway a few minutes ago, well, every time she comes, she tells me the news. My son doesn't tell us so much. He's very serious."

Given the conservatism of her family, it is not surprising to find that she views her daughters' empowerment as tied up with their marriages, and that she favors marriages within the family. Their family has never used a *wacholan* to arrange their marriages. One daughter is married to her *tayazad bhai*, while the other is married to Gulzar Begum's sister's son, the girl's *khalazad bhai*. Gulzar Begum wants to wait 4-5 years before marrying off her third daughter, who she says is eighteen while the daughter claims to me to be sixteen. However, if they can find a very good suitor for her now, they will go ahead and arrange the marriage. Gulzar Begum feels she needs to use the time in the coming years to train her daughter how to be a housewife and to put together her dowry. She feels that her other two daughters' dowry were fair: she had put together some of it, and the remainder was done by her *jaith*. Who her daughter marries, however, will be entirely at her *jaith's* discretion. If her own brother wanted a *rishta* for her daughter, and her *jaith* wanted another one, then the final decision is hers and her *jaith's*, not her brother's, as power to make this decision rests with her late husband's family.

> I want to teach my daughter to stitch clothes, do embroidery, etc. Marriage is the most important thing in life. Her *taya* will decide who the marriage will be with. You ask what if my daughter doesn't want to marry his choice? The girl has no say; she cannot refuse.
> May God's will be done. I had high hopes for my daughters. My heart wants that she should be in a good house, have a car of her own, and a good husband. There should be no restrictions on the girl. The in-laws shouldn't intervene on where the girl goes. Many in-laws stop the girls from seeing their parents. If the husband takes care of his wife, the in-laws don't like it. So they try to blame the girl most of the time, and they complain that the girl has snatched their son from them. They shouldn't be very strict with *purdah*. I hope to be liberal with my own daughter-in-law.

Her desire to be liberal with her future daughter-in-law seems contradictory to the kind of treatment the woman will receive with Gulzar Begum's son as her husband. Regarding her son:

> One neighbor says that he's a *maulvi* himself. He won't be liberal with his own wife. He spends most of his time with very strict people, especially his *taya's* family, and all the girls there are in strict *purdah*. I don't want to marry him into his *taya's* family. My son also agrees that he wants his sister to get married first.

In this family, dreams are reserved only for the men of the house. Gulzar Begum had no childhood dreams, and now sees her future as tied to her son's actions. She sees economic well-being as a necessary reality before she can fulfill her desire to perform the pilgrimage, *hajj*, to Mecca, and this can only come about with her son's success.

He fixes motorcycles now, and wants to be a motor mechanic. I pray that my son becomes a rich man, that I will be able to perform *hajj* at God's house. I have no other wishes. The first is that my son should become rich; the second, that I should have my own house and car; and the third, is to perform *hajj*. I would like my son to go abroad. Financially, that would be better, though I'll miss him. My father-in-law's brother's wife has just left for *hajj*. She went with her *malik's* brother in a group. One of her sons is abroad, and sent a draft before she went for *hajj*. He doesn't send money regularly.

Her use of "*malik*" here is most interesting, as the word means owner or controller; she is referring to the woman's husband.

When we asked her daughter what her dreams for the future are, she said: "I have none, just work, work, work. I wanted to study beyond matric, and was going to get admission, and then my brother didn't give me permission. My dream was smashed by my brother."

Gulzar Begum almost happily affirmed, as if this too were a sign of respectability, "My daughter has no dreams." Her daughter then reiterated, "I have no dreams, none."

It seems important to consider the dramatic transition which Gulzar Begum has undergone in her life. For many years she lived with her own fairly liberal husband, but since his death must defer to his conservative brother, one with whom she does not even share a consortial relationship. What strategies does she use to overcome this scenario? First, her dreams for the future do not include him and indeed enable her to have some independence from his dictates. This enables her to psychologically bear her current circumstances. Second, she intends to delay marrying off her third (and last) daughter. Perhaps her *jaith* will die first, and she would not have to marry her daughter to a conservative man of his choice.

Farida

Farida's encounters with health issues spans the underside of the market for illicit drugs that has been growing in Pakistan during the last decade. She alleges that her husband has become addicted to drugs as a way to overcome problems he was having with women.

We didn't sleep together on our wedding night, on the *valima* (the bridegroom's celebration), not even during the *muklava* (when the new couple stays at the bride's parents' home). He then talked with one of his friends about his sexual problem. He had gone to so many ladies, and that is why he's used up. He got an injection, then he was O.K. Every time we had sex, he had to have an injection. I didn't get any joy out of this marriage.

> Now my husband is a mandrax addict. He smokes a pack of cigarettes
> early in the morning, then takes pills. That's why his health is bad. His
> body has gotten weak; he hasn't been to a doctor.

Farida makes a strong connection between unhappy marriages and ill
health. She had a sister who died in childbirth seven years earlier. She
describes her sister as charming and attractive, but her sister's husband
was old and not good-looking. Her sister had a very unhappy life with
him.

> She had become very sick. They thought it was tuberculosis, but she
> couldn't be treated. We took her to a *pir* in Sheikhupura, Habibullah, and
> he said she's become possessed by an *aseb* (spirit) and that's why she got
> sick. But it was too late then, and she died.

Farida feels that her parents had always put too many restrictions on
her, that she couldn't go outside and that she should live within *chadar
aur char diwari* (the veil and four walls of one's home). If she went out,
they became suspicious of where she was going and feared she was
going to "a wrong place."

> My brothers put a lot of restrictions on me. They wanted to beat me for
> going out to work. They suggested I get divorced from my husband and
> come back to them. They want me to come back to their house and then
> they'll take care of me. My father-in-law gave me permission to do this
> work. In my in-laws' home, there are fewer restrictions on me. I wear a
> *chadar* without a *nikab* since I have been married.

Farida's experience with purdah since she has been married differs
from that of most women for whom restrictions have become more
severe. However, she does not enjoy good relations with either her
husband or her in-laws, so it is difficult to discern what has actually
occurred and what is her interpretation of events. For example, as bad as
she describes her life is with her husband, who she claims is a drug
addict, she would rather live in his house than return to her natal
family's, which she claims as being tantamount to social death. "I prefer
to be either in my husband's house or in an orphanage. I don't want to
go back to my parents' home. They won't allow me to wear fancy clothes,
comb my hair or wear make-up."

Farida was probably more rebellious of social norms than her parents
could tolerate, hence the poor relations which exist between them. A
fiery, strong woman, she had dreams of what she could become when
she was young, and feels that her parents had not done for her what they
could to enable them to have been realized.

Given the events of her life, it is not surprising that she prefers to be independent, if possible. If she ever does follow through and get a divorce from her husband, remarriage would not be the first thing on her mind.

> If I could find a good man, I would remarry. Mostly, I now want to have my own beauty parlor. I am willing to leave my husband now. I went to my parents and spoke with them. They went to arrange another marriage for me. I went and saw the man: he was seventy years old, and I refused.

While the age of the suitor might be a bit exaggerated, her reaction to being placed once again in another man's home and under his control seems in line with her desire to be independent and make her own decisions concerning her life. That she doesn't really know how to take command of this situation and make allies out of her parents is also not surprising, as she has probably been rebelling against all forms of control for a long time.

Aside from someday owning her own beauty parlor, her other dreams lie in her son's future. Her parents felt that her son should become an apprentice somewhere, but she wants to educate him well, preferably in an English-medium school. She sees ample benefits in a good education.

> Education is a guarantee of a better future. It's good to have children, but it's also difficult. My husband isn't doing any job, and it's difficult for me to feed my son. It's good to have a son, but only the expenses of the family are difficult. I want to see my son as a doctor, engineer, in the airport, a bank officer, etc. A real mother wants to see her children in a better place, as a bank officer, etc., not as a film star. If I had a better education, I would be like you, teaching in one of the universities. Whatever work I have been able to do, I did it with my own senses and put it in my mind. That's how I learned to read and write. My husband is illiterate. My father-in-law was educated, but he didn't educate his son.
>
> My old dream was that I had wanted to be a very popular figure, even after my death. But childhood dreams of a good house, good husband, fame and all remain unfulfilled. Now, I just hope to save up money to buy a refrigerator so I can cook *handi* (curry) and store it.

She pays fifty rupees per month tuition -- a hefty price, given her salary -- for her son to study at Najaf Ideal School, inside Delhi Gate, where he is in the third class.

Jamila

Most likely because of her experiences as a trader during the last seventeen years, Jamila appears to be a very practical person and one who can quickly adjust to changing circumstances when necessary. She clearly appreciates freedom. She commented that the first few years of her marriage were happy in that her husband had not tried to control her in any way. For example, he had no objections to her using birth control when she realized that they could not afford to have all the children they were having. Aside from her four children who are still alive, they had lost twin daughters, and later a son when they could not afford to buy necessary medication for him. She, primarily, used birth control pills while her husband, on occasion, used condoms. Someone she knew had told her about the birth control pills. She didn't learn about them from any education she had nor from the media.

Now that she is separated from her husband, she has to provide for herself and her children. She thinks that whether she works or not should be her own decision -- any woman's own decision.

> Although Islam says that a woman should remain confined to the house, if circumstances justify it then it is all right to work, and I do to it support myself and my family. I will tell Allah on the Day of Judgement that he had not left me a choice. Other women do not understand this as they do not have to face the same situation. They have their husbands providing for them. People tend to give me a harder time because they do not realize that I am poor as I dress well when I go out.

Jamila has observed *purdah* since puberty. She wears a veil with a *nikab* whenever she leaves her *kucha*. She is not orthodox in her religious orientations: though she is a Sunni, she has also been influenced by Shi'a ideas from her sister and closest friend who are Shi'as. "I don't wear a *burqa* if I go as far as three *galis* over. I was born here, and I'm a daughter-in-law here. I wear a *burqa* if I'm going elsewhere."

Many people, including her sister, have been telling her to stop wearing a *burqa* as she is no longer young. She said she would stop wearing one only when she stops living in the *kucha*, where everyone has known her most of her life.

When she went to Iran on business, she was uncomfortable that society there was much more strict. She had to wear either a *burqa* or a *chadar* with a *nikab* as soon as she crossed the border. She wears a *chadar* whenever she travels in India or elsewhere in Pakistan.

Her dreams for the future are tied to her hope that her eldest son will be successful and thereby her financial situation will improve. He has completed his matric (tenth grade) graduation, and works in one of the restaurants in the Lahore Hilton Hotel. His friend who works there helped him get the job. He took English classes at the hotel after being hired.

She feels she has had a difficult and unhappy life, and that "having four or five happy years in a lifetime is not really living." She would be happy to leave her *kucha* and even the country. She would like her eldest son to get a job in the Gulf. She, like many Pakistanis, considers a job in the Gulf a way to escape from poverty. She hopes that her brother in Kuwait will help her son to get a good job. If her son works there for a few years he can save enough to buy a nice house and have a good wedding. Once he is well settled, he will then be able to help his younger brother get settled too -- and, by implication, the entire family will benefit. It would not be so important if his future wife went to the Gulf with him or not; in her opinion, earning the money is the most important thing.

Hasina

Her being unable to sew (and hence earn no income) and the interminable arguments she has with her husband are not the only major difficulties Hasina has faced during her married life. The health problems that her family has endured display the problems associated with overpopulation throughout Pakistan, where the average family size remains over six persons. At least she has the confidence of knowing that her family doctor lives nearby (she never goes to a *hakim*), and she patronizes Lady Wellingdon Hospital when necessary.

> After seven years of marriage I had four children. We never used any kind of birth control. My husband was so strict he wouldn't permit me to look into the street. I wasn't allowed to go out, leave alone use birth control devices. I couldn't talk to any neighbors. I couldn't dream of taking any pills or anything to control having children. My youngest daughter is five. Before her, I had two miscarriages, one after three months and one after four months.
>
> Four days after my daughter's birth, I had an operation. They took something out and now I can no longer have children. When I was admitted to the hospital, my mother-in-law arranged for the operation. I didn't know what was happening. We didn't have money for bread or milk. I had a fever before my daughter's birth, and had a temperature of 106 degrees, just before the birth. So the doctors put in an intravenous drip five days before the birth. At the time of the delivery, my mother-in-law told the doctors about the operation.
>
> Since then, I've gained a lot of weight and have gases. I can't wear any of my nice clothes. I still have my menses, but they're very light and come only periodically. A lady doctor has said there's no blood there (she's anaemic) so I should eat eggs, meat, etc., but my husband can't afford such food. If I can't give this food to my children, then how can I eat it myself? Sometimes I suffer from low blood pressure, headaches, and weak nerves.

My eldest son who is now nine years old was sick when he was very small, and is still thin. Though there was medicine, he couldn't be looked after properly. My husband was only making three hundred rupees monthly. My son threw up often, and had a high fever and diarrhea when he was two months old. He was hospitalized then for 10-12 days. He was always sick until he was four years old. This was very expensive, and there was a lot of emotional strain too. Whenever he cried, I used to cry also. My mother-in-law gave me money to take him to a good doctor. I only care for his good health; no other children can replace him. Once, a cousin brought me some American medicines, about eight years ago.

My eyes have been bad for ten years; they itch and get red. It's because I've been crying for ten years.

Her sister's father-in-law died two weeks ago. The coming Thursday, they would all go together to visit the sister's in-laws because "these are things which women must do." According to Hasina, a Muslim woman should care for *adab* (customs), her husband, and for her elders. She should also pray.

Children should also pray by the age of 8-10, even if you have to hit them and force them. Women should cover themselves and not be seen by other men. However, men are free. The only restrictions are on women. A man only has to care for his parents, not even for his wife.

I go to Hazrat Syad Suf nearby, in Masjid Wazir Khan, if I have any problems or worries. I become calm there. When I go there and say my prayers, my prayers are granted. For example, one day my daughter got lost. She had gone off with some children and I didn't know it. I went there to pray, came back home exhausted, and she was at the house! Another time, I was looking for a house to rent and was very worried. I went and prayed there, and then found this house shortly afterwards. *I* found it — my husband doesn't do anything like this.

Hasina has been in *purdah* since she was nineteen. She wore a *burqa* before marriage, after which her husband and in-laws told her not to wear it.

When I go out with my husband, I wear a *dupatta,* though not on my head. If I go out alone, I will put a big *dupatta* over my head. At first, it felt strange not to wear a *burqa*, but now I'm used to it. In this *kucha*, most of the women wear *chadars*. Many are Shi'as, and they tend to wear *chadars*. Women in this *kucha* are becoming freer. They are taking off their *burqas* and wearing *chadars* instead. It is also becoming more fashionable. Women like this kind of freedom.

In terms of freedom, there is a big difference between wearing a *burqa* and a *dupatta*! Sometimes, they (some other women living in this *kucha*) take their *burqas* off on their own, and their husbands curse them. But they put up with this because they want to live like this. I go with my husband in a *dupatta*, so no one says anything.

Hasina's visions of freedom were perhaps the most unconventional that we found, while also the most thought-provoking.

Freedom means, if a woman can have a bad relationship with another man -- a sexual relationship -- then that's freedom. These two things -- taking off the *burqa* and having a sexual relationship -- are the main things that·mean freedom to me! Men prevent women from becoming free. Even *sharif* men, brothers as well as husbands, can restrict freedom. It's mainly men, not women, who restrict women's freedom.

Upon further questioning, the meaning of freedom for women comprised three major dimensions for her: being able to study; being able to dress in the latest fashions; and taking off the *burqa* and replacing it with a *chadar*.

She does not view women's communication with each other as particularly empowering, and does not regard women's networks as central to how she hears about news.

I hear news from other people in the neighborhood, mostly. I read either *Jang* or *Nava-i-Waqt* (Urdu newspapers) on Fridays. We have no television. I wanted to buy a television on installments, but the shopkeeper wanted about two hundred, two hundred and fifty rupees monthly, and I felt I could only get a hundred rupees per month It would have cost eighteen hundred rupees. I would have earned the money from working.

But as we saw in Chapter 3, Hasina only works occasionally and has not reached an agreement with her husband that would enable her to work.

My husband makes all the decisions. I wanted to have my say at first, but now I don't bother about it, because I know I don't have a say and that he won't listen. I could have more power if I could have some of my own money, that could make a difference. My husband says "you don't earn for me." What I want is that he should go abroad. I had thought that I could do some sewing with my new machine, but he won't let me do that. While I'm working, he's always stopping me, "make me tea, massage my legs, do this or that for me."

Sometimes it happens that I have to attend a function or ceremony. My husband doesn't inform me about it, he just says to get ready, we're going out. When I ask where we're going, he gets angry and says, "*Bas* (enough), you have to go out -- get ready!" And you ask what is the most important thing to my husband? Freedom is the most important thing for him.

Hasina feels that her lack of an older brother who could protect her enables her husband to take such advantage of her. Younger brothers cannot do much for a sister.

My younger brother is staying with me for two months. He's studying nearby at a tuition center during his summer holidays. He leaves the house or goes upstairs to watch television in the landlord's flat when my husband fights with me. He doesn't say anything -- he was only a year old at my marriage. He gets angry, but puts up with it. I have no older brothers. If I did, life would be different because my husband would realize that there would be someone to ask him about his actions. He would be accountable to someone. I don't think anything will change after my brother grows up, because he's so young. It's difficult. In Pakistan, people pay due respect to their *damaad* (son-in-law). My brother is also brought up in that society. He doesn't say anything, and has to put up with the circumstances. None of my brothers tell me what to do or put restrictions on me because they're younger. If they were older than me, obviously my life would be better.

She has great expectations for her children, but fears also that her sons might resemble their father.

My children are the most important things to me. I put up with my husband only because of them. I have locked up my dreams in my sons. If my sons should turn out like their father, I won't marry them off! I worry a lot about this. As educated as my husband is, he doesn't want to send his children to a good school -- he says he cannot afford it. For this reason, I want him to go abroad to work.

My life is a drama; we always fight. My only hope is that he'll go abroad. I tell my husband to go outside (to leave Pakistan), but he hasn't gotten the chance and no one in his family has gone and done this. My in-laws live nearby, so it wouldn't be hard. My life would change if he went. It would be difficult for me, but it's necessary to improve our financial condition. I want my children to study in a good school, and to have my own home. My husband has to go out to work -- it's very hard to fulfill this in Pakistan. If he remains in this job, there won't be any chance. If he could get another job, maybe conditions could improve, but it's almost impossible to get another job. I want to educate all my children but I do realize that my husband is not good. He curses and abuses me most of the time. The atmosphere of the house isn't good, so it has a bad influence on the children.

I can't even dream that my sons will become doctors, as they'd have to speak good English, study sciences, etc. I don't have that much money so that I can help them settle in a business. I can't even provide them with good food. The ambition is there, but I'm not hopeful and my husband is not cooperative.

Her thoughts about what a woman can contribute to a family and what she ultimately can become are ambiguous, but no more so than what the expected norms and roles for girls actually have become in today's Pakistan.

If I could do some work, it could make a difference. But how much difference can a woman make?

In the past, people used to have a poor opinion of education and didn't send their daughters to school. Now we send our daughters to school. Girls should study well. I want my daughter to study as much as possible. (She states this emphatically, three times.) A matric degree is nothing nowadays. She should be well-educated. It's good for a girl to do a B.A. The best benefit is that she can get a good *rishta* in marriage. There is no working woman in our family, and I don't necessarily want my daughter to work. I want to train my daughter in different skills after her matric. After her marriage, if necessary, she'll be able to earn some money. If she has a hard time, she could do some work.

She has less of a clear idea on how to work out a strategy to solve the existing problems with her husband.

The five thousand rupee *haq mehr* (promissory bridewealth) is the only chain between us, husband and wife. There is no mental understanding between us; our thinking is very different. He has a hot disposition and our traditions are very different. He is very stubborn, and whatever he says to me, I don't like it. For example, my husband is very *ayash* (hot-blooded). He wants to see me in make-up and good dresses, but he doesn't give me these things. He demands it, but there's a lot of misunderstanding between us. He gives himself too much importance. He doesn't like me to be talking when he is around. We argue all the time. He is a *pukka* Kakazaiya, a real fighter. (His *qaum* has a reputation for fighting.) He curses me in front of the children, so the environment in the house isn't good.

When we question her if he has ever accused her of adultery, she replies:

No, he knows that I have no chance to do this. Sometimes he just says that you are not interested in me, and I try to make him realize that it's not so, have you seen me interested in any other man? I have ruined myself for this man. I have given all my money, my gold, my savings, to this man. I have borrowed money for him. He presses me to go get money. Now I have nothing in my hand: no money, no land, nothing. It's not possible for me to leave him. If I didn't have children I would have left him, but I have children and I am also too old. I had gotten pregnant at once after my marriage. Many people were saying don't do the marriage, that the boy isn't good. But that's it, that was my fate.

Will I divorce him after our children are all married? No, because then they'll do everything for me, and there's no purpose in getting divorced then. This is the right time to get divorced, so I can live a good life. I don't want to take a divorce, but he just might. I have to always live with this fear. Nowadays, I am having a very bad time with this man. I have told him to have a talk with his sisters and mother. There won't be a divorce; I just want my mother-in-law and *nund* to talk with him; they're with me.

Kanize

Kanize, sitting at home and making *samosas* for her family's business, enjoys fairly good health.

I get sick maybe only once a year. I was sick with malaria for about two weeks last year. It was during the month of fasting, Ramadan. I went to Dr. Ramzan, nearby. I also went to Gunga Ram hospital last year.

I think my parents had me inoculated against smallpox when I was a child. My brother's son has been inoculated. He was born here in our house. Our midwife, Gigi, lives nearby. We gave her about two hundred fifty rupees -- no clothes or anything, just the money. When he was born, we informed the public health office that a child is born. We went to the one in Rang Mahal. There are so many in the city. The address is on the card that the midwife gives when a child is born. The midwife also informs the public health officials.

The only Shi'a who shared her life history with us, Kanize relies on many Shi'a religious symbols for support and succor.

When people in our family are sick, we first go to the doctor. Our *murshid* (religious teacher) is in our own home – his symbol is our *alim* (a pole topped by a black flag), which we keep in our house. If the doctor isn't successful, then we go to our *murshid*. My *murshid* is Hazrat Abbas Alamdar, the *alimwala* (who held up the flag of Islam at the battle of Karbala). Hazrat Abbas was the half brother of Hazrat Imam Hussain. He was a soldier at Karbala and died there.

I question Kanize, that I thought that all *murshids* have to be alive to be relied upon.

Absolutely, he is alive. I also go to Pir Gama Shah's shrine when I'm sick. Gama Shah was the *mutwali* (religious caretaker) of the *imam bara* (Shi'a religious sanctuary) in that place. He himself is not my *murshid*. I also go to Bibian Pak Daman once a month or sometimes more than that. I go there because I believe those women, the women who are buried there, are holy and noble. We offer sweet cooked rice and rice pudding when our prayers are answered. Their gravestones are covered with green cloth, and *qawwalis* (devotional singing) are held periodically. There are many stalls selling religious items such as brass bowls with Qur'anic verses written on them. When you drink water from one of these, you will be healed. Whenever I am in trouble I go to Gama Shah or Bibian Pak Daman, and then I feel my prayers are answered. I went to Bibian Pak Daman and asked that I wanted to have a house of my own, and within two years time, I got the house in which we're living now. Two years after I had asked for the house, I went back and thanked them. But in that period I went many other times as well, along with my brothers and sisters.

The difference between the two places is that at Gama Shah's shrine, there is a *taziya* (replica of Imam Raza's shrine at Karbala) which is fixed in there. At Bibian Pak Daman, the daughters of Hazrat 'Ali (who are said to have traveled to Lahore) are buried there. There's no difference in reason why I might go to one or the other. In fact, we can even have everything while just sitting at home. We can remember them at home, and our prayers can be granted. We go to show our gratitude. There's a special area where men are not allowed. They used to not allow pregnant women into that area because it was sacred and you couldn't predict if the baby would be a girl or a boy.

Purdah and maintaining respectability are extremely important to Kanize, who has been wearing a *burqa* since she was twelve or thirteen. She regards her father's brother as having made the decision that she should wear a *burqa* back then. The *burqa* has become part of her habit. She feels she would be uncomfortable to go to the bazaar without it. Her father said she can wear a *chadar*, but she is used to the *burqa*. Her older sister, who is twenty-two, has worn a *chadar* since she was about sixteen. Her twelve year old sister doesn't wear a veil yet at all.

When we asked her questions about herself, she always answered in reference to other people. She doesn't read or watch television, and doesn't appear interested in anything promoting her own imagination or thoughts. She works for the whole family, either cooking, cleaning, or making *samosas* for the stand, from morning to night. She has no articulated desire to further empower herself as she envisions no change in her future.

Erum

Erum, the best educated woman (now a teacher) of all those with whom we spoke at length, appears to be no better off -- nor any worse off -- healthwise than any of the other women. In the past year, she experienced excessive bleeding while menstruating which caused her to have to stay home seven or eight days from teaching in her school. She had become very anaemic and couldn't work. Other than this problem, her major health concern has revolved around birth control.

> My husband and I, we were very careful not to have children at times. In the beginning, I took medicine, and we didn't meet (engage in sex). I was scared that maybe another daughter might come. I had excessive bleeding during my menses from the medicine, and went to a lady doctor.
>
> Then, we used FL (French Leather, a brand of condom) for men. FL gave trouble to me; I've heard it's harmful to the ladies sometimes. We also use foam; sometimes my husband discharges outside.
>
> My sister had the opposite problem. She had no children, after six years of marriage. We all went to the shrine of Sultan Bahu: me, my husband, my sister, her husband, and her mother-in-law. We prayed to God there. Old ladies told us "you have to go and pray there for children. The saint will pray for you to have children." That very year, a *baba* (old man, with religious connotations) came to their house in Gulberg, and gave both my sister and brother-in-law medicine. Very soon after that, they had a baby boy. He is now seven. Then they had a son who died, then a third son. Then she stopped having children: she had her tubes tied or something.

Erum usually hears about events in the Walled City from the female sweeper who works for her part-time. The woman sweeps the interiors of many of the homes in this neighborhood as well as others in the Mochi Gate area and hears about news from many different people. Erum's children also inform her about things that are going on in the vicinity, as they did when there was a riot near Shah Alami Gate. In addition, the boys who play outside or else other people in the neighborhood tell her about news in their locale. Interestingly, she never cited her husband as a source of news.

Erum has worn a *chadar* (without a *nikab*) since she was about fifteen. Her father had put her into *purdah*. The first day she ever wore a *burqa* was just after marriage, though not on her wedding day. One had come in her dowry, the other came from her in-laws. In those days, it was the custom to wear a *burqa*. Other people regarded that it was better that she wore it over her bright clothes, and she didn't mind it.

> I wore a *burqa* for two years after my marriage. Many of the women here wore *burqas*, though they now go with *chadars* or *dupattas*. The old, strict *purdah* is finished; none of the women here observe it anymore. Young girls hardly observe *purdah*. When they are with their parents, there is no *purdah* -- no *chadar*, just a *dupatta* on the head.
>
> The *chadar* is not as strict as the *burqa*. A *chadar* with a *nikab* is equal to a *burqa*, but most don't wear a *nikab* with their *chadar*. You can also use cheaper cloth for a *chadar* (than a *burqa*), and you save on tailoring.

When we travel to Gulberg on the motorbike, I wear my *chadar*. It doesn't get in the way, and I wear my *dupatta* on my head. My daughters move freely, unveiled, in our *kucha*. I've told them that if anyone passes a remark, they should just move straight ahead. But no one bothers them.

She feels that replacing the *burqa* with the *chadar* is just one physical manifestation of the increased freedom which women now have.

In the previous generation -- and even now, at times -- husbands were very strict. Now women have more public power. In my father-in-law's time, every man used to listen only to his mother. They would listen to their mother over their wife. My mother-in-law's mother-in-law was very strict. My mother-in-law and her *bhabis* couldn't do anything, not even send for medicine on their own.

Now it's different. I and my *bhabis* are freer to do whatever we want. We meet each other, but we don't interfere with each other. It's not just education. My *bhabi* only studied to eighth or ninth class. My mother-in-law gives me so many examples of very strict women. Some of them were very loving too. My mother-in-law has complained about her own mother-in-law to me. My husband's uncles wouldn't go to a doctor with a child's high fever without their mother's permission. And then once, a child died. One of my husband's brothers died when he was ten or eleven. My father-in-law said to his mother that I was depending on you, and I don't want my children's lives to be like this. So, we go to buy everything: clothes, shoes, etc. We just don't go to the bazaar for food.

This last comment by Erum must be noted, for *what* a woman goes out to shop for also denotes status and respectability. There is an important differentiation made between going out to the bazaar on a daily basis to buy staples -- why can't the men or children of the family do this instead? -- and periodically going to the bazaar (generally with others) to purchase personal goods for one's use.

While she regards that women are free as long as "you aren't doing anything wrong," she doesn't have an answer to define what are the limits to correctness. She implies that the limits are understood. Political changes, television and enhanced education have all contributed to women enjoying greater freedom now within their households than previously.

Our daughters still cannot go out without a purpose, but they are free to go with a purpose. We don't let them go to their friends' houses whenever they want, but they can go sometimes. My daughters, studying in ninth or tenth class, aren't so *samajdar* (understanding; mature) yet.

There are other girls living in this *kucha*, but I don't like my daughters to go to their homes. It is the custom here that girls don't go to each other's house for nothing, to play or to gossip, though they do go for functions. There are six girls nearby. They don't come to my house, and my daughters don't go there. Three girls nearby have done their Intermediate Degree, and others are very educated. My own friends used to come to my house. We'd gossip together and their mothers would pick them up. The atmosphere here is different than where I grew up in Mughalpura. The roads and all are cleaner there than here, and the people are different.

My daughters have friends in their school. These girls are from Samanabad and Gulberg (wealthier areas outside of the Walled City), and are freer than my daughters. But my house is not as nice as theirs. Girls in other areas, they can go out and nobody will tease them. But here, they're not so free to walk about. There is no space to walk about. Girls just don't go out here. This is a drawback.

It has changed a lot. In previous years, girls were hardly seen. They were just dumped into their house. My *nund* had always worn a *burqa*, even when she went to school and after her marriage. But 17-18 years ago, she gave up the *burqa*. Now her daughter studies at Queen Mary College, without a *burqa*.

Two of her daughters go to a tuition center in the afternoon. They spend four hours there, reviewing their assignments and learning other things from the tutor. Erum teaches her daughters herself during the summer, though the girls want to fool around too much with her. The older ones want to gossip, watch television, put on the tape recorder or play caremboard.

Given Erum's career as a teacher, she has been able to provide her daughters with an excellent education at her school. She has no specific dreams for them except that they can take care of themselves if need be.

I hope my daughters will have good husbands, and that they will come and visit me often. But I also want them to get educated. They can be a help for me and my husband when we are old. I wouldn't mind them working someday. That is better than just sitting at home. I miss not having boys now. Boys are a great help; they look after the house and their old parents.

Erum considers that she is broad-minded despite living in the Walled City. However, while she would encourage her daughters to work, she doesn't want them to be working with men as that is not acceptable in her family.

Chand Bibi

Chand Bibi's experiences epitomize the brutal difficulties that poverty and illness can wreck upon women in the Walled City. One wonders who will care for her daughters when she is no longer capable to sew or make artificial earrings given her frailty and her tuberculosis. Medical problems seem endemic to her life. She never knew her mother, her father died when she was a child, her uncle had gone mad and it seems her husband was handicapped and often ill:

> Six months after we were married, my husband had an operation on one eye, and it became okay. As he was about forty-seven, the doctor said he was too old to have the other eye operated on. The hospital is behind Data Saheb. The operation cost twenty rupees.

It would appear that as they were poor, the operation was virtually free. The clinic had probably agreed to the necessity of one operation, but the second operation was not deemed to be critical. Not only was her husband's health never very good, but many people in his family died young. His late mother used to live in the downstairs flat, but now no one does.

> My husband died a year ago. He went crazy. He had been crazy three times, once before marriage. I lived with my husband sixteen years. For the first fourteen years, he never hit me. But the last two years, he beat me a lot. He used to throw stones and pebbles. I was afraid he would hurt or kill someone. He used to grab our daughters by the neck. When he did that, I used to send them outside.
>
> Dr. Chaudhry in Shah Jamal (a wealthy part of town, near Gulberg) treated him. The first time, he charged a hundred rupees in fees from my *dewar*. When I took my husband the second time, I told the doctor that this is the family's bread-earner. Then, he took no fees. But the medicine was expensive.
>
> I used to have to take him (her husband) everywhere: feed him, dress him, take him to the latrine. I took him to the hospital, dressed him, and did all those sorts of things for him.

She wants to sell the house in which she lives, but has mixed feelings about living elsewhere as she thinks that could be dangerous. At least, in this neighborhood, she is not afraid that there is no man in her house or that she doesn't have male children. However, she and her daughters sleep inside their house and not on the roof during the hot season as do many others in the Walled City because all the other homes on all four sides of their house are higher than theirs and people could see them sleeping. This is not respectable for either her or her daughters.

She says she has been sick for the last ten years, and that her health has dropped considerably in the last year. Everything about Chand Bibi, from her tuberculosis to her decaying teeth to her skeletal arms, reminds us of her extreme poverty.

There isn't any day in my life that I can call a "best" day. My life is too hard. My children can't dress as well as others. There was no great day. Mondays are the worst day. Everyone in my family died on that day, my father-in-law, mother-in-law, *jaith*, *dewar*, and my husband. If anyone's sick and a Monday comes, they die. The worst day in my life was the day I became a widow, despite all the problems my husband gave me. I have never seen happiness. I don't know what happiness is. My story is very sad.

When I feel sick, I take different medicines. I go to Mayo Hospital, mostly. I've been to Chitta Hospital for tuberculosis. I've also gone to Gulab Devi hospital, Gunga Devi hospital, Dr. Ahsan in Wachowali bazaar, and to *hakims*. I have consulted as many doctors as I could. I've never overlooked any doctor. *Hakims* are the best. Medicine from a doctor makes you feel hot; the *hakim's* makes you feel easy. And it soothes you while the doctor's makes your head spin.

She is concerned about her *nund*, the one who takes care of her third daughter, because she had recently been admitted to a hospital. No one understood why there was blood in her urine and everyone was worried. Her preoccupation with her *nund's* illness is consistent with the tradition that there is virtually an interlude in one's own life when there is a medical problem with any relative.

At least, she had minimal problems giving birth to her children:

All my four daughters were born in my house. A *dai* (midwife) came for the first three. For the fourth, a lady doctor came, as my daughter was born at seven months and was very weak. Once, a neighbor came by to help. My *dewarani* was here once, and another time, my *chachi* came. I cooked the evening meal then, as my mother-in-law was very old. The fourth time, my *dewarani* was at her mother's house and my *jaithani* was at a wedding. My mother-in-law was here; my husband sent for the lady doctor.

My children go to a regular doctor, who sits at a dispensary in Wachowali. They have all been vaccinated. None of my children have died.

The wealthy people in the neighborhood have opened "Bismillah Dispensary" and they don't take anything from me as I'm a widow. Usually, it's two rupees per prescription. When I was sick, my hair got ruined. If I had money, I still wouldn't cut my hair.

If I had money, I still wouldn't forget about God, because you have to die someday. Because of money, one can forget about God. The rich ladies just sit in their cars, have their luxuries. They don't fast during Ramadan. If you look around, it's the poor people who are particular about fasting. There's no way out; poor people have no prestige of their own. Rich people are becoming richer because, like the seven *marla* scheme that was supposed to give land to people like me, poor people couldn't get it. So poor people have no place here.

As a widow completely on her own, Chand Bibi must make all her decisions. As she has extremely limited purchasing power, she is dependent on the charity of others for major goods, such as the used black and white television a neighbor gave her family when he purchased a new one a few years ago. Her daughters had been going to other people's homes to watch television. She asked this neighbor, who she regards as "very *sharif* (honorable)," if she could have his old television set, and he gave it to them. On television, she enjoys watching two serialized dramas (*Sona Chandi* and *Andhera Ujala*) and a variety game show (*Nilaam Ghar*). When I asked her if she ever thought of participating on *Nilaam Ghar*, she completely dismissed that possibility and said "No, I'm not educated. What will I go there and do?"

Chand Bibi wears a *chadar* around her neck, like a *dupatta*. She no longer observes *purdah* as she gave it up when her husband had become very sick, just before he died. Religion and respectability, however, remain central to her values.

> What does Islam say about women? Pass your life in respectability, with modesty. Live in *purdah*; don't show your hair in front of men. But nowadays, girls hardly wear a *dupatta* and they get their hair set. General Zia (the government) says he's bringing Islam, but when a woman leaves her home, the men tease her, and young girls are chased by young boys. If you get a tonga or a rickshaw, there's a problem when people see you.

She is ambitious, especially in her aspirations for her four daughters. While we are informally talking with her, her youngest daughter comes in complaining that her skin is too dark, prompting Chand Bibi to give her some "Fair & Lovely" cream. She herself takes a ready-made *pan* out of her brass *pandan*. Chand Bibi continues to tell us that she wants her daughters to be able to stand on their own feet and have a better life, especially as she has no son. She wants them all married into well-to-do families. The eldest, in the eighth class at age sixteen, is not too bright and Chand Bibi hopes to find a good husband for her soon. The second, now thirteen, wants to become a doctor. The third daughter is ten, in class three and lives with Chand Bibi's childless *nund* and wants to be a schoolteacher. The youngest, at seven, is in her first year at school and very small for her age, perhaps due to malnutrition. Chand Bibi jests that perhaps she will become a hairdresser when she grows up.

We thought that there must be some time, some holiday, when she puts her problems out of her mind and relaxes with her family. We ask her to describe how she celebrates *Eid*, the feast commemorating the performance of the pilgrimage, *hajj*, in Mecca:

Poor people can't do anything for *Eid*. I won't go to my relatives, just to my daughter's *phuphi's* house. I have no other relatives in Lahore. There are two *phuphis*. The husband of one is a railway worker; the husband of the other one works in Murree as a customs superintendent. His wife, my second *nund*, lives with her sister in Lahore.

While we talk, she keeps reminding her daughters that it's time for them to go off to tuition. They go for this extra help in their studies throughout the year. The monthly tuition fees are costly: eighty rupees for the eldest, sixty for the second and twenty-five for the youngest (her *nund* pays the fee for Chand Bibi's third daughter who lives with her). An unmarried girl who has completed her matric exam and lives in the neighborhood tutors them in the afternoons after they return from the Forman school where their classes are held in the mornings. Chand Bibi sends them to the private tutor because, since her eldest daughter has failed her exams twice, she doesn't think the school is very good. Her teacher had said that the eldest daughter didn't study sufficiently and should be taught at home but as Chand Bibi is illiterate she had to hire a tutor.

Durdana

Durdana's life has not been the ordeal that Chand Bibi's has been. She lives largely within a traditional context and has good relations with her in-laws and her husband who retain power and control over most circumstances affecting her life. Durdana neither questions this arrangement nor the existing authority thresholds within it. From our conversations with Durdana, however, there emerged an implicit assumption that even to question this arrangement may indeed jeopardize it.

If there is any important decision to be made, our elders -- my mother-in-law, father-in-law, etc. -- they do it.

The worst time of my life was when I was fighting with my mother-in-law. My *dewar* was saying that I ate well, dressed well, and he wanted the same for his wife. My mother-in-law wanted us to stay and live there with her, but my *jaithani* told us to get out. My parents told us it was best. What was necessary they helped us with, especially with moral support.

This house is in my husband's name. For this area, it's large, about 2 1/2 *marlas*. The factory is on the ground floor, we live and work on the first, and the second floor is for the storeroom and where the help stays. My husband bought a house nearby and put it in my name. I've let my mother-in-law live there now. My father-in-law died twelve years ago. When my mother-in-law dies, the house is mine.

This acceptance extends to her ideas about *purdah* and power. While it seems that as a young girl she waged her small rebellions against being put into strict *purdah*, in no way does she question that a family's respectability revolves around a woman's honor. Therefore, the safest way to secure it is through observing *purdah* and early marriage.

> I believe in early marriage because at that age, a girl can leave her house with *izzat* (respect). Also, her mother and father can be free from worry.
>
> *Dadi* used to keep herself in *purdah* from her own husband in front of others. Only when *dada* used to go to say his prayers in a mosque some distance away, could we then be able to go outside to play. Otherwise, we were, even as children, confined within our home. My mother used to keep her *dupatta* over her head in front of her father-in-law at all times, despite the fact that they lived together in close quarters. My *chacha* was very strict. My mother also had a strict tradition with the girls. But my brothers could go out to play at anytime.
>
> When I was 11-12 years old (at puberty), total restrictions were put on me. I was then put into total *purdah*. Through age ten, I could at least sneak out. After eleven, I was in total *purdah*. I would only play on top of the roof after I turned eleven. Since then, I have worn a veil with a *nikab*.

She considers her brother, more than anyone else, as the person who decided that she should be put into *purdah*. She identifies her husband as the person mostly responsible for keeping her there now.

She views the work she does, assembling plastic toys, as helping her family, but hopes that her own daughter would not have to work after she gets married.

> Would I want my daughter to work after marriage? No — God forbid! When I die, God will give me his judgement for my life. "Why did you make her work?" he'll ask.
>
> There's a lot of *purdah* in our family. I wear a black *burqa*, with a *nikab*, when I go out. The top and bottom are separate. I doubt my daughter will wear a *burqa* when she grows up, not in ten or twenty years. Nowadays, girls put the *dupatta* over their heads, that's all. I sometimes do it too now. There's no freedom in a *burqa*. With a *chadar*, there's more freedom, and there's the most freedom with a *dupatta*. But I don't believe in freedom for girls.

Durdana blames males for chasing and teasing young girls. She feels that it is usually not the girls' fault, but that it is the inequity of the system which causes such actions. Wearing a veil can help a girl avoid this treatment.

Her four sons are fifteen, fourteen, eleven and five. Her daughter is seven. She regards the happiest day in her life as the day her eldest son was born. She sees her own future as tied in with the fortunes of her sons -- and outside of the Walled City.

> I want a big house, so my sons' future will be good. It should be one *kanal* (land measurement equal to twenty *marlas*) -- and outside the Walled City. All my six brothers and seven sisters' live outside the City. They all live in Gulshan Ravi, in their own separate homes. This *kucha* is dirty -- we should live outside. We have just bought a plot of land in Gulshan Ravi also. Someday, we'll build a five *marla* home there. We have just cleared the title to the land and everything.
>
> I want that my sons should have their own shops to sell the plastic goods, and they shouldn't have to make them in their homes. They should study to tenth class and finish their matric degree. This work of making plastic toys should be finished. Work shouldn't be done in the house. It's a problem if guests come, and it doesn't look good. I would like to see better working conditions for my husband and children.
>
> My daughter should get married. She should also study to tenth class so she can read and write. If there's any problem she'll be able to write to me and tell me. She can get a better *rishta* if she studies to eighth or tenth class. In our family, people just don't study further.

As her family makes a reasonable income, none of the male members have sought to go abroad in search of work. She is also fortunate that they can afford good medical care. Durdana complains that she has often feels a general pain in her body. She has also had a problem with a kidney stone recently and has been going for treatment at the new, very expensive, western-standard hospital built by the Amir of Kuwait in Lahore, Sheikh Zayed Hospital. Treatment is considered to be far better than at Mayo Hospital or even the other Christian hospitals in Lahore. Sheikh Zayed Hospital lies near the Punjab University New Campus, very far from the Walled City in very many ways.

Amina

Amina's world virtually revolves around activities in her household, which generally includes stitching *sehras* at every chance she gets. She only leaves to visit relatives and an occasional *pir* or shrine maybe once every other month. She doesn't go anywhere else.

She considers that she has a healthy, "smart" body, despite having some sort of glandular problem in her throat and diabetes. Her doctor has suggested she have an operation to remove something, though she doesn't know what it is (from her description, it is most likely a cyst). The problem has persisted 3-4 years; she can't tolerate eating hot spices anymore. She attributes her diabetes to her life circumstances: "I think I got my diabetes from being worried. It's God's will."

Some years back, she had to have a gall bladder operation. When they went to talk with the doctor about it, he said that if she had the operation at the government-run Ganga Ram Hospital (on Fatima Jinnah Road), it would cost five thousand rupees, but if it was done privately in his own clinic, it would cost ten thousand rupees.

> I had it done at Ganga Ram. It was less than five thousand rupees, about three thousand. I had it about six years ago. If I had done it privately, in the doctor's own clinic, they take better care of the patient, but we could not imagine being able to afford it. I went to see a doctor in a private clinic, but had the operation in Ganga Ram Hospital.

About three years ago, her oldest daughter who is still living at home had to have a nose operation to clear her nasal passage. They were told to consult with a doctor at Mayo Hospital; it took them three or four months just to meet with him.

One day when we were visiting with Amina, her youngest daughter was ill with a stomach pain. Amina told us of how she had waited on line at Mayo Hospital for hours a few days earlier, only to be told that the time was up and they had to go home. She then went to a doctor in Wachowali Bazaar who told her to get certain x-rays done, for which she had to pay eighty rupees. Feeling that this was a small way I could repay Amina for taking so much time to talk with us about her life, I arranged for them to meet a doctor at Mayo Hospital the next day. An old friend of mine from Gulberg, now a doctor herself, had a friend from medical school who was working at the hospital, and she was able to arrange this appointment for me over the telephone. The next day, when we arrived and went inside the hospital, we were quickly escorted into the doctor's office. The doctor examined the girl, and said she could have the x-rays done for free in the hospital's clinic. He took no money, and gave us fruit juice to drink to combat the 120 degree heat. After a thorough examination, he gave the girl a prescription and we left. But when we reached the street, both the mother and daughter were in tears: they had never been treated so well in a hospital before as we were treated that day.

> Normally, we have to wait and wait. The doctors don't pay such good attention. Usually we have to wait at least three hours to be seen. Without influence, it is hard to see a doctor. If you see a doctor, they ask the patient to come to their private clinic. When you go there, you have to pay fees, often a hundred and fifty rupees.

It turned out that the daughter had a urinary infection which was then successfully treated with medication.

Amina's approach to dental care does not lend itself to sustaining healthy teeth and gums. She now has false teeth.

> When I was young, if I had a problem with my teeth, I'd take them out myself. Sometimes I went to the dentist to get them extracted, or to consult him. I'd go when I had a bad pain in my mouth. He'd give me an injection and extract the tooth.
>
> I had a lot of pain in my teeth, went to a dentist, and he advised me to have my teeth taken out. I had my teeth taken out three years ago. Two years ago, I had the false teeth fixed. I ate a lot of rice with milk, bread with milk, rice with soup, and porridge for that year!
>
> No, I've never gone to a dentist to get my teeth cleaned or for a check-up. We only go when there's pain or the teeth become bad. The same is true with our health. When health is good, we never go to see a doctor. When people are in trouble, only then do they need to see a doctor. When my daughters were born, I didn't know about inoculating them. I only knew about smallpox, nothing else.

One of her daughters shows us the scar from an injection which she received when she was in fifth class. The two younger daughters received only one smallpox shot each while the eldest had three shots, probably due to differences in medical advancements between those periods. Today, the situation is very different, and inoculations have become a matter of course, and Amina is very familiar with the routine.

> A pregnant woman gets an injection in the seventh or eighth month for the security of the baby. When a woman gives birth to a child, then she is advised to have an operation if she already has seven or eight children. When a child is born, and someone from the health department comes to give an injection -- at five or ten days old -- we give them five or ten rupees because we're happy. Otherwise, they don't ask for anything. When we go to get the birth certificate for a new baby, a doctor comes to the house for the first inoculation. We get the birth certificate from an LMC (Lahore Municipal Committee) center. There's one in Wachowali bazaar, and one in Shah Alami. I know we're supposed to go because I saw it on television and it's written about in the newspapers. We all also talk about what we have to do nowadays when a child is born, and we tell each other what to do.
>
> In the warm monsoon season, the government people come around with injections against cholera. We sometimes get them, sometimes we don't. The people at the girls' schools are very particular. My daughters have had all their shots. Since they've left school, we haven't paid attention to it.

But Amina does pay close attention to ensure that her daughters' actions are respectable, and considers that they are all in *purdah* as they keep separate from men. As she did before marriage, her daughters wear a *chadar* when they have to leave the house, though on occasion they only take a *dupatta* to drape over themselves. Amina never wore a *burqa* until her wedding day. It was a white *topiwala*, the old style that looks as if a woman has a shuttlecock draped over her. She had never worn one before, and wearing it upset her. She tells us that she wanted to throw it away, but she couldn't as she was the bride and the center of attention. She was being married into a *purdah*-observing family, which presumably implied a rise in status.

> When I spoke with my husband about it, he said I have to wear a *burqa* as it is his family's tradition. I talked with him once about it, and that was enough for my whole life. When diabetes began and my vision became weak about 2-4 years ago, I myself put the *chadar* away.

Honor and status are intertwined with marriage, for herself as well as for her daughters. She has eight daughters and one son; five of her daughters are married, most to relatives. We met one of her married daughters, all dressed up in her finest clothes, who came by to visit her mother and sisters. She was wearing six gold bangles on her left hand, two thick traditional gold bangles on her right hand, and a gold necklace with matching gold earrings. She had been engaged to her husband, Amina's sister's son, when she was 8-10 years old, and was married shortly after she began to menstruate. Circumstances and hence values within this family are indeed in flux; the eldest unmarried daughter at home in 1987 was in her early twenties, and Amina was hoping to wait a year or two longer before arranging her marriage.

Amina's only son, an apprentice in a curtain shop, is about twenty years old and she is very proud of him.

> Sons are a source of happiness for parents. After the girls get married, they leave. The son is the only property of the parents. It never happens in Pakistan that a girl performs the role of a son. If a girl starts playing that sort of a role, there would be a lot of complications with her husband and in-laws. It's a male-dominated society, and the girls have to say yes to their husbands. A son-in-law is very different from one's own son.

Her daughters never go out alone, and never visit any neighbors. In their leisure time, her daughters enjoy listening to cassettes and watching their large black and white television. Amina fears that if her daughters go out, the neighbors will talk that the girls aren't good. Related to this issue, she contends that the main reason she did not send her daughters to college is that boys stand outside the school gates and tease the girls.

When this dynamic, active woman contemplates the events in her life, thinking if she would have done anything differently, she concludes that her own actions and desires were virtually irrelevant to her fate.

> If I could have gotten a better husband, my life would have been better, but that was out of my control. When my son becomes older and he gets better work, my life can become better -- God only knows.
> The happiest days in my life were when my daughters were married, and the day my son was born.

The symbolism involved in these two events are of a very different nature. When her daughters were married, she had successfully fulfilled her obligations to them and to her family and gave them away with *izzat*. But the birth of her son was the day her provider in her old age was born. And, true to her speculation, her life has indeed improved since her son got a sales job in late 1990 in the large wholesale market by Sheranwala Gate, Azim Cloth Market, and supplies her and her daughters with curtains to hem. They no longer stitch *sehras* for the middleman, and their income has dramatically improved. She now contemplates buying the necessary dowries for her remaining unmarried daughters...and hopes to marry them off as soon as possible.

Bilqis

Bilqis, whose family makes shoes together in their house near Wachowali Bazaar, is rather uncertain about what medical facilities she can avail upon and apprehensive about the ones with which she is familiar. In most instances, she relies on traditional methods of health care, such as giving birth at home with the assistance of a *dai* (midwife). She does, however, value preventive vaccinations for children which are now accessible.

> All of my children were born in the house, with the help of a *dai*. I heard about the *dai* through relatives.
> All the children were inoculated after birth for 2-3 diseases, but not for the whole course. Now it's five diseases. I know they were inoculated against smallpox. My children went for three injections only, smallpox and two others.
> Two of my girls died, one at six months and one at three months. The first died for no reason, in her sleep. The second one - *suk gaya* (dried up; dehydration from diarrhea). I know now about ORS (oral rehydration salts), but in those times, I didn't know. If a child is dehydrated nowadays, he is admitted to hospital, and doesn't come back. In the hospital, we have to

spend a lot of money, whenever we have to buy medicine. There is no free medicine. It's very difficult to see a doctor. Poor people are badly treated in the hospitals. I have to spend all day in the hospital just to see a doctor. Most of the time, the doctors scold us.

When I was about twenty years old, I fell down the stairs in the house, and injured my head. Because of that, I lost some strength in my right eye. The doctor says it's incurable. Recently, I went to Mayo Hospital because my eyes were hurting. I went there, waited for my turn all day. I went so many times and at last, the peon said "the time is over now, you have to come some other time." I came back home and went some other time. I had to leave home very early. They won't give me any medicines, they just write it down.

I have gases; look at my bloated stomach. I'd like to take medicines because it looks bad. I can't work easily because it bulges. Sometimes it hurts a lot, and I have to lie down on my bed. Otherwise, thankfully, we're all healthy.

Her conception of health, however, only concerns physical aspects. The family has been confronting a serious mental health issue for some time in that her *jaith* is a heroin addict who has little to do with them now. His addiction disrupted his family entirely, and led his wife to leave him; she has since remarried. She, however, left her four children with Bilqis as she didn't want to take responsibility for them at the time without a husband. Bilqis cares for them as her own.

Bilqis is somewhat pious, though she would not consider herself very religious.

I pray regularly, though five times is a lot. In Ramadan, I pray five times daily, but usually I just go for *fajar* prayer (before sunrise). I wake up about at 5 a.m., just in time to pray.

I go to Data Saheb about every other month. It's important to go there. I don't go to any other shrines though.

Connected with her view of religion are her views on *purdah*. The elders in her family made the decision to place her into *purdah* when she was thirteen. She feels strongly that women should observe *purdah*.

Islam says that women shouldn't go in front of other men. While Zia ul-Haq had said this in the beginning (had initiated his Islamization program in 1979 and advocated that women should observe *purdah*), the result now is that women walk around freely, without observing *purdah*. I used to wear a *burqa*, but I now wear a *chadar*, without a *nikab*, when I go out. I took the *burqa* off six years ago. I copied everyone else; they were taking off the *burqa*, and so did I. In the beginning, I had an uncomfortable feeling, but now it is comfortable. I feel freer in a *chadar*.

Every woman in Pakistan is covering herself with a *chadar* instead of a *burqa*. No one wears *burqas* nowadays. I don't like those women who still wear *burqas*. If you go somewhere in a group, and two of them are wearing *burqas*, it looks odd. They're not necessarily more religious if they wear a *burqa*. When women are married, for the first few years they wear a *burqa*, then they switch to a *chadar*. My married daughter wears a *chadar*.

She feels that there is little difference between wearing a *burqa* or a *chadar* in terms of being able to do something or go somewhere. The real consideration seems to lie in the power paradigm existing within a family. For example, her late husband used to intervene in her activities and tell her not to go somewhere, but her sons would never do so. This is not the case in other families, such as Gulzar Begum's, where sons have equal license in curbing their mother's mobility as do husbands, brothers and fathers.

Before her husband's death, Bilqis considered that she had helped her husband make important decisions concerning their family and home, but also acquiesces that he had the final say.

I make the important decisions with my husband. We don't fight. We bought a black and white television seven years ago. We have no fridge or washing machine, or other expensive things in the house. My husband decided to buy the television. My husband also decided on my eldest daughter's marriage.

Her sons, since the death of her husband, now play that pivotal role in making definitive decisions. This is not surprising given that she has been dependent on them for some time regarding her knowledge of the world outside their home. They have been key players in her information network, reporting back to her about news they read in *Jang* and *Mushriq* newspapers in the bazaar and returning with news told to them by local shopkeepers.

However, Bilqis has been frustrated with her sons. Of the four, only the youngest, age ten, is still in school. The eldest -- with her prodding him -- completed his matric exam and then wanted to run his own shoe shop. She became annoyed by his attitude, that he didn't want to use the degree he had earned nor continue studying, and so she was disheartened about sending the others to school. Her second son only studied until sixth class; he often failed, and just gave up. The next son gave up after seventh class.

While she remains disappointed that her sons did not study up to her expectations, this is immaterial regarding her daughters' fates. She regards all her sons as being bright, but not her daughters.

My oldest daughter had been enrolled in school,' but she didn't want to study – she never did. She just is not bright. My sons are all bright. My younger daughter, Zahara, also didn't study because she was scared of going to school. She was afraid she would be locked in when they locked the gates. She never studied.

Now, her brothers don't want Zahara (about sixteen years old) going out of their house because they don't like the *mahaul* (social atmosphere) in the *kucha*.

That's how our *mahaul* is. They have locked Zahara inside the house. Sometimes she has gotten furious and wants to go out. Zahara has said that she would prefer to die than live her life like this. She is not allowed to go upstairs on the roof, not allowed to go to the main gate of the house.

When I first came to Pakistan, all these restrictions were put on me too. We think that Punjabis are not good, we can't trust them with out daughters. Here in Punjab, 15 or 16 year old girls are not permitted to go outside.

Bilqis completely blames the *mahaul* of Wachowali for these restrictions, and not her family's traditions. She doesn't regard adhering to these restrictions as necessary for preserving a woman's respectability. However, rather than blaming the system directly, she regards "fate" as being a major actor.

There don't have to be such restrictions. I envy the life of you Americans because you are free, you study a lot, have good jobs, and are liberal-minded women.

I wanted to educate my daughter, and I tried a lot, but she could not continue with it. When Zahara was three, she fell from the third story of the house; her brain hasn't been the same since. When she fell, she was admitted to hospital. I wasn't allowed to stay there. Sometimes, the nurses even threw me out! They wouldn't let me stay or sleep with my daughter at night because we were poor.

Interestingly, the same kind of story, a child falling from three flights at a young age, was told to me by another woman in the Walled City. But in the second instance, the child was the woman's son, and there was no mention of any kind of permanent damage. As the circumstances were almost identical, we must surmise a similar outcome. But here, gender differences surface in influencing perceptions. Either both children suffered some major handicap, in which case it was covered it up in the case of the boy, or both survived without permanent impairment, in which case it has become an excuse for the restrictions placed on the girl.

When we were talking with her in both 1987 and 1988, before Benazir Bhutto had become Prime Minister, Bilqis was an avid Pakistan People's Party supporter. She regarded Benazir as an important symbol for women in Pakistan, and having the power to improve conditions for women if she came to head the state. "What needs to be done to lift the restrictions on Zahara? If (Zulfiqar Ali) Bhutto was still in power, there would be more freedom. If Benazir comes, it will be much better."

Bilqis believes that women's conditions could be improved, though she never had thought about how that could be done. In the course of the time we spent with Bilqis, she surprised us one day by telling us she had enrolled Zahara in a *Nai Roshni* school in her *kucha*.[1] She said that she did this because a few other girls from the neighborhood have also joined the *Nai Roshni* schools.

> Zahara said she wanted to go. I take her at 2 p.m. everyday, and bring her back at 5 p.m. Our neighbor took her today; when she goes, I don't have to go. We heard about the school last winter, six months ago, when two teachers came from the school to persuade us to send Zahara. At first, her brothers objected, and said she's grown up now and she should stay home all the time. But now, my oldest son made the decision that it's O.K. I convinced him that Zahara should be permitted to study. But only sharp, intelligent students can do all the five classes in two years, which is how they teach it in the *Nai Roshni* schools. I don't know if she will finish all the classes, but look - she's going to school. Let's see if she can qualify on the tests. The teaching is good there, and the teacher earns a thousand rupees per month. This school is only for girls. The teacher told me that there is a *Nai Roshni* school for boys as well, but I don't know of it, and no one I know in Shah Alami goes to it.

We thought that her actions might signify a change in her attitude about her daughter. Did she think it was possible that Zahara might someday become a *Nai Roshni* teacher? "It's not possible. Her brain isn't so big." She does not regard studying in the *Nai Roshni* school as an option for her other daughter as she is already married and has a son.

While it appears that Bilqis' family provides a supportive unit and that she derives happiness from its smooth functioning, she was unable to discern the most special, happiest day in her life. "There was no special day. I have to always work. I pray to God that every day is a good day." She fears tragedies that they cannot overcome, outside of her control.

Itrat

In some ways, Itrat is very isolated from the world outside of her family. She spends most of her time working in her house near Bazaar

Syad Mithha. She hardly ever visits neighbors or relatives, and only travels to Data Saheb's shrine two or four times a year. On the other hand, she usually does the daily shopping for her family. This is unusual, since most of the other women interviewed rely on a child or male family member to go to the bazaar daily. We must recall that Itrat, working at home making artificial jewelry, earns a better income than her husband at this time. But her encounters in the bazaar are limited to purchasing essential goods, and she has no other communication with the shopkeepers.

> I decide on my own and go to the bazaar to buy things. I just have to inform my husband. My husband bought the ceiling fan on his own. For this pedestal fan, I decided myself, but then my husband went to the bazaar to make this purchase for the house. If I want to buy something and don't have enough money, he gives it to me. The money I have, I spend on daily expenses like food and clothes. Sometimes I go to attend a marriage, and I spend from my own pocket. We don't have anything else, no television, no refrigerator, nothing.
> We sit in our house, and we have no idea about what is happening outside. We don't go out so much.

She is used to not going outside much as she was put into *purdah* by her parents when she was thirteen. Her in-laws placed stricter constraints on her movements after her marriage when they made her wear a *burqa* instead of her *chadar*, but she no longer feels it is restricting. Indeed, when she first became sick with diabetes, her lady doctor told her to stop wearing the *burqa*, but Itrat did not want to set it aside. Women who do so are considered old, and she doesn't yet identify herself as such.

> I have a lot of body pain and my vision has grown weak, because of the work (making artificial jewelry) and my diabetes. Sometimes it hurts to talk with the pain. I got diabetes in 1986. I went to Mayo Hospital, to a doctor, and then to a lady doctor. I don't drink tea, eat almost no sweets at all, and eat a lot of vegetables. I feel suffocated and when I talked to the doctor, she told me to stop wearing the *burqa*. But I would feel ashamed to go out and not wear it.
> Today, a lot of women are wearing *chadars* without a *nikab*. It looks strange for people to wear a *chadar* without a *nikab*. It doesn't cover enough. My daughters all wear *chadars*, except for the oldest one who is married and wears a *burqa*. She always wore a *burqa*.

On a return visit a couple of years later, she no longer wore the *burqa* at all, and used a *chadar* instead. She says that she has really been too ill from the diabetes to wear the *burqa*, and so no one objects to the change.

Her life, now, is focussed on her children's futures. Being able to educate them and arrange their marriages are two ways in which she might exert power, but she has been ineffectual in being able to follow through on what she would like to do.

Now, all my dreams, hopes and wishes have been transferred to my children, and I hope to marry them off into good families. A "good family" is one which can earn enough to provide food and housing. That's enough... that's a lot.

I had my eldest daughter married outside of the family because I am not on good terms with my *susural*. My daughter was married when she was nineteen, seven years ago. We had thought of engaging her to her *taya's* son since childhood. But the boy was in Karachi, and his parents refused because they said he wanted to marry somewhere else.

Her use of "somewhere" is indicative of the meaning that marriage holds for her, that it is a bond between families more so than a bond between individuals. Her nephew had indeed wanted to marry a girl he had met in Karachi, and his father allowed it saying he didn't want "to ruin the boy's life." Bilqis still doesn't accept that action, resents that her husband's family did not oppose that marriage, and therefore no longer considers herself as having good relations with her *susural*.

So, we married our daughter outside also. My nephew is uneducated. My daughter, at least, can read the Qur'an; she had studied until eighth class. Her husband is illiterate. He works in a cycle shop in Main Market, Gulberg.

But after eight years of marriage she still had no children, so they adopted her cousin's son. Right after that, they had a daughter and then a son of their own!

Another daughter is seventeen and studied to third class. Some relatives didn't understand why she should study. It became a question of prestige, so I decided to stop her from going to school. But I believe it's up to the parents whether to send their daughters to study or not. Poverty is what really stood in our way. My daughter still wanted to study more, and I think girls should study. She was married a year ago, when she was sixteen, and now has a son.

My sons, however, didn't have the chance to study. One only stayed in school until sixth class, the other to eighth class. We needed them to earn money to help the family survive: one works in a welding shop, the other makes shoes in that small factory on our roof.

I've heard about the *Nai Roshni* schools. The education is free, and books and a uniform are also provided. My middle daughter is already grown up now, thank God. She's 15-16, and we're hoping to marry her next year. Her menses have begun, and there has to be someone to escort her to the school. She can't go alone. But I can't spend my time taking her to school. I have work to do, clothes to wash, and I have this work with the jewelry. I hear they do primary education in two years. They go up to the fifth class in the *Nai Roshni* schools. She has already studied nearly that far. I have to do my work. If my house was in good order, then she could study more.

I want to keep sending my two youngest daughters to school. Education is helpful, but poverty stands in the way. It's poverty -- to pay the fees, books, etc. We have no money for our children to study. We have to make uniforms for them to study in, light blue *kamizes*, white *shalwars*, and a *mal-mal* (light cotton) *chadar*, and we have to pay for books.

Despite her poverty, she now feels that she must make whatever sacrifices are necessary to ensure that her youngest daughters can continue their studies, for that is the girls' only real opportunity for a better lifestyle. While her sons may someday be able to improve their economic condition by joining her *nund's* son who went to work in Saudi Arabia, working abroad -- or simply work itself -- is not the answer for her daughters' lives. She considers that they will have more secure lives if they are also educated, but as she confronts the double-barreled forces of poverty and sentiments of respectability, she submits to them.

We have seen in this chapter that women in the Walled City recognize the ways in which they can wield power and some are indeed in the process of trying to renegotiate new authority parameters in their lives. Recognition of these forces is not all these women discern; both abstract and concrete alternatives were raised, as discussed in the following chapter.

Notes

1. The "new light" schools were part of a controversial program of adult education established by the Zia ul-Haq government.

5

Empowerment and Social Change

Social change is an ongoing reality in the Walled City of Lahore. Many women expressed their desire to have a voice in those changes, as opposed to being passively affected by them. In this chapter, we explore the kinds of changes both imagined by women -- what they dream could happen in the future -- and envisioned by them -- what they see actually occurring. To some extent, these visions of what is and is not desirable are tied in with changing political realities in Pakistan. The symbolism which Benazir Bhutto held for women, first as leader of the opposition against Zia ul-Haq and then as Prime Minister, has given way to concerns that the government of Pakistan has shifted its focus away from women's empowerment once again. However, the bulk of views offered by women in the Walled City, except in those instances where they might be affected by specific laws, tend to be independent of these national political shifts.

This chapter concludes with some concrete recommendations for development projects to empower women in the Walled City. The recommendations attempt to give a public voice to women who have felt they have none. They have been influenced by what has been gleaned from the women's narratives, existing development programs and objectives in Pakistan and the body of literature on the experiences of women-in-development projects elsewhere.

The act of women in the Walled City removing the *burqa* in favor of the *chadar* and the even more liberating *dupatta* symbolically reflects increased degrees of freedom. With this, evident in women's expanded economic activity and aspirations for the future, we can see a great potential for them to play more active roles in various dimensions of social life. Nevertheless, women recognize that social values are the most powerful constraint on their activities, even when practical needs force women to break away from traditional norms. For example, Amina underscored to us earlier the constraints facing women who need to earn an income. It is not only the issue of a woman leaving her *kucha* and

161

thereby bringing her morality into question, but the larger social issue of her family's status being problematic when it becomes known that she is earning an income and feeding the men in her family. Home-based work therefore, despite the problems associated with it, becomes the labor of choice for most women in the Walled City who aspire to engage in work for remuneration.

Envisioned Dreams and Aspirations

Women here appear to acknowledge their dreams and aspirations for the future only during adulthood, when they have enough personal power that they might indeed be able to act on their hopes. Young girls uniformly insisted that they have no goals or dreams; older women could recall no childhood wishes, not even regarding a future husband as that decision was completely outside their control. Women who articulated their dreams and aspirations generally have intertwined them with the actions of the males in their lives: they hardly ever envisioned themselves as the social actor who would accomplish the stated goals nor include any role for their daughters in the scenario. While often being well informed on political issues, few women perceive a change in the personnel or ideology of who runs the country as making much of a difference in their lives. However, having more of a say in what happens to them and gaining either the cooperation of other women or some degree of financial independence gradually emerges as the cornerstones of how these changes are coming about.

Laila

Our youngest informant, Laila, is still unmarried and works at home doing *salma sitara* embroidery for a middleman in the hopes that her dowry will be well augmented by the time of her marriage. As expected, her dreams for her future are tied up with her hopes for a good marriage. But unlike many of the older women we interviewed, Laila does not see herself as a passive actor. She and others in her generation are also gradually becoming more a part of the process of making the marriage choice, though they must still be very subtle in acknowledging a preference.

> A husband should be beautiful and well-educated. Just beyond the city of Sheikhupura is a small village. There's a boy there, my distant cousin's son. We met at a family wedding. We had met a lot before that, but had never spoken. At the wedding, we spoke, and he wanted to take my picture. He did, and later spoke to his elders about our marriage. Everyone agreed, except for my father. My father thinks that very well-educated men become

wild womanizers. I'm hopeful, because the negotiations are still going on.
A letter arrived for my father from his father nearly two weeks ago. I
wanted to write a reply, but I've just placed it away.

A reply to the boy would be evidence of interest and of possible
involvement, risks that Laila will not take as it could jeopardize both the
rishta and her *izzat* (respectability).

Unlike the endings of so many similar stories which we heard, Laila's
father finally agreed to the marriage in 1990. The elders in the boy's
family had come to visit Laila's father on a number of occasions and
emphasized that the marriage would bring the two families closer
together. They were engaged after the boy completed a three month
course in engineering and took a job at a factory in Sheikhupura, a town
not far from Lahore. His family had wanted the wedding to be held
shortly after the engagement, but Laila's mother insisted it be postponed
until the entire dowry was ready, which she predicts will be sometime
in 1993.

Laila's pragmatic attitude about day-to-day necessities is reflected in
her views of the potential that political change might hold for her life.
Working class support for the Pakistan People's Party (PPP) is evident in
the enthusiasm her family -- as well as her neighborhood -- had for
Benazir Bhutto when she returned to Pakistan in 1986. An important
Walled City PPP candidate, Jehangir Badr, who emerged during the PPP
tenure (1988-1990) from his working class roots into the national arena,
surprised her family when he lost his election bid in the October 1990
elections.

> A new government might be better, it might be worse, who knows? Most
> of the people in Chuna Mandi like Benazir Bhutto and Jehangir Badr (the
> local PPP candidate). When her father was in power, things were not so
> costly. My father was looking forward to Benazir coming into the
> government, so maybe things would get less expensive. All the men in my
> family, and all the men from around here, went to the big gathering at the
> Minar-e-Pakistan (across from the Badshahi Mosque) when she came in
> 1986, and they all still support her. Jehangir Badr brought a water pipe to
> our *haveli*, and he had the ground paved nearby. Everyone in our *kucha*
> voted for Jehangir Badr in October 1990, but he lost and Shahbaz Sharif, the
> brother of Nawaz Sharif (who became Prime Minister following that
> election), somehow won. We don't really understand what happened. We
> think that Benazir's party is better for people like us, *awam* (common
> people).
>   I think that, obviously, being a woman, Benazir understands women's
> problems better than men and she could do something for women. But
> those people who believe in Benazir believe in her politics, not in her

personal life. They'll still do what they want in their personal lives, they keep women in *purdah* and limit what they can do. A lot of people didn't want a woman to be prime minister. Nowadays, the *mahaul* (social environment) in Pakistan has gotten much worse. A woman can't go outside, people worry too much about her.

Laila's visions for her own future, therefore, have little to do with formal political matters. Her concerns center on where she will be living, whether she will have to earn an income, and the size of her family after her marriage. She is used to city life and does not want to live in a village. While she would prefer to do embroidery for fun, she realizes that she will probably be doing it for payment even after she is married.

> Women have to work hard. A husband and wife must both work hard to make ends meet, and still it's hard. Things have gotten too expensive.
> I want to live in a city, not in a village. I don't like villages. I've lived my life in Lahore. I don't have any special city in mind, just any city. It should be a beautiful house, more beautiful than this one in Chuna Mandi. I don't want *to have to* do so much *salma sitara* work. I want to do it at my pleasure. I don't want to do any other work.
> I want two girls and two boys. If you have fewer children, their life will be better. If you have too many, there are more liabilities and responsibilities.

Laila, as is increasingly becoming the norm in Lahore, desires to have a small family consisting of only four children. We are reminded that Pakistan's fertility rate (the number of children a woman is likely to have) of 6.8 in 1986 is one of the highest in the world, nearly double that of the average of all low income countries (3.9 percent) and one third higher than the average for lower middle-income countries (4.7 percent) (World Bank 1988: 274).[1] Therefore, a family with only four children is indeed smaller than average.

Gulzar Begum

Typical of the visions of many older women, Gulzar Begum views her future -- and the prospects for her daughters as well as for her son -- through the prism of her son achieving some sort of financial success. Until then, she perceives that her hand-to-mouth subsistence which she derives from stringing flowers will have to continue.

> If my son can learn his work well and earn a lot of money, then a change can happen. Marriages will be done, and he'll be able to spend his money lavishly and have children. I'd like to stop doing this work, if my son can earn enough money. We work during the day and eat from it at night.

Once, she did aspire that she could improve her circumstances herself. She had heard that the Zia ul-Haq government was going to distribute seven *marla* plots of land to widows and the poor through a lottery. Her *bhabi* went with her when she applied for the land; they were unaware that a video was being made of the application process when they were at the government office filling out the forms. Her strict *taya* was furious with them when, going to the cinema with some friends, that video was shown before the feature film and he saw them in it! No precautions had been made to protect the identity of women in the video, including those who observe *purdah*. She contends that her lack of understanding how to fill out the application form properly is the primary reason why she failed to get any land; she does not know of anyone who indeed received land through the lottery.

> When I applied, I forgot to write if I was applying for three *marlas*, five *marlas* or seven *marlas*. Widows and other helpless people could apply for seven *marlas*. People are supposed to come from the government department to see if the applicants are deserving, but no one has come to see me. Why not? I couldn't sign the form correctly. I filled the form, sitting by the side of a man who sits in the district court. He's an experienced man, and he made a few mistakes. He is my daughter's *nund's* husband [daughter's husband's brother-in-law]. That man forgot to write seven *marlas*, five or three. I didn't return to correct it because the date had expired, and my son wanted to have the land through his own efforts. He doesn't believe in the seven *marla* scheme.
>
> We don't know anyone in Delhi Gate or Yakki Gate who has gotten any land, though we heard on television that some people have. We don't know anyone who has gotten any land, because we have no contact with people outside of our *kucha*. Poor people deserve the land that the government was saying they were going to allot, but they couldn't get it. Without money, there is no power. With money, there is power.

Gulzar Begum regards the only affect that the government could have on her life would be if it gives her son a job. Even so, she sees little security in this as she fears that many employees lose their jobs whenever the government changes due to patronage.

Farida

Farida hopes to someday own her own beauty parlor. That would be the key to being able to have her own house and find some happiness. If she were to meet a good man, she would consider divorcing her present drug abusing husband and marrying him, but she has reservations about the prospects for success of that route: "There's no way out now. I'm looking for a man of my own choice. If I can't find one, I'll stand alone in this world. Love is deceiving. Women can love, but men cannot. Men are frauds." The only solutions she sees is by changing society and changing men's thinking. As she does not see such changes on the horizon, she feels she is going to have to fend for herself, despite social criticism, to improve her life.

Jamila

Jamila, the trader, is in a difficult social situation. The very identity of most women in the subcontinent rests in their husbands, and her husband has abandoned her. Not only is the situation emotionally difficult, but it is also economically difficult. Of course, her situation would have been even more onerous were it not for her sons. They assist her economically, travel with her as witnesses to her *izzat* (respectability) as well as give her status. Without them, she would find it arduous to run her trading business as it is socially unacceptable for a woman to travel alone so extensively.

She is compelled to work to support her family, despite having to bear with others' disapproval. It troubles her that her daughter is given a hard time by her *susural* because of what Jamila does, and that her own father did not approve of her working. Her brother is supportive of it in that he thinks she should not live off of other people; if she had no independent income, she would most likely be dependent on him.

Not surprisingly, she makes her own political choices, given her degree of independence. These decisions, from her account, are impulsive rather than consciously thought out. In voting for Zulfiqar Ali Bhutto and in supporting other candidates, she had simply taken a spontaneous liking to them. She did not study their political philosophies or their policies. She also did not care who others voted for; instead, she followed her own instincts. She had voted for Zulfiqar Ali Bhutto even though many of the others in her *kucha* were going to vote for the more conservative Jamaat-i-Islami. She was also an early supporter of Benazir Bhutto. She thinks that most people like Benazir but they are hesitant to admit it in public. However, she does not think that women politicians necessarily do anything special for women.

Jamila has the expectation that she will have a direct personal gain from supporting a given politician, though that has never yet been realized. Accepting the system of patronage as a given, she believes politicians only do things for people they know. For example, she did not apply for the seven *marla* scheme as she did not believe that anyone without the proper amount of influence could get anything out of it. She had once publicly taken a stand supporting a female candidate from Bhati Gate by putting a shawl on the woman's head when she visited Jamila's *kucha*, but was later disappointed when the politician did not remember her nor did anything to get her nephew admitted to a particular school when she requested the help.

In effect, Jamila holds a very personal view on politics, as opposed to considering the larger social effect of political events. She thinks the position of women has improved minimally in recent years. As people become more affluent, only then do women have access to more freedom as restrictions -- such as *purdah* and having to remain indoors -- are lifted.

Hasina

Hasina regards women's lack of education and having no particular interests outside of their families as the fuel which drives them to be competitive and gossip about each other in Kucha Kakazaiyan, her neighborhood in the Walled City.

> People in this neighborhood are illiterate, and watch over every activity of women. An educated woman can do everything, but an uneducated woman can't do anything. A skilled woman can contribute to society, to her home. She can make sweaters, sew, and have an independent income.
>
> I have seen that the women in the Walled City are very clever and street-wise. Kakazaiya women here are domineering and strong, and their husbands go along with them, and don't interfere in their wives' affairs. But I have not been able to be like this with my husband, and no one from here comes to tell my husband to stop what he's doing when he fights with me.
>
> It's a good thing for a woman to take an active part in politics, if she's understanding and clever. No Kakazaiya women are active in politics, because they are clever in another sense. They know how to handle their man, dominate, quarrel and fight. But as far as politics are concerned, they are the least interested because they don't have a mind for politics.

Many of her relatives, including her mother and mother-in-law, applied for either three or seven *marlas* in the government's land lottery giveaway. The only people she knows who have ever received land from the government were distant relatives from Karim Park, where she grew up. They had received some land just past Data Saheb's shrine during Zulfiqar Ali Bhutto's period in the 1970s. She has heard that people have been allotted land more recently, but does not know of any. She is apprehensive that the *zakat* program can make much of a difference in poor women's lives, either.

> I know that the chairman of *zakat* in my sister's neighborhood gives out one hundred, two hundred, sometimes two hundred fifty rupees to widows. If

the chairman gets funds to distribute, he gives a little of it to the widows, but most of the rupees he uses for himself. There is nothing for poor people here; it's all for the rich. They don't take care of orphans, but if somebody is rich, they try to please them.

In our *gali*, most people support the PPP. I don't support anyone. When Zulfiqar Ali Bhutto was in power, he did nothing for us. He distributed land, but we got nothing. When General Zia was in power, we were still weeping, day in and day out. He also distributed the lands, but we got nothing.

Kanize

Kanize does not reply to the question of what are her aspirations; instead, she calls her father to respond. Her concerns are confined to the running of her natal household and preparing *samosas* for her father and brothers to sell. She fears that, given her advanced age (she is in her late twenties), when her father finally marries her off the bridegroom will be an old man, but she will not refuse her father's choice.

I'm completely illiterate, and I'm not hopeful about getting a good *rishta*. But first I'll get my sister married, because I'm like her mother. Whatever type of man my father proposes for me, I have to get along with him. I'll have to spend the rest of my life with that person, so my father is looking for a good man. One *rishta* has come recently. I don't know what work that man does. God knows better how old he is; he is older than me. He's never been married before.

Kanize recalls having no aspirations when she was a young girl, and hesitates to envision her future. She regards her options as being products of a combination of other peoples' wishes and God's will. Similar forces are at work in the outcome of elections: "I didn't vote in the 1990 election, but my father and brother did, for Benazir's party. Everyone I know voted for them, but they didn't win."

Erum

As a child, Erum had wanted to tour the world, and regrets that she has not had the opportunity even to see the whole of Pakistan, given her full-time workload at her school. From an early age she thought that being a teacher was something she could do that could help out her family. To her, access to a good education holds the key to a myriad of positive social changes which view women as important social actors.

More women nowadays are going out as teachers. There is a new generation of women like me who are not backward and narrow-minded.

Some women, mostly elderly ones, are still backward and narrow-minded and don't even allow their sons to send their daughters to school.

Pakistani women remain dependent their entire lives. They start out dependent on their families, and they remain emotionally dependent. It is uneducated women who say and do things... for example, my mother-in-law is in the habit of interfering in each and every thing. My *nund* tells her not to interfere in my affairs. My mother-in-law gets annoyed very quickly.

Erum perceives that better economic prospects due to improved education are responsible for the important changes in people's lives.

First, few houses even had televisions; now everyone has televisions, tape recorders, many even have VCRs. People believe in education. That has changed people's lives. People used to burn stoves with wood, then coal, then kerosene, now gas. There were no desert coolers (humidifying and cooling the summer air) in the past; now, in every home there are coolers.

While knowledgeable about the political situation in Pakistan, Erum concludes that whoever is in power makes little difference for the majority of people. She considers that most people are politically apathetic.

Notwithstanding, she concludes that there are times when women have to take a public stand. They should not, however, always do this, but only for a certain time around particular issues. Indeed, some women *have to* talk for other women, and they might have to talk with men to accomplish their objectives. Under certain circumstances, she would not mind going out and protesting, seeing this as consistent with Muslim women's history in South Asia, as "even before Partition, women came out and fought for general rights. Given a chance, women will take part in politics."

Despite her teaching at a large girls' school and being supportive of the idea of women standing up for their rights, Erum was not familiar with most of the women's groups (e.g., Women's Action Forum; Pakistan Women Lawyers' Association) which played important roles in the country's politics in the 1980s.[2] The only group she knew of was the All Pakistan Women's Association (APWA), and that was for the schools and training programs which it runs. She had not heard of the Ministry for Women's Development nor the Women's Division in the Punjab government. "I've never heard of their names even."

Chand Bibi

Given her poor health, Chand Bibi had difficulty considering larger social problems; all discussions would ultimately return to the particular

ones she, a widow, is facing. She has no recollection of ever having the
freedom to hope for a brighter future, as she has been impoverished her
entire life. Indeed, hers are problems representative of the poor in the
country, especially of illiterate women who are forced to survive on their
own.

> I can't solve my own problems, so what can I think of others'? I can't go
> anywhere. To fill my stomach, I have to do the work I do, embroidering
> *dupattas* and making earrings in my house. I have to think of my four
> daughters' futures, arrange their marriages, bring them up, etc. I can't earn
> enough. If I go to a shopkeeper, he'll give me ten or twenty rupees, that's
> all. So I have to wait for other women to bring me work. If the husband
> isn't there, or there is no male member, then life becomes a problem.

Chand Bibi has taken the initiative to act independently when required:
asking a neighbor for an old television, contacting shopkeepers for more
work and applying to the government for both *zakat* and for land. Her
frustrating experiences have left her quite alienated from all political
solutions. In 1987, a year before the demise of Zia ul-Haq and the
subsequent elections which saw Benazir Bhutto's party come to power,
she concluded that no political solution can strive to empower the poor
if democracy is not a part of it.

> I applied for the seven *marla* scheme, but I couldn't get it. I applied, but my
> name wasn't on the list. I don't know why. I don't know of anyone who
> has received land under it. They prefer to give it to their own people, I
> suppose. They just eat everything up.
>   Before martial law, there were no bomb explosions and things weren't
> so expensive. If Benazir comes to power, things will be a bit better. Martial
> law demolished peoples' lives. If we have Benazir, life would be better,
> hopefully. During Zulfiqar Ali Bhutto's time, a thing was for ten rupees;
> now you can't buy anything for ten rupees. All the prices have gone up, for
> food, homes, everything. Poor people don't live. All the lotteries are won
> by the rich — it's their own conspiracy!
>   If Benazir comes, it benefits everyone, not just women.
>   Society wasn't always this bad. We can only hope it will get better.
> People are going wild and Zia can't stop it, but democracy can. The bomb
> blasts will stop if Benazir comes. When her father ran the government, no
> one objected. With Zia, there's a lot of objection.

Her optimism for the prospects of Benazir Bhutto's government proved
unfounded as ethnic clashes, erratic bomb blasts and anonymous violence
continue to percolate in the country in the 1990s.

Durdana

Despite living only a few *galis* away from Chand Bibi, Durdana's life -- and hence her aspirations and views on social change -- has been dramatically different. Her responses were among the most conventional we heard from women in the Walled City. Durdana enjoys a warm relationship with her husband as she and their children help him assemble plastic toys in their home. She considers that the worst problem she faces is that her children do not pray sufficiently.

> That is, thankfully, the only problem we face. I have been trying to teach them the Qur'an. When we die, we'll be accountable to God, not to this work we've done in the world.
>
> Most people in this *kucha* make shoes. Their women are more free and their children don't listen to their elders. It is a very bad thing. Children should be respectful, the house should be calm, no anger.

Durdana is largely removed from political concerns, leaving that arena to her husband. While governments may change, she sees no prospect that the internal workings and orientations will.

> No, there will be no change. There never is any real change.
>
> What Benazir is doing, being so active politically, is wrong. A woman shouldn't mix with men like that and think she can run things. I don't usually vote, because there's too much of a rush where you have to go to cast your vote. I have voted twice; I've had my husband go cast my vote.

Amina

Amina's dreams for bettering her family's position have rested on her one son. She is relieved that five of her daughters are happily married, and hopes for the same for the remaining three. Feeling her responsibilities to her daughters are nearly fulfilled, her attention is turning to religious matters and fulfilling one of the pillars of Islam, that a Muslim perform the pilgrimage, the *hajj*, to Mecca at least once if possible.

> I wanted to get married into a big family, have a bungalow, a big car, have my son become an officer, lawyer or judge. I wanted to learn English... now, I want to perform *hajj*.
>
> My eldest daughters are married. After they were married, my husband installed a flush latrine and bath upstairs. It was a lot of trouble to bathe within the home, and guests would come just as someone was beginning a bath! This is cleaner. We finally installed it when we had enough money,

we didn't have any way to take out a loan for it. We also finally bought a washing machine last year.

Women have gotten more freedom. They were all wearing *burqas* in Bhutto's time, now they've taken them off! But the common people are becoming worse off, they are becoming poorer day by day.

I inquired as to whether Amina had applied for land from the government under the seven *marlas* scheme, as some of the other women had done. She is apprehensive about both this and the *zakat* program.

We don't believe in this. On television, they tell us that villagers have gotten land but we don't know of anyone actually getting land, and haven't been told of anyone getting land by anyone. I didn't apply for any land. We aren't in such dire need, so why bother? Everyone says it's a fraud.

I don't know of anyone getting *zakat* either. I read about it in the newspapers and hear about it on television. Some people think it's a fraud; some people think it's okay and functioning.

Not surprisingly, she also expresses apprehension about the prospects that a change in government might make a difference in her life.

If there's any other government, what will they do? The government doesn't do anything -- they make things expensive. They have nothing to do with our job or work. A woman politician canno: be successful in a country like Pakistan. But whoever comes, they will only go to feed their own stomachs. The government changes now and then, but a good leader isn't possible. We supported Nawaz Sharif in 1988 and in 1990, but even we know that something happened in the 1990 elections.

However, Amina is an optimist about her future and that of her children. She believes that if they continue to work diligently, someday their lives will become a bit easier.

Bilqis

Today, her dreams are in her four sons who work with her at home making shoes and her unmarried daughter. But when Bilqis talks about her hopes for herself for the future and where her children fit in, she's really talking about her sons. She hopes to find a good husband for her daughter, and that she will live in a better house, and she envisions giving her daughter away sometime -- and hopefully soon -- to her in-laws.

Thank God, we have no major health problems in our home. Poverty isn't a problem. The problem is fate. My eldest daughter was married to a fine man who was perfectly alright. He had an appendix problem, had an operation, and now he can't walk properly -- he slumps. I'm sorry she married him. She has become a problem for the family. It would have been better for them if she hadn't married, though she did marry within the *biradari*.

When asked about her ideas that a government -- any government -- might be able to create a better life for her and her family, Bilqis responses changed dramatically between the period before the PPP came to power and after it lost the 1990 election. By 1991, her earlier enthusiasm for the prospects of change had been replaced by the same disillusionment with which we had become familiar.

I have no dreams. I hope for peace in the world, prosperity in the world. But since Pakistan was made, there have been so many new governments and there is little difference. Our forefathers faced the same sorts of difficulties as we do.

Benazir's people are hard-working; we thought that if she comes, everything would be better. In 1988, people wanted Benazir back. We thought that if Benazir comes, there would be liberty and freedom in the country. People wouldn't stress so much on Islam and Islamization as they had done. What was Zia's government doing? There were bomb blasts in the cities, and they couldn't find out who was behind them. But when her government actually came in, they also did nothing.

In this whole area, most everyone supports Benazir and the PPP. The benefit of Benazir's celebrity is there, but I'm not certain about it. Even before she was elected, I thought that if Benazir's government comes, people who have to live by working won't get any profit. I said, "Let's wait - she'll come and we'll see what she does for women."

Zia ul-Haq had been in power for ten years, and had no intention of leaving his seat. He did nothing for women. There were only advertisements on all the buses and wagons that poor people could apply for plots to make houses in Rana Town, Iqbal Town, and other places. I don't know anything about them; no one I knew got anything.

While she hopes that Nawaz Sharif, elected as Prime Minister in October 1990, might help turn Pakistan's economy around in that he is an industrialist, she has no expectation that this will actually happen.

Itrat

Itrat feels that she hardly has any time to think about the future, between having to cook and care for her family and make the artificial jewelry whenever she can. She doesn't have much to do with people or events outside of her immediate circumstances. "Being poor, my ambition is to get my children good clothes, food and education. But poverty prevents me from doing what I'd like to do."

Itrat hopes that the middleman who provides her with work will pay her more in the future so she can provide for her children better, but she doubts this hope will be realized soon.

Women's Empowerment and Development Planning

There are various ways in which many of these situations can be rectified. Shahid Javed Burki (1984: 406) has observed from the vantage point of the World Bank that "social developments" have lagged behind in Pakistan, and that

> in many cases, [it is] even worse than that faced by countries with much lower per capita incomes. This situation needs to be changed not only for humanitarian reasons, but also because social development is one of the important preconditions for sustained economic growth... There is now agreement among economists that without social development it is not possible to break out of poverty and economic backwardness.

The 1991 *Human Development Report* (UNDP, 1991) features Pakistan's development experience. It argues that Pakistan's neglect of various social development issues has compromised the country's chances to cross the World Bank's "poverty threshold," which many people had expected was possible just a few years ago. It urges increased attention to improvements in literacy, health care and in incorporating women into the benefits of the development process.

We can gain a great deal of awareness of possible arenas for development planning by reviewing what the women have said and placing their aspirations in a development-oriented context. For example, Laila, Gulzar Begum, Chand Bibi, and Itrat all recognize their dependence on a middleman but see no alternatives to their current situations. Laila hopes to limit the number of children she will have after marriage, but is uncertain of birth control options. Hasina has a skill, sewing, and desires her own income, but needs some catalyst to get her started. Farida hopes to own a beauty parlor someday, but lacks access to capital and training in running a business. Jamila is anxious about what others think of her because of the traveling she must do in connection with her trading, but recognizes it is necessary for her family's maintenance. She could benefit by becoming integrated into a support group comprised of women who share similar problems of separation and divorce. Erum places great emphasis on the benefits that education bestows on a girl's life, but as yet has not been integrated into on-going education programs sponsored by the Punjab Government's Women's Division or the federal Ministry for Women's Development.

Recognition of the significant place of religion, culture and tradition in women's lives remains central when we contemplate ways in which problems confronting women in the Walled City can be overcome. Nadia Hijab (1988: 164), writing on women's position in the Middle East, reminds us that "[a] society in transition is one where traditions are still alive, and where many different kinds of social systems are in force." Consequently, the only viable way of modifying women's circumstances -- according to women in the Walled City themselves -- is to recognize which traditions remain important and then operate within permissible cultural arenas. Undoubtedly, acting outside of acknowledged acceptable social parameters too quickly will cause fears to surface of women losing their respectability and no gains will be made whatsoever. Nonetheless, there are ample social arenas in which changes can be encouraged, particularly in the establishment of good secondary schools for girls (including scholarships), vocational education, and moving beyond skill improvement to all-female collectives and cooperatives. When development practitioners recognize what is both possible and respectable in this sociocultural environment, not only will women become empowered but Pakistan's dreams for a satisfied and prosperous future may well become realized.

It is not enough to simply state that women living in the Walled City are either working at low-paying jobs or would like to work but cannot find employment. Rather, given this reality, as well as the existing constraints on their working outside of their homes, their limited education and lack of financial resources, what kinds of possibilities can we envision which might increase the likelihood that those seeking gainful employment may will find it?

Needless to say, a major first step towards increasing women's options lies in increasing education prospects. Only 13.7 percent of the Pakistani female population in 1981 could "read a newspaper and write a simple letter" (Government of Pakistan, 1983: 178). Out of the total population who have completed primary school, only 30 percent are female; of those matriculating (about tenth grade), only 24 percent are female. While literacy rates in urban areas are much higher, a large number of women remain uneducated. For example, in our survey, 41 percent had studied beyond seventh class (achieving basic literacy), and only 14 percent beyond matriculation. While nearly all find being a doctor the best possible profession for women, none had studied for a professional degree in any field nor had any imagined that they might have been able to have become a doctor.[3]

There are a growing number of urban technical training programs in Pakistan, although there exists no statistical breakdown as to female participation rates.[4] Until very recently, it was generally assumed throughout much of the Pakistani bureaucracy that "manpower" training programs should be focussed on men, thereby leaving women's training needs largely to non-government organizations such as APWA's carpet weaving projects. However, these kinds of projects, despite their good intentions, serve few long-term goals. In recognition of this certain programs, such as the National Vocational Training Project, are now receiving funding from such sources as the United Nations Development Programme, Canadian International Development Agency, the European Economic Community and the World Bank to strengthen their women's training component. The International Labor Organization has sponsored research on the working conditions of home-based women in Pakistan. The emphasis of these and other agencies, as occurring elsewhere in the world, is on women's technical training is shifting from crafts projects to those containing more tangible benefits for both women and the country's industrial infrastructure, such as to poultry education, civil drafting and maintenance of water pumps. Increasing such kinds of technical education for women, with or without the goals of establishing separate but equal work facilities, must certainly be encouraged as a means to fairly and equitably integrate women into formal industries.

Another important step for women is to acquire some degree of control in the economy. Alejandro Portes (1989: 309), in exploring how the informal economy can function "in ways other than as a reservoir of overexploited labor" suggests that "support must go well beyond exclusively economic measures" and that innovative state responses are necessary. The likelihood is that the process of incorporating women into these innovative state responses will in turn lead to a greater awareness of other social issues.

The way in which the state and development practitioners think about home-based work can have major implications on what those innovative responses could be. Ela Bhatt (1989: 1060-61), founder of the Self-Employed Women's Association (SEWA) in India, finds that most people's perceptions of home-based workers' economic contributions is unfounded.

> Our experts describe them by various names, including "unorganized," "informal," "unprotected," "unregistered," "peripheral," "marginal," and "black economy" workers. But it is grossly unfair to describe such a vast and active workforce in terms that imply an inferior and insignificant position, while in reality they are central to the economy and make a major contribution to it.

It would, therefore, be advantageous to help strengthen women's informal associations and networks and recognize their value and applicability to the modern workplace.[5] We see such associations and networks time and again playing crucial roles in the lives of women within the Walled City. For example, women have usually learned whatever skills they possess from a close relative or a neighbor. If they are engaged in cottage labor, it is invariably because a close relative or neighbor introduced them to the relevant middleman. That 38 percent of the women surveyed have had a close female relative work inside the home implies that a precedent has been established and that they could likely do the same. In addition, the fact that 29 percent of the women have had a close female relative work *outside* the home implies that even within the Walled City, an area closely identified with traditional norms and values, society is undergoing an upheaval and substantial changes are occurring.[6]

State policy in Pakistan, therefore, could respond to a number of suggestions. March and Taqqu (1986) argue that if the obstacles are not too great, women's shared economic strategies, networks whose roots lie in traditional relationships, can demonstrably improve women's position, not simply maintain it. In India, such ties have proved successful in women's urban trade union participation (SEWA; Working Women's Forum); in Egypt and Bangladesh, they have been valuable in urban credit ventures. Strengthening women's informal associations and networks in poor urban areas such as the Walled City would tie in well with efforts being made by the Ministry for Women's Development, the United Nations Development Programme and the Aurat Foundation, a non-government organization (NGO), in establishing community groups. This could also provide support to women's informal sector economic activities, for we have seen that financial viability is one of the greatest problems confronting women in the Walled City. In their recommendations to the Asian Development Bank, Nigar Ahmad and Shahla Zia (1989: 46) urge the bank to assist in developing "flexible procedures, decentralized control systems, participatory mechanisms and innovative arrangements within the government outreach systems to incorporate the special requirements of the programmes and projects for women." Attempts to promote networking between NGOs working within the Walled City as well as the establishment of women's cooperatives and community groups would fit in well with new programs established within provincial Social Welfare departments. These ventures could also be linked with the newly established Women's Bank. This linkage would facilitate NGOs' and community groups' attainment of small loans which the Women's Bank intends to distribute on a pattern similar to that of the Grameen Bank in Bangladesh. In addition, closer ties could be built with the International Labor Organization in its efforts to consider adopting standards regulating home-based work.[7] Needless to say, further research on the conditions, scope and contributions of home-based women workers in Pakistan is essential to all of the above.

A preliminary effort in the Walled City may be the establishment of a sewing cooperative network, perhaps under the auspices of the Small Industries Corporation. A great number of women already can sew, and ample opportunities exist, as we have seen, for those who would like to learn. Barbara Rogers (1980) cautions that such cooperatives should emphasize the manufacture of goods whose economic importance to the larger economy are popularly recognized -- in this case, clothes and household necessities -- and should shy away from craft items and other goods made for tourist and overseas specialty markets. The latter kinds of enterprises sustain the invisibility of women's labor by perpetuating the idea that women do such work in their "free time."

Another important component would be to pursue the establishment of a small loans program for enterprising women resident within the Walled City who already are trained in some field and would like to start their own business. A training program covering such issues as small business management, taxes and marketing might be included as a requirement for getting the loan from the Women's Bank. For example, Farida has the requisite skills for cutting hair and providing other beauty treatments, but has no access to borrowing capital either from her parents or her *susural*. Jamila, who buys and sells cloth, could make more profit if she could make her purchases in larger bulk, but that also takes an initial capital investment. Widowed Chand Bibi feels she could earn more if she sells already-embroidered shirts rather than making them on order, but needs money to purchase the cloth and threads to get started. All three of these women are self-supporting, but being without a male wage-earner is not so unique anymore. Many women find themselves in this position at some stage in their lives. These women would prefer to earn for themselves rather than rely on their husband's family for their sustenance. While the nature of the work these women propose is simply not an option for married women like Durdana or Itrat, or for those with other close supportive male relatives such as Gulzar Begum and Bilqis, such independent work is vital for the survival of this group and their dependent children. A small loan program recognizing this has the potential to contribute to a marked improvement in their lives.

A more comprehensive project would be to establish a central cooperative/clearing-house which could draw on the existing and varied expertise of women living in the Walled City. It could keep lists of skills which women have and of unskilled women willing to do some sort of cottage labor in their homes. Businesses could be given incentives, such as import tax credits, to participate in the program. They would provide the raw materials to the cooperative and market the finished goods. Studies of women's work cooperatives throughout the Third World (Huston, 1979; Rogers, 1980; Tinker & Bramsen, 1976) have shown that the greatest stumbling block confronting such enterprises is *not knowing what to manufacture*, followed by their inexperience in raw materials acquisition and marketing. Therefore, if private enterprise becomes involved, these pitfalls can be eliminated. The cooperative would then be responsible for distributing the raw materials to those women in their homes qualified to work on them, collecting the finished goods, and providing quality control checking. Initially, the cooperative would need the voluntary assistance of members of a woman's group or an NGO, but should ultimately become self-sustaining both financially and in internal management. Under this system, the work women would do and the place in which they do it would not differ much from the present situation. The major differences is that they would not be living under the threat, as Laila and Itrat do, of having work arbitrarily withheld from them, and they would earn far more than they currently do when middlemen control the entire operation.

Part of the ongoing process of sociocultural transition which is occurring within the Walled City involves a reevaluation and often a redefinition of tradition.[8] Within that reevaluation process, idealized myth must be separated from reality. Certain strategies have already been devised within traditional contexts for dealing with the transition. For example, most women refer to the middleman as a brother or cousin, despite the lack of a biological relationship or, in most instances, a long-standing friendship between their families. This process can be strengthened with the establishment of women's community centers, which could be expanded to include a variety of educational, health and technical training activities as well as provide childcare. Trained women could counsel others regarding coping with personal dilemmas and economic hardship. Ultimately, an area could be set aside where women could work within the building. Rather than the alienating conditions found within private sector factories, this kind of women's community center could facilitate a pleasant working environment where women could meet with each other, similar to when Gulzar Begum strings flowers in her home. As one of the strongest deterrents to a woman's participating in such a community center would be the possibility of questions being raised about her respectability, needless to say, absolutely no men should *ever* be allowed within the building. Supervisory and maintenance positions could all readily be held by women, thereby also providing employment to women willing and needing to take such jobs. Based on countless discussions with women in the Walled City, it seems that since this building would be housed within a *kucha* under the watchful eyes of all its inhabitants, it is likely that there will be a high degree of public acceptance of this kind of project and families would be unlikely to hesitate to send their female members to participate in it.

These recommendations do not address the underlying contradictions which arise in the process of economic development and sociocultural transformation such as that which Lahore is undergoing. We cannot isolate women's dilemmas from those confronting the larger society. However, this discourse must be left to the people living there and trying to come to terms with these issues. But they are a first step in recognizing the presence and importance of women in the workforce, and a chance that the lives of these working women may be able to be improved just a little bit.

Notes

1. The World Bank (1988: 274) estimates that the growth rate of 3.1% between 1980-86 will decline to 3.0% by the year 2000. At this rate, however, Pakistan's population which is now over 113 million will be a whopping 150 million by the turn of the century.

2. For a history of the women's movement in Pakistan, refer to Mirza, 1969 and to Mumtaz and Shaheed, 1987. Weiss (in press) discusses the impact of state policy on Pakistani women and the response by the women's movement.

3. To Pakistan's advantage, due to considerations of modesty and *purdah*, nearly a quarter of medical school graduates are women, but few open practices in poor slums such as within the Walled City of Lahore.

4. The Seventh Five-Year Plan (1988-93) makes mention of the need to increase female training and provides some statistics on male and female participation rates in polytechnic institutes. Refer to Planning Commission, 1988: 416 for participation rates, and to Planning Commission, 1988: 243-250 for future intentions.

5. March and Taqqu (1986) cite numerous examples of how women's informal associations have been transformed into progressive modern organizations. See in particular their section on formalizing informal associations (1986: 103-115).

6. Refer to Table A.2 (in Appendix) for further elaboration on characteristics of female respondents who live in families where a woman has worked.

7. In her World Bank Report, Ann Duncan (1989: 145-163) summarizes various government, donor and NGO programs targeting women's development in Pakistan. She also provides a an overview of the Grameen Bank in Bangladesh (1989: 187-192). Other recommendations and strategies for ways in which official development assistance (ODA) can benefit women in Pakistan are in United Nations Development Programme "The U.N. System in Pakistan and WID: an Inter-agency Review, 5-30 November, 1989" Islamabad, February 1990: 31-35.

8. Horowitz (1982) writes that of the three dimensions associated with tradition (economic and related processes; the maintenance of religiosity; cultural identification), the worldview established by religion is at considerable variance with "the notion of backwardness as an economic or cultural issue," and that maintaining religiosity does not necessarily impede development. Rather, concepts of traditionalism, modernism and industrialism are linked to ideological statements of power, and thus can be transformed as the need arises.

Appendix

TABLE A.1: Women's Monthly Income Compared to Monthly Income Earned by Husbands or Fathers, and as a Percent of Total Monthly Household Income, by Percent of Earners in Each Income Group

Monthly Income Group (Rupees)	Incomes of Fathers or Husbands (percent)	Women's Incomes (percent)	Women's Earnings as a Percentage of Total Household Income
1-500	8	68	5
501-1000	34	18	15
1001-1500	19	11	29
1501-5000	32	3	43
5001+	7	0	8

TABLE A.2: Characteristics of Women with Some Female Family Member (Including Self) Who Has Worked, by Location of Work

	Female Family Member Has Worked Outside of the Home		
	Percent of Group with Women Working Outside of Home	Percent of All Households with Women Working Outside of Home	Absolute Number
Respondent's Birthplace			
Walled City	24.2	51.7	15
Muhajir (migrant from India)	21.4	10.3	3
Born elsewhere in Lahore	45.5	17.2	5
Born elsewhere	41.7	20.8	6
Family Origin			
Lahore	33.9	72.4	21
Migrant (from India)	21.4	20.7	6
Other	20.0	6.9	2
Sect			
Sunni	27.8	86.2	25
Shi'a	40.0	13.8	4
Educated at all			
None	19.5	27.6	8
Some	35.6	72.4	21
Years of Education			
0-7	25.4	51.8	15
8-10	18.5	17.2	5
10+	64.3	31.0	9
Anyone in Family Gone Abroad to Work?			
Yes	28.8	51.7	15
No	29.2	48.3	14
How Respondent Observes Purdah			
Never leaves house alone	25.5	41.4	12
Wears a veil with a *nikab*	30.8	41.4	12
Wears a veil without a *nikab*	50.0	13.8	4
Keeps separate from men	25.0	3.4	1

(continues)

Table A.2 (*continued*)

	Female Family Member Has Worked Inside of the Home		
	Percent of Group with Women Working Outside of Home	Percent of All Households with Women Working Outside of Home	Absolute Number
Respondent's Birthplace			
Walled City	33.9	55.3	21
Muhajir (migrant from India)	57.1	21.1	8
Born elsewhere in Lahore	45.5	13.2	5
Born elsewhere	33.3	10.4	4
Family Origin			
Lahore	32.3	52.6	20
Migrant (from India)	50.0	35.8	14
Other	40.0	10.6	4
Sect			
Sunni	33.3	78.9	30
Shi'a	80.0	21.1	8
Educated at all			
None	48.8	52.6	20
Some	30.5	47.4	18
Years of Education			
0-7	49.2	76.3	29
8-10	22.2	15.8	6
10+	21.4	7.9	3
Anyone in Family Gone Abroad to Work?			
Yes	42.3	57.9	22
No	33.3	42.1	16
How Respondent Observes Purdah			
Never leaves house alone	36.2	44.7	17
Wears a veil with a *nikab*	35.9	36.8	14
Wears a veil without a *nikab*	62.5	13.2	5
Keeps separate from men	50.0	5.3	2

TABLE A.3: Characteristics of Purdah Observance, of Those Who Observe Some Form of Purdah (96 Percent of Sample), by Type of Purdah Observed

| | *Characteristics of Those Who Wear a Veil (Burqa or Chadar) with a Nikab* | | |
	Percent of All Who Observe This Form of Purdah	Percent of Respondent's Own Group Observing This Form	Absolute Number
Place of Birth			
Walled City	68.1	51.6	32
Muhajir (migrant from India)	10.6	38.5	5
Born elsewhere in Lahore	8.5	40.0	4
Born elsewhere in Pakistan	12.8	54.5	6
Family Origin			
Lahore	66.0	50.8	31
Migrant (*muhajirs* from India)	25.5	48.0	12
Other	8.5	40.0	4
Marital Status			
Single	12.8	25.0	6
Married	76.6	56.3	36
Separated, widowed or divorced	10.6	62.5	5
Age Group			
16-19	0.0	0.0	0
20-29	29.8	41.2	14
30-39	36.2	68.0	17
40-49	29.8	58.3	14
50-59	4.2	28.6	2
Sect			
Sunni	95.7	52.3	45
Shi'a	4.3	20.0	2
Educated at all			
None	53.2	65.8	25
Some	46.8	37.9	22
Years of Education			
0-7	74.5	62.5	35
8-10	19.1	34.6	9
10+	6.4	21.4	3
Wakes up before 6 a.m. (presumably, with the *azan*)	76.6	46.8	36

(continues)

Table A.3 *(continued)*

Characteristics of Those Who Wear a Veil (Burqa or Chadar) without a Nikab		
Percent of All Who Observe This Form of Purdah	Percent of Respondent's Own Group Observing This Form	Absolute Number

	Percent of All Who Observe This Form of Purdah	Percent of Respondent's Own Group Observing This Form	Absolute Number
Place of Birth			
Walled City	59.0	37.1	23
Muhajir (migrant from India)	17.9	53.8	7
Born elsewhere in Lahore	12.8	50.0	5
Born elsewhere in Pakistan	10.3	36.4	4
Family Origin			
Lahore	56.4	36.1	22
Migrant (*muhajirs* from India)	30.8	48.0	12
Other	12.8	50.0	5
Marital Status			
Single	28.2	45.8	11
Married	66.7	40.6	26
Separated, widowed or divorced	5.1	25.0	2
Age Group			
16-19	7.7	50.0	3
20-29	38.5	44.1	15
30-39	20.5	32.0	8
40-49	25.6	41.7	10
50-59	7.7	42.8	3
Sect			
Sunni	82.1	37.2	32
Shi'a	17.9	70.0	7
Educated at all			
None	28.2	28.9	11
Some	71.8	48.3	28
Years of Education			
0-7	46.2	32.1	18
8-10	35.9	53.9	14
10+	17.9	50.0	7
Wakes up before 6 a.m. (presumably, with the *azan*)	82.1	41.5	32

(continues)

Table A.3 *(continued)*

	Percent of All Who Observe This Form of Purdah	Percent of Respondent's Own Group Observing This Form	Absolute Number
Characteristics of Those Who Keep Separate From Men When Outside			
Place of Birth			
Walled City	70.0	11.3	7
Muhajir (migrant from India)	10.0	7.7	1
Born elsewhere in Lahore	10.0	10.0	1
Born elsewhere in Pakistan	10.0	9.1	1
Family Origin			
Lahore	80.0	13.1	8
Migrant (*muhajirs* from India	10.0	4.0	1
Other	10.0	10.0	1
Marital Status			
Single	70.0	29.2	7
Married	20.0	3.1	2
Separated, widowed or divorced	10.0	12.5	1
Age Group			
16-19	30.0	50.0	3
20-29	50.0	14.7	5
30-39	--	--	--
40-49	--	--	--
50-59	20.0	28.6	2
Sect			
Sunni	90.0	10.5	9
Shi'a	10.0	10.0	1
Educated at all			
None	20.0	5.3	2
Some	80.0	13.8	8
Years of Education			
0-7	30.0	5.4	3
8-10	30.0	11.5	3
10+	40.0	28.6	4
Wakes up before 6 a.m. (presumably, with the *azan*)	90.0	11.7	9

Glossary

anna: former system of currency in which 16 annas equal one rupee

aseb: evil supernatural spirit

ayah: a maidservant usually employed to care for children

azan: call to prayer announced five times daily from mosques

baji: older sister

baraat: the marriage procession, when the bridegroom takes the bride from her house to his

behan: sister

bhabi: brother's wife; often used for cousin's wife

bhai: brother

biradari: clan; the next level of kinship beyond the extended family

burqa: fitted veil worn by Muslim women

chacha: father's younger brother; general term used for father's brother [spouse: *chachi*]

chachazad: cousin-sibling through a *chacha*

chadar: loose-fitting cloth worn as a veil by Muslim women

chana/kulcha: cooked garbanzo beans served with a small *nan* common for summertime breakfasts [in Punjabi, *chana* = *chole*]

chana/nan: cooked garbanzo beans and large, flat bread baked in a tandoor oven

chaprassi: low level worker in an office or factory; peon

charpai: string bed

dada: father's father (spouse: *dadi*)

dai: midwife

dal: cooked lentils

damaad: son-in-law

darvaza: door; in the Walled City, the term used for the gateways into it as well

dewar: husband's younger brother [spouse: *dewarani*]

dupatta: diaphanous scarf worn with Punjabi dress by women

Eid: generic term used commonly in the Walled City to denote either Eid al-Azha (also referred to in Punjabi as Bakr Eid, the festival of sacrifice beginning on the last day of the hajj) or Eid ul-Fitr (festival that breaks the fast, at the end of Ramadan)

gali: inhabited alleyway

ghee: clarified butter

gherrara: traditional Pakistani bride's marriage outfit consisting of a shirt covering an embroidered skirt

gota: heavy, thick golden lace embroidery

gurdwara: Sikh temple

hajj: the pilgrimage to Mecca, an obligation for every perform at least once in their lifetime if they can

hakim: practitioner of unani medicine

✓ *halwa/puri*: fried sweet semolina and fried bread, a summertime breakfast specialty, generally purchased cooked from the bazaar

hamam: a vessel, usually in brass, copper or steel, with a faucet at the bottom used for storing water

handi: generic term for curries

haq mehr: promissory gift from bride's in-laws at the time of marriage; a kind of bridewealth, stipulated in the marriage contract, to be paid to the wife in the event of divorce or the husband's death

har: marriage garland

haveli: a residential area enclosed by a wall generally housing an extended family

✓ *hookah*: tobacco-filled water pipe, often shared

imam bara: Shi'a religious sanctuary

izzat: respect; respectability

jaith: husband's elder brother [spouse: *jaithani*]

✓ *jamadar*: sweeper *Most in Lahore at Christian*

jharoka: stylized abutting windows common in pre-partition Hindu areas

kalma: statement which is an affirmation of one's belief in Allah and His Prophet; the affirmation of the Islamic faith

kanal: land measurement equalling twenty *marlas*; 1/20th of an acre

katra: formerly a fortressed area with its own inhabitants and markets; now a haveli which has been divided up into separate living quarters inhabited by 5-10 households not necessarily related to each other

khala: mother's sister [spouse: *khalu*]

khalazad: cousin-sibling through a *khala*

kucha: neighborhood, *muhalla*, usually socially cohesive and virtually economically self-sufficient

✓ *ladoo*: round sweet distributed on joyous occasions

lal roti: a special bread for marriages in the Walled City, very rich and custom-ordered in the bazaar

mahaul: living atmosphere; social environment

mammu: mother's brother [spouse: *mamani*]

mammuzad: cousin-sibling through a *mammu*

marla: a measurement of land, commonly used to measure plots of land for houses (*marla* = 1/400 of an acre)

✓ *masjid*: mosque

matka ghara: clay pot for cold water storage

maulvi: religious practioner who performs various ceremonies

✓ *mehndi*: henna, often used to color hands in intricate patterns for weddings and other happy occasions; the ceremony in which henna is applied to a bride's hands and feet before her wedding

mochi: shoemaker

muhajir: migrant; generally associated with those Muslims who migrated to Pakistan from India at partition

muhalla: neighborhood; commonly used term throughout Pakistan

murshid: religious advisor, teacher

nana: mother's father [spouse: *nani*]

nihari: spicy beef or chicken curry cooked in a large vat, a Lohari specialty

nikab: a piece of cloth which can be attached to a *burqa* or a *chadar* to cover a woman's face so as to hide her identity

nikah: Muslim marriage

nikahnama: Muslim marriage certificate

nund: husband's sister

pan: a treat made of betel leaf enclosing betel nut, tobacco and various spices

pandan: receptacle for holding various ingredients for *pan*

pancha: hem by the ankle of a *shalwar* which helps its fall, often embroidered

palang: western style bed

paranda: cotton strands used to braid into girls' and women's hair

paratha: fried bread, often eaten for breakfast

pehlwan: wrestler; "big" man

phuphi: father's sister [spouse: *phupha*]

phuphizad: cousin-sibling through a *phuphi*

pir: popularly recognized pious individual; saint [fem.: *pirni*]

purdah: lit. curtain; the social separation of men and women

qaum: tribe; stratifies Pakistani Muslims into groupings

rakat: portion of a verse in the Qur'an

rehra: horse-drawn cart

rishta: arrangement made for a marital bond

roti: cooked flat bread; generic term for food

sadqaat: alms given to beggars as a religious obligation

sag: curried spinach or mustard leaves

salma sitara: embroidery using pearls and silver and gold threads

samosa: spicy potato-filled dumpling

saparah: one of thirty verses in the Qur'an

sas: mother-in-law

sehra: a type of wreath used at marriages and saints' shrines

shalwar kamize: Pakistani clothes consisting of baggy pants (*shalwar*) and a long shirt (*kamize*)

shamize: undergarment sometimes worn by women beneath a *kamize*

sharafat: honor

shari'a: Islamic law

sharif: honorable

susr: father-in-law

susural: in-laws, generally implying all those related through marriage

taviz: religious amulet housing Qur'anic verses

taya: father's older brother [spouse: *tayi*, though *chachi* is commonly used]

tayazad: cousin-sibling through a *taya*

tikan: stiff white cloth used for embroidery

tikka: broach hung from mid-section of hair onto forehead

tola: a measurement in weight of a bit under an ounce, generally used to measure silver and gold

valima: final wedding reception, given by bridegroom's family

wacholan: matchmaker
zakat: institutionalized system of religious alms given to poor, unfortunate and
  disabled

Bibliography

Abu Nasr, Julinda *et. al.* (eds.) 1985. *Women, Employment and Development in the Arab World* Berlin: Mouton Publishers.

Adams, Charles, 1982. "Tradition and Legitimization of Social Change in Jessie Lutz and Salah El-Shakhs (eds.) *Tradition and Modernity: the Role of Traditionalism in the Modernization Process* Washington, D.C.: University Press of America.

Ahmad, Nigar and Shahla Zia. 1989. "Women in Development: Pakistan" Country Briefing Report prepared for the Asian Development Bank, Lahore.

Baqir, Muhammad. 1985. *Lahore Past and Present* Lahore: Punjabi Adabi Academy.

Barnes-McConnell, Pat and Dora G. Lodwick. 1983. *Working with International Development Projects: a Guide for Women-in-Development* East Lansing: Office of Women in Development, Michigan State University.

Bay, Edna B. (ed.) 1982. *Women and Work in Africa* Boulder: Westview Press.

Beck, Lois and Nikki Keddie (eds.) 1978. *Women in the Muslim World* Cambridge: Harvard University Press.

Beneria, Lourdes (ed.) 1982. *Women and the Sexual Division of Labor in Rural Societies* New York: Praeger Publishers.

Beneria, Lourdes and Martha Roldan. 1987. *The Crossroads of Class and Gender: Industrial Homework, Subcontracting and Household Dynamics in Mexico City* Chicago: University of Chicago Press.

Bhatt, Ela. 1989. "Toward Empowerment" *World Development* 17, pp. 1059-1065.

Black, Naomi and Ann Baker Cottrell (eds.) 1981. *Women and World Change: Equity Issues in Development* London: Sage Publications.

Boserup, Ester. 1970. *Women's Role in Economic Development* New York: St. Martin's Press.

Bujra, Janet M. 1979. "Female Solidarity and the Sexual Division of Labor" in Patricia Caplan and Janet Bujra (eds.) *Women United, Women Divided: Comparative Studies of Ten Contemporary Cultures* Bloomington: Indiana University Press, pp. 13-45.

Burki, Shahid Javed. 1984. "Pakistan's Sixth Plan: Helping the Country Climb out of Poverty" *Asian Survey* XXIV,4, April, pp. 400-422.

Chapkis, Wendy and Cynthia Enloe (eds.) 1983. *Of Common Cloth: Women in the Global Textile Industry* Washington, D.C.: Transnational Institute.

Charlton, Sue Ellen M. 1984. *Women in Third World Development* Boulder: Westview Press.

Dauber, Roslyn and Melinda Cain (eds.) 1981. *Women and Technological Change in Developing Countries* Boulder: Westview Press.

Duncan, Ann. 1989. *Women in Pakistan: an Economic and Social Strategy*

Washington, D.C.: The World Bank.

Economic Policy Research Unit. 1990. "An Evaluation of the Orangi Pilot Project" Report carried out for the World Bank, Lahore.

Esposito, John. L. 1981. *Women in Muslim Family Law* Syracuse: Syracuse University Press.

Fawcett, James T., Siew-Ean Khoo and Peter C. Smith (eds.) 1984. *Women in the Cities of Asia: Migration and Urban Adaptation* Boulder: Westview Press.

Goulding, H.R. 1924. *Old Lahore: Reminiscences of a Resident* Lahore: Universal Books.

Government of Pakistan, Finance Division, 1983. *Economic Survey: 1982-83* Islamabad: Economic Adviser's Wing.

Gran, Guy. 1983. *Development by People: Citizen Construction of a Just World* New York: Praeger Publishers.

Hafeez, Sabeeha. 1983. "Women in Industry: Phase I, Basic Survey" Prepared under the auspices of the Women's Division, Cabinet Secretariat, Government of Pakistan, Islamabad.

Hijab, Nadia. 1988. *Womanpower: the Arab Debate on Women at Work* Cambridge: Cambridge University Press.

Hooper, Emma. 1985. *Working Women in Lahore* Unpublished Ph.d. dissertation, University of London.

Horowitz, Irving Louis. 1982. "Tradition, Modernity and Industrialization: Toward an Integrated Development Paradigm" in Jessie G. Lutz and Salah El-Shakhs (eds.) *Tradition and Modernity: the Role of Traditionalism in the Modernization Process* Washington, D.C.: University Press of America.

Huston, Perdita. 1979. *Third World Women Speak Out* New York: Praeger Publications.

Irshad, Sairah. 1986. "Inside the Walled City" *The Herald* January, pp. 138-151.

Jahan, Rounaq and Hanna Papanek (eds.) 1979. *Women and Development: Perspectives from South and Southeast Asia* Dacca: The Bangladesh Institute of Law and International Affairs.

Jeffery, Patricia. 1979. *Frogs in a Well: Indian Women in Purdah* London: Zed Press.

Johnson, B.L.C. 1979. *Pakistan* London: Heinemann Educational Books.

Jules-Rosette, Benetta. 1982. "Women's Work in the Informal Sector: a Zambian Case Study" Working Paper No. 3, Michigan State University, Office of International Development Working Papers Series, East Lansing, Michigan.

Khan, Verity Saifullah. 1976. "Pakistani Women in Britain" *New Community* V, Number 1-2, Summer, pp. 99-108.

Lahore Development Authority (LDA). 1982. "Household Survey of Walled City: Area between Lohari and Mori Gate" Lahore: Metropolitan Planning Wing, April.

Lahore Development Authority (LDA). 1984. "Study of Household and Sanitation Conditions, Walled City, Lahore" Lahore: Metropolitan Planning Wing, August.

Lahore Development Authority (LDA). 1979. "Walled City of Lahore: a Socioeconomic Study" Lahore: Metropolitan Planning Wing.

Lahore Development Authority (LDA). 1980. *Walled City Upgrading Study* Lahore Urban Development and Traffic Study, Final Report/Volume 4. Lahore:

Metropolitan Planning Wing.

Latif, Syad Muhammad. 1892. *Lahore: Architectural Remains* Lahore: New Imperial Press (reprinted in Lahore by Sandhu Printers, 1981).

Leghorn, Lisa and Katherine Parker. 1981. *Woman's Worth: Sexual Economics and the World of Women* Boston: Routledge and Kegan Paul.

Madsen, Richard. 1984. *Morality and Power in a Chinese Village* Berkeley and Los Angeles: University of California Press.

Makhlouf, Carla. 1979. *Changing Veils: Women and Modernisation in North Yemen* Austin: University of Texas Press.

March, Kathryn S. and Rachelle L. Taqqu. 1986. *Women's Informal Associations in Developing Countries: Catalysts for Change?* Boulder: Westview Press.

Mernissi, Fatima. 1987. *Beyond the Veil: Male-Female Dynamics in a Modern Muslim Society* Revised edition. Bloomington: Indiana University Press.

Mies, Maria. 1982. "The Dynamics of the Sexual Divison of Labor and Integration of Rural Women into the World Market" in Lourdes Beneria *Women and the Sexual Division of Labor in Rural Societies* New York: Praeger Publishers, pp. 1-28.

Mirza, Sarfaraz Hussain. 1969. *Muslim Women's Role in the Pakistan Movement* Lahore: Research Society of Pakistan, Punjab University.

Mumtaz, Kamil Khan. n.d. "Appendix II: Preliminary Notes on Political, Social and Physical Evolution of Lahore" prepared for Walled City Study Team for Lahore Development Authority.

Mumtaz, Khawar and Farida Shaheed. 1987. *Women of Pakistan: Two Steps Forward, One Step Back?* Lahore: Vanguard Books.

Noe, Samuel. 1977. *A Systematic Analysis of the Islamic City: Lahore, Pakistan* Unpublished Ph.d. dissertation, University of Cincinnati.

Pakistan Environmental Planning and Architectural Consultants, Ltd. 1987. *Conservation Issues and Intervention Alternatives: a Strategic Framework* prepared for the Lahore Development Authority, Conservation Plan for the Walled City of Lahore, April.

Papanek, Hanna. 1981. "The Differential Impact of Programs and Policies on Women in Development" in Roslyn Dauber and Melinda Cain (eds.) *Women and Technological Change in Developing Countries* Boulder: Westview Press, pp. 215-227.

Papanek Hanna. 1971. "Purdah in Pakistan: Seclusion and Modern Occupations for Women" *Journal of Marriage and the Family* XXXIII, No. 3, August, pp. 517-530.

Papanek Hanna. 1973. "Purdah: Separate Worlds and Symbolic Shelter" *Comparative Studies on Society and History* XV, No. 3, pp. 289-325.

Pastner, Carroll. 1974. "Accommodations to Purdah: the Female Perspective" *Journal of Marriage and the Family* XXXVI, No. 2, May, pp. 408-414.

Patel, Rashida. 1979. *Women and Law in Pakistan* Karachi.

Planning Commission, Government of Pakistan. 1988. *Seventh Five-Year Plan, 1988-93* Islamabad: Printing Corporation of Pakistan Press.

Population Census Organisation, Government of Pakistan. 1984. *1981 District Census Report of Lahore* District Census Report No. 54. Islamabad: Statistics Division, February.

Portes, Alejandro, Manuel Castells and Lauren Benton (eds.) 1989. *The Informal Economy: Studies in Advanced and Less Developed Countries* Washington, D.C.: Johns Hopkins Press.

Research Society of Pakistan. 1976. *Extracts from the District and States Gazeteers of the Punjab (Pakistan)* Vol. I. Lahore: Punjab Educational Press.

Rogers, Barbara. 1980. *The Domestication of Women: Discrimination in Developing Societies* London: Tavistock Publications.

Shackle, Christopher. 1970. "Punjabi in Lahore" *Modern Asian Studies* IV,3, pp. 239-267.

Shah, Nasra M. (ed.) 1986. *Pakistani Women: a Socioeconomic and Demographic Profile* Islamabad: PIDE and Hawaii: East-West Population Institute.

Shah, Nasra M. and Makhdoom A. Shah. 1980. "Trends and Structure of Female Labour Force Participation in Rural and Urban Pakistan" in Alfred de Souza (ed.) *Women in Contemporary India and South Asia* New Delhi: Manohar, pp. 95-123.

Shaheed, Farida and Khawar Mumtaz. 1983. *Invisible Workers: Piecework Labour Amongst Women in Lahore* Islamabad: Women's Division, Government of Pakistan.

Swidler, Ann. 1986. "Culture in Action: Symbols and Strategies" *American Sociological Review* Vol. 51, April, pp. 273-286.

Thorbek, Susanne. 1987. *Voices from the City: Women of Bangkok* London: Zed Press.

Thornton, J.H. n.d. *Lahore: 1860-1924* Lahore.

Tinker, Irene and M.B. Bramsen (eds.) 1976. *Women and World Development* Washington, D.C.: Overseas Development Council.

Tufail, M. (ed.) 1962. *Nuqoosh - Lahore* (in Urdu) No. 9, February.

United Nations Development Program (UNDP). 1990. *Human Development Report, 1990* New York: Oxford University Press.

United Nations Development Program (UNDP). 1991. *Human Development Report, 1991* New York: Oxford University Press.

Waring, Marilyn. 1988. *Counting for Nothing: What Men Value and What Women are Worth* New York: Allen and Unwin.

Weiss, Anita M. in press. "The Consequences of State Policy for Women in Pakistan" in Myron Weiner and Ali Banuazizi (eds.) *The State and the Restructuring of Society in Afghanistan, Iran and Pakistan* Syracuse: Syracuse University Press.

Weiss, Anita M. 1991. *Culture, Class and Development in Pakistan: the Emergence of an Industrial Bourgeoisie in Punjab* Boulder: Westview Press.

Weiss, Anita M. (ed.) 1986. *Islamic Reassertion in Pakistan: the Application of Islamic Laws in a Modern State* Syracuse: Syracuse University Press.

Weiss Anita M. 1984. "Tradition and Modernity at the Workplace: a Field Study of Women in the Pharmaceutical Industry of Lahore" *Women's Studies International Forum* VII, No. 4., pp. 259-264.

World Bank/Lahore Development Authority (LDA). 1980. *Walled City Upgrading Study* Final Report, IV, Lahore, August.

Index

197